Books by Peter F. Drucker

Published by John Day
The End of Economic Man, 1939
The Future of Industrial Man, 1942
Concept of the Corporation, 1946, 1972

Published by Harper's
The New Society, 1950
The Practice of Management, 1954
America's Next Twenty Years, 1957
The Landmarks of Tomorrow, 1959
Managing for Results, 1964
The Effective Executive, 1966
The Age of Discontinuity, 1969
Technology, Management and Society, 1970
Men, Ideas and Politics, 1971

Published by Prentice-Hall
Preparing Tomorrow's Business Leaders Today
(edited by Peter F. Drucker), 1969

CONCEPT OF THE CORPORATION

CONCEPT OF THE CORPORATION

With a
new Preface and new Epilogue
by the author

Peter F. Drucker

THE JOHN DAY COMPANY

NEW YORK

Published in Canada by Fitzhenry & Whiteside Limited, Toronto.

Printed in the United States of America

Library of Congress Cataloging in Publication Data

Drucker, Peter Ferdinand, 1909-
  Concept of the corporation.

  1. Corporation. 2. Corporations—U.S.
  3. General Motors Corporation. I. Title.
  [HD2731.D7 1972] 338.7′4′0973 72-000074

ISBN 0-381-98093-6

2 3 4 5 6 7 8 9 10

CONTENTS

PREFACE TO THE 1972 EDITION

The Corporation Revisited

A FAVORITE slogan of the New Left is that of the "Corporate State." Insofar as this—rather vague—term asserts that the Big Business Corporation has these last twenty-five years come to be the "dominant institution" of American society, it is total misunderstanding. Big Business has declined almost precipitately in relative importance in the United States since the end of World War II, that is, since the time when *Concept of the Corporation* was originally written and published.

But if the slogan of the "Corporate State" is read as implying that American society has altogether become a society of big, highly organized and managed institutions—the kind of institution of which Big Business, twenty-five years ago, was in many ways the prototype and first exemplar—there is a good deal of substance to the term. American society—and society in all other advanced countries as well from Japan to Soviet Russia—has increasingly become a society of big, organized power centers: government agency and hospital, large university and research laboratory, trade union and armed services, in addition to Big Business. These institutions have emerged as managerial and managed institutions of great size, formal structure, and systematic decision-making. They have become the very fabric of economically and socially developed societies.

Concept of the Corporation was the first study of a major institution of this new pluralist society of institutions, in addition to being the first study of the constitution, structure, and internal dynamics of a major business enterprise. Since then, the literature on management has come on in a veritable flood. But still this is the one book that looks at a major managerial organization from within and tries to understand what makes it work and what its principles are.

When I started work on the book, I could find practically nothing to prepare myself for the task. To be sure, there were texts galore on accounting and on methods of industrial production, on sales training and on advertising, and on many other business tools. But how a big business was organized and structured, how it functioned, and what its basic problems were—these questions had never been asked before. Indeed, they had not even been seen as questions.

Neither economist nor political scientist at the time concerned himself with institutions, let alone with business and enterprise. And students of management—so plentiful today —were almost totally absent then. In this respect, this book was a "first." It established the study of organization as a major subject.

However, it did not do so without a struggle. Businessmen and other managers such as administrators in government agencies and hospitals (with whom the book has perhaps been even more popular than with businessmen, from its very publication) immediately accepted the book as being of major importance. It has retained its popularity with students and practitioners of management and administration to this day. But neither economists nor political scientists saw, at first, much point to a book that concerned itself with business enterprise, and indeed, with organization altogether. Both were rather baffled—the economist, because the book treats what he considers an "economic subject," that is a business, as a social institution and power center, and indeed as a kind of government; the political scientist, because the book applies what he considers his concepts and methods to a business, that is to an institution which is not "government." I was told repeatedly by well-meaning friends in the academic world that I had ruined a "promising career" as a political scientist or as an economist. And a good friend among political scientists concluded an otherwise favorable review of the book in one of the learned journals with the words, "It is to be hoped that the author will soon apply his considerable talents to a more respectable topic."

What this book tried to say, however, is that an understanding of the structure and constitution of large organizations—"respectable" or not—is indeed *the* topic for students of economics, society, politics, and government in this century. This book was written in anticipation of the dramatic developments of the last twenty-five years, that is in anticipation of the rise of a society in which the major social tasks are all being discharged in and through large, organized, managed institutions: our pluralist society of institutions today.

I did not select the General Motors Corporation to make this pioneering study of management because I was particularly interested in the automobile industry. I did not even pick GM because I was primarily interested in business. I picked GM as a subject for what I knew was an attempt to break new ground, because a study of a big business enterprise in general, and of General Motors in particular, seemed to me the only way to come to grips with big organization. When I embarked on the work that led to this book, early in 1944, in the midst of World War II, I had reached the conclusion that we were facing a period of rapid growth in big organizations in society.

I do not claim any prophetic vision. Nothing would have surprised me more, at the time, than a glimpse of the development of the university since those days. Indeed, the rise of the university into bigness, power, and prominence in society was something no one at the time could have predicted. Also, at that time, no one, as far as I know, would have expected the large military service to remain with us as a constant feature of the political and social landscape. Rather, everyone then expected the armed services, in all countries, to return to a position of relative unimportance—at least, measured against the importance they had during the war, or have today —once the actual fighting had come to an end.

But it seemed to me reasonably clear by 1944—largely as a result of the thinking that had gone into an earlier book*— that the new, large institution was different from any social and political phenomenon we had known in the past. I saw, if only dimly, that the society of large pluralistic institutions which was evolving then was no longer the society which conventional social and political theories assumed. At the same time, it also seemed to me not to resemble at all any of the earlier pluralisms.

Our political and social theories then—and still today— presume a society in which, beyond the family, there is really no "institution" except the central government. In that respect, there is little difference between "liberals" and "conservatives," between "free enterprisers" or "Marxists," indeed not even between "democrats" and "totalitarians." They differ only in the role each of them assigns to the one institution traditional theory accepts, that is to the central government. Otherwise, they are all children of the seventeenth-century theorists, from Bodin to Locke, who hammered out "modern political theory," the theory of the sovereign nation-state.

When business enterprise emerged, in the early years of

---

* *The Future of Industrial Man,* John Day Co., New York, 1942, republished by New American Library (Mentor Paperback #265) in 1965.

the twentieth century, as an autonomous large institution, it was either ignored (by practically all economists) or treated (as it still is by the "anti-trusters") as an aberration.

Like everyone else in my generation, I grew up in this tradition. But by the end of the 1930's, and especially during World War II, it was becoming increasingly clear that this tradition no longer answered the facts. The performance of the United States economy in World War II—and somewhat earlier, that of the British war economy after Dunkirk—argued persuasively that with business enterprise a new, permanent power center had come into being, an institution that had autonomy in its own sphere, its own rationale and purpose, its own governance, and its own dynamics. And by that time we had heard enough also about both Hitler's Germany and Stalin's Russia to know that this new institution, business enterprise, had the same needs and the same characteristics, and indeed the same job, in societies which politically were organized very differently and which either totally "owned" or totally "controlled" the economic sphere. Indeed, it was by then reasonably clear that business enterprise performed only if given autonomy and its own governance, and that both Hitler and Stalin had learned that fact the hard way.

It took only a little observation of reality to see that, while business enterprise was the most visible of these institutions, it was by no means the only one. The full unfolding of the new pluralist society of institutions was, of course, still in the future. But its lineaments were there.

Since then, as everyone knows, the change has been fast indeed. Only a lifetime ago, at the turn of the century, the social world of Western man might have been represented as a prairie on which man and his family were the highest eminence. A small hill—government—rose on the horizon, but while it was larger than anything else around, it was still quite low. Today, by contrast, man's social world, whether West or East, resembles the Himalayas. The individual seems to be dwarfed by the giant mountains of large-scale organization all around him. Here is the Mount Everest of modern government. Next to it there are the armed forces, which in almost every country devour a lion's share of national income. Then come the towering cliffs of the large business corporations and, scarcely less high and forbidding, the peaks of the large, powerful labor unions; then the huge universities, the big hospitals—all of them creatures of this century.

How great the change has been, very few of us appreciate. It is hard for us even to imagine the reality of 1900. There was then, for instance, not a single university in the Western world with as many as 10,000 students; only three or four had student bodies of 5,000. The "large" university of those days was so small that its president or dean was expected to know every student by name and to be available for counsel on the individual's problems or on his choice of a career. Today the United States alone has at least 60 universities with student populations of more than 10,000, and about 150 with more than 5,000 students each. The American military services have a peacetime budget now—some seventy or eighty billion dollars a year—which would have sufficed to maintain the most powerful and most dreaded army of 1900, that of Imperial Germany, for more than a century.

The "giant" business of those days, the huge "trust" which gave our grandparents nightmares, was Mr. Rockefeller's Standard Oil Company. Every one of the eleven companies into which the Supreme Court split the "octopus" in 1911 is today larger than the original Standard Oil Company ever was —in capital, in employees, in production. Yet only four of them rank among the major American, let alone the major international, oil companies today.

When Lord Curzon became British Foreign Secretary at the end of World War I, he found the Foreign Office so swollen and inflated by wartime expansion that, as he complained bitterly, he still had not met every member of the professional staff after working three whole days. Can anyone imagine today's cabinet ministers, even in a small country, as much as trying to meet the tens of thousands of professional employees of a major government department?

Of course there were large organizations in earlier days—the masses of laborers who built the pyramids, the armies that fought the Napoleonic wars or the American Civil War, forces much larger than anything man had till then thought possible. But there is a real difference between these traditional large organizations and those of today. Historically, man has been able to organize on a large scale only repetitive, monotonous, thoroughly unskilled work.

The designers of the pyramids must have been men of tremendous knowledge and ability. A modern engineer would be hard pressed to design such a structure with the degree of precision required by its religious purpose. And no modern engineer would be able to build any such structure without mechanical tools and without heavy earth-moving equipment to transport the huge stone blocks. The Egyptians had neither wheeled vehicles nor draft animals. The execution of the design was done by unskilled peasants doing totally unskilled work. Yet the overseer had only to make sure that his men used their brute strength and pulled together when the command was given. He had, one imagines, little concern with "communications" and none with employee morale or employee motivation. Napoleon's armies still were organized the same way.

These were the prototypes of large organizations down to this century. The largest of them, the armies, were always composed of a tiny group of generals at the top, who made all the decisions, and a vast mass of illiterate soldiers underneath, who were rigidly drilled to obey a few repetitive commands. Frederick the Great, the creator of the Prussian Army in the mid-eighteenth century, was thoroughly ridiculed by contemporary military writers because his soldiers were expected to be able to distinguish among fifteen different commands. "Everyone knew" that this was far too many for soldiers as well as for officers. Men in large organizations could not possibly be that skilled! Seen in this perspective, Henry Ford's assembly line is not a new but an old organization pattern. All Ford did was to bring into the factory the tradition of large-scale organization. But in the post-Ford automated factory of today the work is done by people of very different knowledges, working together for a common purpose and for joint results. It is this, rather than Ford's, pattern, however, that characterizes the modern organization. And it is this very different organization on which all our institutions try to mold themselves today.

The essence of this large-scale organization of the late twentieth century is that within it people of very diverse skills and knowledges work together. This, traditionally, could never be done except in very small groups, teams of four or five at most. Today we do it—or at least try—with very large numbers—thousands of people with different knowledges, coming together in a business, a government agency, or an armed service—under a management with specific knowledge of building and directing the large-scale organization.

This newly gained ability has given man great new capacities, for better or worse. The atom bomb was much less a triumph of science than a triumph of organization. What created it was our new ability to have thousands upon thousands of scientists, each with his highly specialized knowledge, work together under one management and direction. Science by itself could not have done the job. The moon shots similarly are primarily "management" rather than "science" or even "technology." If the capacity to organize has raised our power of destruction, it has also given us the means to work purposefully at works of peace. The development of the polio vaccine was one of the first results of this new ability to organize and to manage large-scale knowledge work of great diversity. That we can today talk of social and economic development as something we can plan and should do springs directly from the capacity to organize. Indeed, what we mean in calling a country "underdeveloped" is not primarily that it is poor. That, we know today, is an effect rather than a cause. The cause is the absence of ability to build and use the large-scale organization that is the instrument of social achievement in the modern world. Large-scale organization is not the accomplishment of one race. The Japanese are as good at creating and guiding large knowledge organizations as any people of the European tradition. And some countries of the European tradition (e.g., in Latin America) are, at best, beginners at organizing.

In this tremendous surge, business has, of course, developed too. One of the important events of these last twenty-five years is surely the development of the "multinational corporation." It is the first institution that transcends the sovereign state. It is the first challenge to the nation-state in three hundred years or more. It is, at the same time, our first transnational institution in a world infected by the most poisonous nationalist virus.

But otherwise, the last twenty-five years have been years in which the nonbusiness institutions—the university, the government agency, the hospital, and many others—have grown much faster than business has. Indeed, as already said, in relative importance business has declined steadily.

Altogether, to anyone who grew up in Europe, as I did, the assertion that the U.S. is or ever was a "business society" has always been rather a joke. The "enemy" for American "liberals" since the days of Andrew Jackson has so clearly been "business," where, in sharp contrast, the enemy of the European "liberal," especially on the Continent, has been "clericalism" with "business" actually supported by the "liberals." The American governmental tradition is that of "hands-off," if not of an adversary relationship between government and business. The great American political invention in the nineteenth century was that of government regulation of business —that is, of political control of business enterprise. The true "business societies"—the societies in which the line between government and business is blurred, and in which government is expected to support, promote, and serve business and the economic interest—have always been and still are the countries of the mercantilist tradition, such as France, Germany, and Japan. And the Soviet Union, while "anti-capitalist," has been as fully "pro-business" as the mercantilist Czars it succeeded.

But even in the U.S. the "golden age" of "business domination" was surely much earlier—between 1880 and 1910. No business leader, today, has a fraction of the power, whether economic or political, that a Morgan, a Rockefeller, or a Harriman had then, let alone their visibility. No business leader could conceivably have the same political importance that Mark Hanna had around 1900, when he organized and founded the modern Republican Party, and did so as a businessman. Indeed, under the most "pro-business administration" that we have had since World War II, business and businessmen have much less say and are given much less attention than under the avowedly "anti-business" New Deal administration of Franklin D. Roosevelt.

This is not because business has become weaker. Other institutions have become so much stronger. In absolute size and importance, American business has stayed about even with the American economy for the last seventy years—the period in which Big Business grew faster than the economy probably came to an end around World War I. Since then, the growth has been roughly parallel. But, in *relative* size and power, Big Business has been going down for at least thirty and probably for fifty or more years. And size and power are, of course, always relative.

Twenty-five years ago, when I first started to be concerned with the problems of the large-scale organization, its structure, its principles, and its direction, Big Business enterprise was the inevitable choice for such a study. Today this would no longer be so. It, however, would still be, in the end, the right choice. For, of all the institutions we have, only Big Business enterprise is accessible to an outsider. Business publishes accounts and records. It is under public scrutiny. No other one of the large institutions is accessible at all. In no other one would it be possible to move in, as I moved into General Motors twenty-five years ago, spend two years or more in extensive study and remain independent and an outsider. Some of these institutions—the university and the hospital are the outstanding examples—simply have not done enough thinking on their own structure, their own principles, and their own direction to tell a student anything about themselves.

Business is no longer the one institution, as it was twenty-five years ago. But for those who want to understand large institutions, it is still the one to concentrate on.

Would it still be General Motors today, if one could pick a

company? After all, GM is a manufacturing business. And the businesses that have grown the fastest these past twenty-five years are not essentially manufacturing businesses, if only because the service and knowledge sectors of a modern economy are growing so much faster than the sectors that supply goods. GM is still essentially an American business, whereas the "growth businesses" have been "multinationals." GM is primarily an employer of blue-collar workers, whereas the growth of the labor force has essentially been in the knowledge work force. And GM is still a one-product business, by and large, whereas so many of the most rapidly growing businesses of the last twenty, and especially of the last ten years, have been "multimarket" businesses and "conglomerates."

And yet, I would still select GM for a study like this—precisely because it is a relatively simple company. Of course, twenty-five years ago, it seemed to be the very embodiment of diversity and complexity. GM was indeed the first of major organizations—whether business or nonbusiness—to organize systematically for the management of diversity and complexity. Yet it is, by comparison, a fairly simple business and therefore a business one can still organize on one principle and understand.

But above all, the attempt reported in this book, the attempt by General Motors to find the principles, the constitution, the concept of order and organization for a very big institution, is still essentially without parallel. No one else has done the job. What GM did—all of fifty years ago—is no longer adequate, as will be discussed in the Epilogue (1972) to this book. It is still, however, the only attempt we have. And if we want to study and understand the large managed institution, GM is still the model we will have to study—if only to be able to decide how to go *beyond* GM.

There is a good deal of talk today about "abolishing" large-scale organizations. It is going to remain talk. Mankind is in no mood to do without the fruits of large-scale organization, whether in education or in health care, in controlling the environment, or in producing goods and services. On the contrary, we can confidently expect a further increase in the "institutionalization" of society, simply because the tasks ahead of us, whether the environment or international order, are tasks which only large-scale organization can tackle. The job of this generation is not to abolish large-scale organization. It is to make it perform—for individual, community, and society alike. This job presupposes, above all, that we understand large-scale organization and know how to make it work. GM tried to do this fifty years ago. The attempt was admittedly a first and incomplete attempt. But it is, so far, the one attempt we have. And for this reason, the study which this book presented twenty-five years ago is, perhaps, even more timely, even more relevant, and even more needed today. We have to learn to manage and to control large-scale organizations. To be able to do this, we first have to understand them.

Claremont, California
January 1972

PREFACE TO THE ORIGINAL EDITION

ONCE upon a time a young man set out to write *the* definitive book on China. He prepared himself by studying all that had been written on the subject. He learned the language. And so great became his reputation as an expert on China that a publisher gave him a most advantageous contract and a big advance. Thus prepared, he landed in Shanghai one fine morning. He spent a pleasant day calling on some people who had been recommended to him as wise in the ways of the country and he was dined and wined wherever he went. He returned to his hotel late at night, but could not go to sleep. His head almost burst with ideas. Finally, in the false dawn, he got out of bed again to jot down a few of these thoughts. When he rose from his desk twelve hours later, he had a most comprehensive, most beautiful outline; the book was done except for the transcription of his mental shorthand. He only needed a few minor statistics on some unimportant point. "Well," said the young man to himself as he read over his outline, "one day's delay won't make much difference; I might as well get those figures tomorrow so that I won't have to interrupt my writing later on." That was forty-six years ago; last heard of the young man—now a very old man— was still looking up a few minor details and figures.

The subject of this book, the social and political problems of industrial society, is fully as big as China and even less known. My qualifications for writing it are vastly inferior to those of the young man in our story. Hence this study cannot and does not claim to be complete or conclusive. It touches upon far more topics than could be adequately treated within the covers of a short book, or be mastered and understood even by a man much better trained than the author. Yet it does not discuss enough topics to cover the field; and the omissions may well be serious enough to affect the conclusions. The subject is so ambitious as to make the author's attempts to deal with it appear journalistic; yet the book is not ambitious enough to do justice to the subject. The only excuse the author has is that the alternative to submitting to the public so sketchy an essay would have been to follow the example of our friend in China and postpone writing and publication if not forever, at least for a lifetime. This may well have been the preferable course. But it seems to me that we cannot afford to postpone any further the discussion of the fundamentals of our industrial society. There is no more urgent, no more immediate topic for America—and none which is less known and less discussed. This book does not attempt to give the answers; it hopes only to raise questions. It does not pretend to be *the* definitive book on the relationship between the big-business corporation and a free industrial society; it is an opening statement in what I hope will be a lively and fruitful debate.

*   *   *

My interest in the social and political approach to the problems of an industrial society—as distinct from economics —goes back a considerable time. Nevertheless I would not have been able to work out even this preliminary sketch but for an invitation received in the Fall of 1943. The General Motors Corporation asked me to study and to report on its managerial policies and organization from the standpoint of an outside consultant, in which capacity I served for eighteen months. This invitation not only made possible this study financially; it also made available to me the records and the plants of General Motors as well as the rich experience of its executives. Needless to say the opinions expressed and the conclusions reached in this book are exclusively mine, and do not reflect the opinions and conclusions of General Motors Corporation or of any of its officers. But it would be ungrateful not to admit how much clarity and understanding this book owes to members of General Motors' management in the central offices in New York and Detroit as well as in the manufacturing divisions. That the end of my investigation means necessarily the end of the close contact with this group which it has been my privilege to enjoy for almost two years, fills me with real regret.

I also want to record the great debt this book owes to many other friends—in the government service, in trade unions, in business, who abundantly gave of their knowledge and experience.

PETER F. DRUCKER.

Bennington, Vermont
January 1946

CONCEPT OF THE CORPORATION

CHAPTER ONE

CAPITALISM IN ONE COUNTRY

1

THIS book on the central problems of American industrial society rests on the one assumption that nothing could induce the overwhelming majority of the American people to give up the belief in a free-enterprise economic system except a major catastrophe such as a new total war or a new total depression. This does not mean that history will necessarily prove the American people right or make their beliefs prevail. But it means that there is only one course open to American political and economic statesmanship: the attempt to make a free-enterprise system work. For it is obvious that any attempt at organizing our economic and social system on another than the free-enterprise basis—either because the free-enterprise system fails to work or because it is considered undesirable—will introduce into American society a tension between political belief and social reality, between the will of the people and their actions, which would compromise our national unity and paralyze our political and economic faculties. The central questions of American statesmanship must thus be: how does the free-enterprise system function and what are its problems; what can it do, what can it not do; and what are the questions yet to be answered?

On America's ability to make the free-enterprise system work depends not only her stability at home but world peace. Peace in the postwar world will not rest, as it always has in the history of the modern West, upon the homogeneity of political, social and economic beliefs and institutions, transcending national boundaries, but upon the ability and willingness of radically different political and economic systems to live together peaceably. This—an unprecedented task—can only be achieved if each of the major countries can prove her particular system to be stable and successful. We have gradually learned that the ability of the Soviet Union to realize a stable and successful "socialism in one country" is the prerequisite for Russia's collaboration in the maintenance of the peace. Should she fail in this attempt she would have to resort to isolationism, world revolution or imperialist aggression; for every development anywhere except in the direction of a communist dictatorship would have to appear to her as a direct attack upon her national security. We will now have to learn that similarly the ability of the United States to participate in the maintenance of peace in a world of Great Powers based upon competing principles of political and social order, depends on our ability to create a successful, stable and confident "capitalism in one country." Thus to make our free-enterprise system function—as the basis of domestic strength and unity and as a model for others—is the most important and the most immediate contribution Americans can make to international peace.

In accepting this approach this book does not intend to become an apology for free enterprise. On the contrary, we shall often be a great deal more critical of the existing order than are its enemies. We shall demand of it not only the performance of economic functions but the discharge of heavy social and political tasks. But the purpose of this study is not to prove that free enterprise is good or bad but to find out the extent to which it does its job and the most promising line of approach for the performance of those jobs that remain to be done. And if only because the American people do so, we have to assume that free enterprise can function.

But what do the American people mean by "free enterprise"? The term has become so loose that even the American Communist Party in one of its giddy gyrations could declare itself in favor of "free enterprise." Yet, I think that it is quite clear, on the whole, what the people have in mind when they use the term. It does not exclude government regulation or government limitation of business; but it sees the function of government in setting the frame within which business is to be conducted rather than in running business enterprises. It does not, however, exclude government management or government ownership of natural monopolies or of industries producing exclusively for national use such as armament plants; it is quite obvious that the American people do not regard the Tennessee Valley Authority as incompatible with their belief in free enterprise, and that proposals for the nationalization of public utilities, railroads and even of natural resources, while not received too cordially, are not felt to violate a basic principle.

But public enterprise is seen not as the rule but as an exception that needs special justification and special safeguards. And outside of this limited sphere of public enterprise, business, according to the American tenet of free enterprise as popularly understood today, is to be in the hands of men who are neither appointed by the political authorities nor responsible to any political agency other than courts of law. And the productive resources of the country are to be owned privately.

The popular concept implies further the acceptance of profit as motivating and controlling business actions. It implies that the consumer decides what he wants to buy, and that prices are based on supply and demand in the market rather than politically determined. Finally included in the concept of free enterprise is the acceptance of the privately-owned, independently-managed corporation producing for profit goods to be sold on a competitive market. It is in this sense that the term will be used throughout this study; and it is out of this definition of free enterprise that the large corporation emerges as the focus of any study of American industrial society.*

---

* *NOTE ON TERMINOLOGY.* The phenomenon of an industrial society is so recent—or rather our awareness of it is so recent—that we have no generally accepted terms to describe its representative institutions. What we have to describe and to analyze is (a) the large technically integrated unit which our technology demands, and (b) the specific legal and economic institution in which the technological unit is organized, and by means of which it becomes effective socially and economically. The first of these is independent of the specific social, political or economic system of a specific country—it is a technological fact which is the same wherever and under whatever conditions modern industry exists. The second is determined by a country's specific political and economic order. The terms available and in general use are vague, misleading and full of emotional overtones. For the first concept we have the choice between the clumsy "integrated unit of large-scale production" and the emotionally charged "Big Business." In spite of all its obvious shortcomings this book will use the term "Big Business" consistently to describe the *physical* and *technological* unit of production, whether organized in a privately-owned corporation under a competitive free-enterprise system or as a goverment-owned trust as in Russia. I feel justified in this because the term, apart from being short and in common usage, means originally and literally what I make it mean. The emotional overtones are not in the term but were added by a half-century's struggle against abuses of modern industry.

Much more difficult was the decision on a term to describe the social and economic institution in which Big Business is organized under the American free-enterprise system. There is only one term in common usage: corporation. Usually it is quite clear what it means as in the title of the book by Berle and Means, *The Modern Corporation and Private Property.* It is also clear, however, that this use may be extremely confusing as the term has a very different legal meaning which is by no means extinct or confined to the legal profession. Berle and Means, for instance, do not intend to include the corner cigar stores in their discussion even though in many cases they are corporations. Nor do they mean to exclude a large business that—as may well happen—is owned by an unlimited partnership. We have no separate word, however, for the large-scale business enterprise—usually, if not always, owned in corporate form. Hence I find myself constrained to follow common usage and to use the term "large corporation" or "corporation" (wherever context permits the dropping of the adjective) in spite of its obvious shortcomings.

2

LESS than ten years ago it still seemed to be a vital issue of American politics whether to have Big Business or not. To-day the very question is meaningless if not frivolous. It has become obvious that no modern society can maintain its existence or independence except as an industrial society using modern industrial technology; and it is as true as ever that survival is the first law of any society. It has also become obvious that modern industrial technology requires some form of big-business organization—that is large, integrated plants using mass-production methods—for its operation. Therefore Big Business is something that must be accepted in any modern industrial country. It also has become clear that the large industrial unit is not just a concomitant of modern industrial technology but the very center of modern industrial society. The large industrial unit has become our representative social actuality; and its social organization, the large corporation in this country, our representative social institution. In other words, Big Business is the general condition of modern industrial society irrespective of the forms of social organization or the political beliefs adopted in particular countries. Even to raise the question whether Big Business is desirable or not is therefore nothing but sentimental nostalgia. The central problem of all modern society is not whether we want Big Business but what we want of it, and what organization of Big Business and of the society it serves is best equipped to realize our wishes and demands.

The fact that the large corporation has become America's representative social institution is often obscured in our political discussion today by that fallacy—so easily indulged in by democracy and so dangerous to it—which identifies the representative and determining with the numerical majority.

Thus, statements are current which try to explain the dominant position of the large corporations by asserting that they employ a majority of our industrial workers, that they handle the major part of our industrial production, control the bulk of the country's productive resources, etc. Of course every single one of these assertions is refuted by the most elementary statistical evidence which makes it very easy and seemingly plausible to assert that the large corporation cannot be the representative institution of our society because of its minority position.

But what determines the structure of a society is not the majority but the leaders. It is not majority behavior that is the typical behavior in a society but that behavior that comes closest to the social ideal; and that, by definition, can only be the behavior of a small minority. Only a minute fraction of the inhabitants of Victorian England were "gentlemen" in the social sense. What is more, the great majority of the people, the lower middle and working classes, would not have wanted to be "gentlemen." They very definitely refused to regard this social ideal as valid and as binding on them. Yet they not only accepted the leadership of the "gentlemen"; they expected members of their own class who had risen to positions of leadership, to become "gentlemen." What made the "gentleman" the representative type of Victorian England was his acceptance as such and his actual role in setting standards for the non-gentlemen, not his numerical weight.

What we look for in analyzing American society today is therefore the institution which sets the standard for the way of life and the mode of living of our citizens; which leads, molds and directs; which determines our perspective on our own society; around which crystallize our social problems and to which we look for their solution. What is essential in a society is, in other words, not the static mass but the dynamic element; not the multitude of facts but the symbol through which the facts are organized in a social pattern; not, in other words, the average but the representative. And this, in our society today, is the large corporation.

This assertion should have been self-evident even before the war; but the war has supplied proof beyond any doubt. Some time ago a statement was given wide currency in which a government official asserted that a handful of large corporations which, before the war, had controlled only a small part of America's production, had, during the war, managed to increase their share to almost three-quarters of the total. This statement was not only in flat contradiction to all the known facts; it also tried to prove its point by a statistical sleight of hand which came close to sheer demagogy.*

What was interesting was, however, not the statement but the fact that it was generally accepted even though its logical fallacy was so obvious as to be spotted normally at once by any adult reader. For it showed the general awareness of the fact that the war has brought out the large corporation as the representative institution of American society today. The only reason why the general public could be fooled by a statement purporting to prove that the large corporation had become first in quantity during the war was that the general public

---

* The statement itself ran as follows: "Before the war the largest American corporations handled about 30% of the nation's industrial production; the same corporations held 70% of the war contracts. Therefore Big Business doubled its share in the American economy during the war." Obviously this is on the level of the attempt of a grade school child to subtract three apples from four cows. In the first place, war business, even at its peak, never amounted to more than 50% of the national business; 70% of the war contracts thus equaled only 35% of the total national production at the most; and nothing was said about the development in the civilian sector of the economy in which, according to all evidence, the share of small business increased considerably during the war. Secondly, to hold a contract is not identical with production. As is generally known, a very substantial part of the war contracts held by the big corporations was subcontracted to medium-sized and small businesses; and every large corporation reported that it subcontracted a much larger share of its war-contracts to small and medium-sized firms than it used to do in peace times.

had already realized as a result of the war that the large corporation had become first in importance. The miracle of conversion to war-production was clearly wrought by the large corporation. The war showed that it is the large corporation which determines the limits of productivity of an economic system. It showed that it is the large corporation to which we must look for the lead in technological research and product improvement. In other words, the war made clear that it is the large corporation which determines the economic and technological conditions under which our economy operates. The large corporations do not employ more than a minority of industrial labor but their labor relations set the standards for the nation, their wage scale determines the national wage scale, their working conditions and working-hours are the norm, etc. While the large corporations do not control a majority of the nation's business, their prosperity determines the prosperity of the nation. If we talk about economic opportunities in America we have in mind above all the opportunities offered in the modern mass-production factory and the modern large corporation. If we talk about the American technology, we do not think of the statistical average but of the standard established by the leaders. If we look upon the two other new social institutions of basic importance that have emerged in our society during the last half-century, the labor union and the administrative government agency, we see that they are nothing but social responses to the phenomenon of modern Big Business and of the corporation. In fine, it is the large corporation—the specific form in which Big Business is organized in a free-enterprise economy—which has emerged as the representative and determining socio-economic institution which sets the pattern and determines the behavior even of the owner of the corner cigar store who never owned a share of stock, and of his errand boy who never set foot in a mill. And thus the character of our society is determined and patterned by the structural organization of Big Business, the technology of the mass-production plant, and the degree to which our social beliefs and promises are realized in and by the large corporation.

The emergence of Big Business, i.e. the large integrated industrial unit, as a social reality during the past fifty years is the most important event in the recent social history of the Western world. It is even possible that to future generations the world wars of our time will seem to have been an incident in the rise of big-business society just as to many historians the Napoleonic wars have come to appear incidental to the industrial revolution. Even today, there are observers who interpret the conflict between the ideologies of Western Democracy, Russian Communism and Fascism as primarily a conflict between different concepts of a big-business industrial society; and unless misinterpreted so as to make it appear a denial of the reality of the moral issues at stake (as does, for instance, Mr. James Burnham in his *The Managerial Revolution*, so widely read a few years back), this view makes a good deal of sense.

Certainly, the problem of the political, social and economic organization of Big Business is not unique to one country but common to the entire Western world. And this means that there is a wide area where it makes little difference whether we discuss conditions in the United States or in Russia, whether we assume a free-enterprise society, Communism or Nazism. For the entire realm of social engineering is an objective realm. Profit and profitability, for instance, fulfill the same function under any system of economic organization; they are respectively the risk premium and the yardstick without which economic life simply cannot go on. And it is therefore an objective question—at least from the point of view of business organization—what is more efficient as a basis for measuring profitability: a system based on a free market or cost-accounting based on planned prices?

Yet, social engineering alone determines nothing—except the limits of possibility. The question always remains to what purpose the machinery is to be used. The social engineer may, for instance, decide that profitability based on free-market prices is the most reliable yardstick; and his society may still decide to use the less reliable system of cost-accounting based on planned prices as the only one compatible with its social beliefs and purposes—which is precisely what happened in Soviet Russia. It is indeed the first question of any analysis of a social or political institution: what is necessary to make it function efficiently, to make it survive, to provide adequate leadership? For the first thing society demands of an institution is that it function. But also and at the same time we must ask what requirements must the institution fulfill in order to make society function and be stable? For the first thing the individual demands of his society is that it function. And both questions are only posed to enable us to ask: what is the purpose for which we want to use this institution and how does it fulfill it?

In this book we will be vitally concerned with social engineering; and that part of our discussion would be as applicable to Sweden as to the United States, to a Nazi trust as to a corporation in a free capitalist economy. But we shall focus not on general principles applicable anywhere at any time, but on the United States of today and tomorrow; not on business organization in general but on the large American corporation. Our problem is not just how Big Business functions but how the large corporation functions in America's free society. This is a new problem—it hardly existed before 1929 and was totally unknown before 1914. Hence we cannot demand a final answer—we should actually be highly suspicious of anything that pretends to be that. Promising approaches are all we can reasonably expect to find.

Our study has to start with the principles involved. Yet a discussion confined to the purely theoretical would be aimless and useless unless its conclusions were checked by, and applied to, an analysis of the concrete conditions of American social life. Therefore, this study of the corporation as our representative social institution is focused on the analysis of one specific corporation: General Motors.

There are several reasons why General Motors seems most suitable to serve as a representative example of the American large corporation. In the first place, it is the biggest industrial corporation in this country, employing in prewar times about two hundred and fifty thousand people, and twice that number during the peak of World War II. It is the largest unit in the automobile industry, which is the pioneer of modern mass-production industry and therefore most representative of the conditions and problems of modern industrial society. The main reason is, however, that General Motors—to my knowledge, alone of all American corporations—has for almost twenty-five years been consciously and deliberately working at basic problems of policy and has consciously and deliberately based its policy on the conception of the modern corporation as a social institution. Hence, the policy decisions of the General Motors Corporation, its successes, difficulties and failures, have a general relevance for American industry.

It is not intended to claim that General Motors has gone furthest in every single direction in the exploration of the social issues of modern corporate life. On the contrary, the management of the company itself would be the first to point out that, for instance, in employee training the Bell Telephone system has done the outstanding job, that many of the financial principles of policy control which play such an important part in General Motors derive from the experience of Du-Pont's, etc. But as the result of prolonged investigation, I have come to the conclusion that while other companies may have gone farther in specific directions, none has worked on the problem as a whole as consistently and has been as conscious of the central issues as General Motors. Hence, General Motors can be fairly considered as representative of the achievement, possibilities, problems and perils of the large corporation.

3

THE questions we shall deal with in this book are the traditional questions of politics and political analysis. What is new in this book is their application to the large corporation. Not that we do not have a tremendous literature dealing with business and industry. We have more material than any man can read—often of a high order—on economic problems such as monopolies, business cycles, prices, etc. We have a large and steadily growing literature on business management which has been freely drawn upon in this study; and while much of it deals with purely formal or with purely internal questions, the writings of such men as Chester I. Barnard, James D. Mooney and Ordway Tead, or the work done at the Harvard Business School have contributed greatly to our knowledge of the corporation as an organization. But neither the student of economic policy nor that of business management analyzes the corporation politically, that is as a social institution organizing human efforts to a common end. Our study, however, sees the essence and the purpose of the corporation not in its economic performance or in its formal rules but in the human relationships both between the members of the corporation and between the corporation and the citizens outside of it.

Any social and political analysis of an institution has to proceed on three levels.

It has to look at the institution as autonomous—governed by the rules of its own structure and determined by the desire for survival—capable to be judged in terms of its own purpose.

Every institution has to be analyzed in terms of the beliefs and promises of the society which it serves. Does the institution strengthen the citizen's allegiance to his society by furthering the realization of society's ethical beliefs and promises? This is particularly important if we deal with an institution which is central to a society as by this very fact its performance in the realization of the basic social beliefs and promises is regarded as indicative of the performance of society itself.

It has to analyze the institution in its relationship to the functional requirements of the society of which the institution is a part; what organization of the institution is most conducive to the survival and stability of organized society, and what conflicts exist between the purpose of the corporation as an autonomous body and the needs of the society in which it lives.

There are three main problems on the *first* level, that of the corporation as an autonomous institution. There is the problem of policy: An institution must have a long-term program and rules of behavior and operation. Yet its policies must be flexible enough to allow for adaptation to new problems and to changes in conditions. There is a whole complex of problems centering around the question of leadership: how to insure an adequate supply of leaders; how to train and to test them. Perhaps the most difficult and most pressing of these problems of leadership is that of the conversion of the specialized technician needed in the day to day conduct of business into the well-educated personality capable of judgment who is needed for the policy-making positions. Finally, the corporation needs an objective yardstick by which to measure the success of its policies and of its leaders—a yardstick appropriate to its business, yet independent of short-term business fluctuations and incapable of manipulation.

The *second* level of analysis is perhaps the most difficult and most important. It too deals with relations within the corporation but it projects internal relations against the broad canvas of social beliefs and promises. The corporation as a representative institution of American society must hold out the promise of adequately fulfilling the aspirations and beliefs of the American people. A conflict between the requirements of corporate life and the basic beliefs and promises of American society would ultimately destroy the allegiance to our form of government and society. Hence, we must analyze whether the corporation is satisfying these basic demands: the promise that opportunities be equal and rewards be commensurate to abilities and efforts; the promise that each member of society, however humble, be a citizen with the status, function and dignity of a member of society and with a chance of individual fulfillment in his social life; finally, the promise that big and small, rich and poor, powerful and weak be partners in a joint enterprise rather than opponents benefitting by each other's loss.

On the *third* level, finally, that of the relationship between corporate purpose and social function, we analyze the corporation in society. The central problem lies in the relationship between profit, which is the purpose of the corporation as an autonomous unit, and the maximum production of cheap goods, which is the purpose of the corporation from the point of view of society. Is there a clash between these two premises of purpose, as has been asserted in the traditional theory of monopoly or in the more recent juxtaposition of production for use as against production for profit? Or can the self-interest of the corporation be harmonized with the interest of society in the corporation? Connected is the question of social stability: is there anything in the rationale of the corporation that makes necessary and even likely the recurrence of economic crises?

The three levels on which we shall conduct our analysis of the problems of an industrial society are co-ordinated and equal in weight and importance. Neither of them has priority over the others. But while equal, the three levels are not independent. Failure to solve the problems on one level leads automatically and inescapably to collapse of the entire structure however brilliant the achievement on the other levels might be. In an industrial society in which the large corporation is the representative social institution, it is equally important and equally essential that the corporation be organized in such a way as to be able itself to function and to survive as an *institution*, as to enable society to realize its *basic promises and beliefs*, and as to enable *society* to function and to survive.

All too often this interdependence of the three levels on which society and social institutions function simultaneously is overlooked; and nothing is more common than the belief that a solution confined to the problems on one level will prove the social panacea. Indeed we would get around most of the problems of politics could we thus proclaim one of the fields of social life to be superior to the others. Nothing is simpler than to find perfect solutions on one level only; and nothing is more difficult than to establish a political "harmony of the spheres." In this difficulty lies the endless challenge and the endless adventure of true statesmanship.

The concept of harmony thus emerges as a basic concept of political action. The problems of political order and organization presented on each level of politics are indeed autonomous. But to have a functioning society they must all equally be answered by the same basic principles and policies. It would make social life impossible if the problems of one level could only be solved by means which were inimical to the best solution of the problems existing on the other levels. Such a society would be hopelessly torn and incapable both of survival and of the fulfillment of its basic ideals. For no society can give up the stability of its central institution, its own stability, or its own beliefs.

It follows from this that we cannot base a successful economic policy on the assumption that the interest of the corporation and the interest of society are in conflict—at least not as long as we have a society whose representative institution is the corporation. To justify the needs of corporate survival as "concessions" and as a "lesser evil" is really to give up the claim for a free enterprise industrial society. If the private profit system is necessary for the survival and stability of the corporation, it is a contradiction for believers in the free enterprise system to apologize for profits. And to demand—as do a good many apologists for the large corporation—of an industrial manager that he use, out of "social consciousness," policies which run counter to the interests of his corporation is rather ludicrous. At the same time it is impossible to look upon society's needs, whether functional or ethical, as "concessions" or as the "lesser evil"—the manner in which, for instance, social reforms and policies were justified during the Hoover administration.

This does not mean that the corporation should be free

from social obligations. On the contrary it should be so organized as to fulfill automatically its social obligations in the very act of seeking its own best self-interest. An industrial society based on the corporation can only function if the corporation contributes to social stability and to the achievement of the social aims independent of the good will or the social consciousness of individual corporation managements. In the ideal society even a Simon Legree, whatever the blackness of his heart, cannot but help to promote social ends either because it is to his interest to do so or because he is so integrated into society as to be able to act only in the interest of society.

At the same time the demand for harmony does not mean that society should abandon its needs and aims and its right to limit the exercise of economic power on the part of the corporation. On the contrary, it is a vital function of rulership to set the frame within which institutions and individuals act. But society must be organized so that there is no temptation to enact, in the name of social stability or social beliefs, measures which are inimical to the survival and stability of its representative institution. Failure to see this difference between the necessary task of setting the frame—genuine regulation—and violation of the functional requirements of society which, for instance, underlay Herbert Spencer's attacks on popular education, professional fire brigades and meat inspection as "socialism," is responsible for much of the confusion of our present day political thinking.

Harmony was the great discovery—or rather rediscovery —of nineteenth century laissez-faire, enabling it to overcome the sterility of both the eighteenth century political theory of "pure reason" and the eighteenth century practice of pure Machiavellism. It enabled the nineteenth century to develop at the same time the new beliefs and aims of secular democracy and the new institutions of the market system. But while laissez-faire proclaimed harmony as the basis of society, it made the fatal mistake of considering harmony as established automatically in nature instead of as the final end and finest fruit of statesmanship. To its emphasis on harmony, laissez-faire owed its tremendous vitality and attraction; even its enemies had to measure themselves against the promise of harmony which has remained, to this day, the conscience even of the dissenters. But at the same time, the fallacy of looking for harmony in nature instead of in organized society was responsible for the refusal of practically all practicing statesmen and business leaders to act according to laissez-faire. Above all this fallacy made it impossible to justify the laissez-faire system against those critics who concluded from the absence of harmony in nature the fallaciousness of making harmony the foundation of society.

As a result of the crude and fallacious naturalism of the laissez-faire doctrine, political thinking during the last 75 or 100 years has largely lost again the basic understanding of the meaning and necessity of harmony. It is not my purpose in this book to write a history of modern political thought. But as an aside—and hence in the technical language of political theory—I should like to mention that the two rival schools which have dominated our political life since 1850 have both given up the insight that the three levels of society are co-ordinated—all equally important, all autonomous and yet all dependent on each other. They have instead raised one level to first rank and subordinated the others to it. In *Idealism* the basic aims and beliefs of society became the only level of politics in the name of which the autonomy of individuals and of their institutions is denied. This leads inescapably to the denial both of the functional autonomy of institutions and of the ethical autonomy of the individual; and it makes enslavement, destruction and annihilation of the individual for the sake of the idea not only permissible but laudable. At the same time *Pragmatism*—and its European twins such as *Syndicalism*—threw out all concern with the aims and beliefs of society. Functional efficiency was raised to the rank of an absolute. This leads straight to a concept of society as permanently on the brink of civil war, to a concept of politics as a ruthless game played only for the spoils—*Who Gets What, When, How,* as a popular American textbook of government is called—and ultimately to a glorification of force as the legitimate ruler of society.

Today we know that neither concept is compatible with a free society. Both lead to totalitarianism; and in the ideological fanaticism and pragmatic cynicism of the Nazis both have found their final fulfillment. Today, therefore, it is the first job of the leaders of a free society to go back to the concept of harmony and to a philosophy of society which is neither monolithic nor pluralist but which sees the one and the many, the whole and its parts, as complementing each other. And in this country this means that both our statesmen and our business leaders have to find solutions to the problems of the industrial society which serve at the same time equally the functional efficiency of the corporation, the functional efficiency of society and our basic political beliefs and promises.

CHAPTER TWO

THE CORPORATION AS HUMAN EFFORT

1

ORGANIZATION FOR PRODUCTION

LIKE every institution the corporation can—and must—be analyzed in terms of the society it serves and in its relation to the individuals who constitute the society. But first it has to be understood in its own terms; in order to work for society and for the individual it must be able to function according to its own rules. Survival as an organization is the first law of the corporation as of any institution; and ability to perform its own purpose, to produce goods with the maximum economic return, is its first yardstick of achievement.

When we say that the corporation is an institution we say that, like any institution, it is an instrument for the organization of human efforts to a common end. This common end is not just the sum of the individual ends of the human beings organized in the corporation. It is a common but not a joint end. Though we have largely abandoned it in legal and political practice, the old crude fiction still lingers on which regards the corporation as nothing but the sum of the property rights of the individual shareholders. Thus, for instance, the president of a company will report to the shareholders on the state of "their" company. In this conventional formula the corporation is seen as transitory and as existing only by virtue of a legal fiction while the shareholder is regarded as permanent and actual. In the social reality of today, however, shareholders are but one of several groups of people who stand in a special relationship to the corporation. The corporation is permanent, the shareholder is transitory. It might even be said without much exaggeration that the corporation is really socially and politically a priori whereas the shareholder's position is derivative and exists only in contemplation of law. This, for instance, is the position taken in our bankruptcy laws which put the maintenance of corporate integrity above the rights of the shareholders. We would not have needed the experience of the Great Depression of 1929-39 to show us that society must insist on the maintenance of the "going concern" and must if necessary sacrifice to it the individual rights of shareholders, creditors, workers, and, in the last analysis, even of consumers.

It follows from this that the essence of the corporation is social, that is human, organization. This might appear like a redundant assertion. Actually for far too many people the essential in modern industrial production is not the social organization but raw materials or tools. In our popular concept of industry we suffer from a rigid economic determinism —the legacy of the early nineteenth century emphasis on natural resources as the determinant of the division of labor— and from a blind admiration for gadgets. As a result, most of us—including a good many people in industrial production itself—fail to understand that modern production, and especially modern mass-production, is not based on raw materials or gadgets but on principles of organization—organization not of machines but of human beings, i.e. on social organization.

This misunderstanding has very serious consequences. It is

to a considerable extent responsible for the labor problems of modern industry. And it hampers both the layman in an industrial society and the industrial manager in the understanding of their responsibilities as citizens. This book is not concerned with the principles of industrial production—only with the social problems of the industrial enterprise; and the author lays no claim whatsoever to competence in technical matters. Nonetheless it is so important to realize that even the *technical* problems of modern industry are not technical in the sense of gadgeteering but are primarily problems of *human* organization for a technical end, that a short explanation may be in order.

The experience which directly shows the true nature of modern mass-production was, of course, the American industrial conversion to war in 1942 and 1943. It has by now become clear that most of the experts in this country, including the majority of industrial engineers and managers, underestimated our productive capacity so completely in 1940 and 1941 precisely because practically all of us failed to understand the concept of human organization which underlies mass production. We argued in terms of *existing* raw-material supplies and *existing* plant capacity and failed to realize that we are capable of producing new raw materials, of designing new machines for new purposes and of building new plants in practically no time *provided the human organization is in existence.* Even today, when we have realized the potentialities of the mass-production principle we usually fail to see that it is a principle of organization that achieved the production miracle, and not a principle of gadgeteering.

Thus the popular story of a war production success usually read as follows: immediately after Pearl Harbor it became apparent that the Navy would need huge quantities of a particular weapon, say a carrier-based fighter plane. The

Navy had a very good plane, but before Pearl Harbor it had been produced more or less by hand, in batches of two or three, and by skilled mechanics in a small shop. Now it had to be turned out by the thousands. The XYZ Company which never had produced anything resembling planes, accepted the job. It took half a dozen of its plants which up to that time had been making lamp shades or buttons or assembled automobile bodies, moved in with a wrecking crew, cut its old machinery to pieces with blow torches, tore down the old buildings, the foundations of which were not strong enough, and built new ones, etc. In the meantime its engineers had designed the machine for the new job—here's where the gadgets come in. On May 20th the wrecking crews left, on June 1st the new machines moved in, on June 15th the first plane rolled off an assembly line geared to the production of two hundred planes a month.

This story or something like it was told a thousand times these last few years. It was even accepted as a fair description by people in industry who took a leading part in the conversion to war production. Yet it is a grotesque parody of the truth. Every detail in the story is correct enough—but all the important facts are left out. The wrecking of the old machinery, the new buildings, even the designing of the new machinery, were more or less incidental to the real problems and the real achievements of conceptual and human organization. First came the design—not of machines but of the plane as an assembly of identical and interchangeable parts. Then came the analysis of each part as a problem in mass production, as something that is being produced in a sequence of elementary and basic operations, performable fast and accurately by an unskilled or semi-skilled worker. Next came the task of merging the production of each part into a plant producing the whole—a task involving three distinct problems of organization: one of people working as members of a team to a common end, one of technical processes, one of materials-flow. Finally came the job of training thousands of new workers and hundreds of new supervisors many of whom had never seen the inside of a plant before. On those four pillars, design of the final product as a composite of interchangeable parts, design of the production of each part as a series of simple, repetitive operations, design of a plant to integrate human labor, machines and materials into one whole, and training in skills and in teamwork, rested every achievement of our war production.

Wherever, because of ignorance or urgency, the attempt was made to slight one of these four tasks of organization—and the temptation to do so was great as each of them is time-consuming and can be speeded only with difficulty—the result was failure to produce. For instance, in the example which I had in mind in describing the popular war-conversion story, the management tried to get around the job of designing step-for-step the production of every one of the many thousands of parts which would have taken at least six to eight months, which the Navy could ill afford to wait. Instead one of the planes was borrowed from the Navy and each foreman was asked to make his own designs directly from the actual part. This attempt was a complete failure; no plane was produced until each and every little part had been designed from the ground up and its production planned thoroughly. Once this was done, however, at a prodigious cost in money and time, planes were produced in large quantity and at a fraction of the cost of the old one-plane-at-a-time method of production.

Outside of mass production too it is organization, that is, the arrangement of human work on material resources according to a concept, which determines the social structure and economic function of an economic enterprise. That the machines and plants of a business are of very little value separately—for instance if they have to be disposed of in a bankruptcy sale—and that the real value-element is their arrangement and combination into a whole, is known to every accountant and every lawyer. That most modern inventions are not the result of a "flash of genius" but of the organized effort of a research organization working according to a plan laid out carefully beforehand, is also well-known. Incidentally the recent legal difficulties of squaring this reality of invention with the popular nineteenth century concept of invention as gadgeteering underlying our patent laws, is a good illustration of the difficulties arising out of the failure to understand that industry is based on organization. But while human organization is essential to all industry* and the characteristic that distinguishes industry from the craftsman's shop, it is the very basis, the very meaning of modern industry, particularly of mass-production industry. Mass production does not rest on the assembly line, the conveyor belt or on any other gadget or technique, but on a conscious, deliberate and planned order of relations between man and man, and man and mechanical process. The one thing in modern industry therefore that cannot be improvised but must be worked out carefully and beforehand is the social structure of the corporation.

In this respect the large corporation is in no way different from an army; it must have the equipment but also, as in the army, equipment is of no avail without the functional organization of human effort. And like the army or like any other social institution, the things that really count are not the individual members but the relations of command and responsi-

---

* This point is made with great force and felicity by Mooney and Reiley in their book *Onward Industry* (New York and London, 1931), to which I am indebted.

bility among them. To borrow a metaphor from modern psychology, an institution is like a tune; it is not constituted by individual sounds but by the relations between them.

It is this organization which the corporation must maintain and the survival of which is its supreme law. Of course the corporation is a human institution and thus incapable of ultimate survival. To prevail for even as short a historical period as fifty years or a century is so difficult for any man-made institution that the Catholic Church with profound wisdom points to its own survival over the ages as a proof that it has been instituted not by man but by God. But this only makes the problem of survival all the more urgent for any man-made institution such as the corporation, and makes survival all the more the measure of all its actions and decisions. Unlike man, an institution has no natural end, no natural life span, no "retirement age." It is always engaged in a race against time.

Leadership

As with every other institution, the survival and successful functioning of the corporation depends on the solution of three interdependent problems: the problem of leadership, the problem of basic policy, and the problem of objective criteria of conduct and decision. Of these problems the decisive one, particularly in the corporation, is the problem of leadership.

No institution can possibly survive if it needs geniuses or supermen to manage it. It must be organized in such a way as to be able to get along under a leadership composed of average human beings. No institution can endure if it is under one-man rule. Industrial dictatorship like any other dictatorship threatens the survival of the institution in the event—an inevitable event—of the dictator's death. It also leads inescapably to extreme factionalism within the institution as, in the absence of accepted criteria of legitimate succession, senior executives are forced to subordinate the welfare of the institution to the desire to be in the most advantageous position to seize the throne when it falls vacant. Moreover under one-man rule there will be nobody in the corporation who has had the opportunity to be trained and tested in independent leadership. The future of the institution is thus staked on the gamble that the right man will emerge from a fight for power rather than on the rational selection of a well-known and well-tested successor.

From these twin dangers, that of depending on the "indispensable" leader, and the danger of depending on one-man rule, follows first a demand for a constitution under which there is legitimate rule and legitimate and quasi-automatic succession to the rule. It must be clear who is in command and on what his title rests. It must also be clear and settled in advance from what group his successor is to come, on what criterion he is to be selected and who is to select him.

The second prerequisite for a satisfactory solution of the leadership problem is that the institution must be able to arouse the loyalty of its members. To produce leaders an institution must have an *esprit de corps* which induces its members to put the welfare of the institution above their own and to model themselves upon an institutional idea of conduct. No institution has solved the problem of leadership, no matter how good its formal constitution, unless it gives the leader a sense of duty, of the importance of his trust and a sense of mutual loyalty between him and his associates; for these enable the average human being—and occasionally somebody well below average—to function effectively in a position of trust and leadership. In other words an institution must be able to make useful the good and to neutralize or deflect the bad qualities in its members, to be able to dispense with the superman or the genius, and to organize a systematic and dependable supply of reliable leaders.

It is typical of the most successful and the most durable institutions that they induce in their members an intellectual and moral growth beyond a man's original capacities. The popular respect and reverence for the United States Supreme Court rests on the fact that appointment to the Supreme Court has time and again made model judges out of average politicians rather than on the assertion that justices are supermen. It is an old saying that the most astonishing feat of that most successful organization, the Catholic Church, is that it obtains the best leaders from the worst raw material. Whoever first made this statement certainly did not consider it a criticism but the highest praise. Similarly it was on this ability to bring out more than was in a man on which rested the strength of institutions such as the British House of Commons and of the Prussian Army. The corporation, to fulfill its function as the representative institution of industrial society—and it will not survive otherwise—has to solve the same problem of arousing loyalty to a code of conduct, of training and selecting not only men but their individual abilities. The efficiency of an institution depends both on the efficiency with which it organizes individuals for a community effort and on the extent to which it organizes man for his moral victory over himself.

Next, any institution has to be organized so as to bring out talents and capacities within the organization; to encourage men to take the initiative, give them a chance to show what they can do, and a scope within which to grow; and finally, to offer them rewards in the form of advancement and of social and economic standing which put a definite premium on the willingness and ability to assume responsibility.

Further, the solution of the problems of institutional functioning and survival depends on the ability of the institution to develop independent leaders below the top who are capable of taking top command themselves, and to devise a system under which succession will be rational and by recognized merit rather than the result of a civil war within the institution and of force, fraud or favoritism. This implies also—a very important point—that the institution must be so organized as to be able to test a promising man in an independent command while he is still young enough to learn and so subordinate that his failure will not endanger the welfare of the whole enterprise. Nothing is more dangerous, and nothing is more common than the appointment to the top command of a brilliant lieutenant whose emotional and intellectual capacities for an independent position have been neither developed nor tested.

Finally the problem of leadership also demands an organization in which power and responsibility are divided in balance between final authority and lieutenants, and between central management and executives in the field. Without strong central leadership no institution can itself be unified; but without a strong and autonomous local leadership, willing to assume responsibility on its own, no institution could properly function. The division of power is thus a problem which every institution has to solve.

In the modern corporation, the problem of leadership is not only more important than in other institutions, it is far more difficult. For the modern industrial enterprise needs many more leaders than institutions normally do, and of high quality. At the same time, it does not automatically produce leaders either in sufficient numbers or of sufficient quality and experience.

It is not generally realized that modern industrial and technological conditions have increased tremendously the demand for leaders. It may be said without exaggeration that there has never been an institution in which there is greater need for abilities and greater opportunities for them than modern mass-production industry. This follows from the very concept of mass production. This last war has shown that mass production is a method which can be applied to the most complicated and most precise as well as to the simplest product. It does not matter whether the producer has had any experience with the particular product he is asked to turn out; even if he has never heard of it before he can turn it out faster, cheaper, and more reliably than the experts who have worked in the field for years without, however, using mass-production methods. In other words, mass production is not a technique but a basic concept of industrial organization that is generally applicable. Its essence—to repeat what has been said before in different words—is the substitution of co-ordination and organization for individual skill. The skill of the individual craftsman is replaced in mass production by the understanding of a basic production-concept and the leadership qualities of the supervisor. Sure, there are far fewer supervisors than there used to be skilled workers; mass production can employ a high proportion of unskilled labor. But the ability and knowledge demanded of the individual supervisor is infinitely greater than the skill formerly needed by the individual craftsman. Intellectual energy like any other form of energy cannot be eliminated; and what is saved at the bottom must be added at the top. Moreover the ability needed by the supervisor is of a different and higher order than the skill of the individual craftsman. It requires a much higher degree of abstraction: the skilled craftsman of yesterday knew his tools, the foreman or superintendent of today has to know his principles. And he has to be able to apply these principles to the organization of men as well as to that of material, neither of which was expected of yesterday's master mechanic. At the same time, however, mass production can be learned whereas skill can only be acquired through years of experience.

Any statistical analysis of the development of American industry over the last thirty years would show a tremendous expansion in the number of managerial employees, especially of the middle ranks, together with a considerable increase in their individual incomes. And the process is by no means at an end. On the contrary, the war again increased the opportunities for advancement to leadership in mass production; and the postwar period should continue this trend. Indeed it may be said that the rate of industrial expansion in this country depends very largely upon our ability to recruit and train a sufficient number of potential leaders in mass production industry. The need for leadership has been growing almost geometrically while the production of experienced and tested leaders has shown a tendency to decrease with the expansion of modern mass-production industry.

It was perhaps the greatest asset of a small-business society that it provided adequate proving grounds for leaders while keeping the sphere of the individual manager so small as not to endanger society in case of failure. Hence a good many big businesses of today still look to small businesses rather than to their own organization for the supply of top management. This, however, is clearly not the solution; an institution which cannot produce its own leadership cannot survive. Hence it is the first problem of the large corporation to arrange intentionally for the leadership selection small business made automatically. To quote one of the leading authorities on this subject: "The most 'natural' opportunities (*to acquire* *experience in leadership*) at present formally available seem to me to be the small general business, political party work in communities and perhaps to a less extent, labor union leadership. These are insufficient sources for the supply of general leaders. Hence we need to develop the artificial methods of giving wide experience which are now attempted to some extent in large organizations." * This involves obviously two things: the development of the maximum of independent command at the lowest possible level and the development of an objective yardstick to measure performance in these commands.

The difficulties inherent in its nature which the large corporation has to overcome are fourfold. There is a tendency towards one-man rule and towards a system under which only one man—the President or the Chairman of the Board—is not confined within departmental lines but sees and knows the whole of the business. It is a situation not unlike that of a cabinet in which every member has departmental duties while only the Chairman—the President in the United States, the Prime Minister in England—has a view of the whole and responsibility for it. In England the dangers inherent in this situation have been overcome by the more or less formalized rule that a candidate for the Prime Ministership must have proved his qualities of leadership as leader of his party in Parliament, and his qualities as an administrator in the successful management of several ministries. Contrary to the intentions of the Founding Fathers no such requirements are imposed on a candidate for the American Presidency. That a President can be elected in this country without having given any proof of his ability either as a leader of men or as a maker of political and administrative decisions is probably

---

* Chester I. Barnard, president of the New Jersey Bell Telephone Company, in *The Nature of Leadership,*—p. 21 (Harvard University Press, 1940).

the most serious weakness of our political system. Nevertheless we have an approximation to such a requirement in the tendency to recruit Presidential candidates from the ranks of U.S. Senators or state governors who both hold independent commands though the first are usually without administrative experience and the second often without experience in national affairs.

In the modern large corporation, however, not even such one-sided test in, and acquaintance with, an independent command as is given by the governorship of a state or by a U.S. senatorship is necessarily available. Hence opportunities for such a command in which a man's abilities for leadership are tested and in which he acquires a view of the whole, must be created in the corporation.

In every large-scale organization there is a natural tendency to discourage initiative and to put a premium on conformity. Moreover, there is the danger in any large-scale organization for the older men at the top to be afraid and suspicious of talented or ambitious subordinates. Sometimes there is a fear that the young man is out for his superior's job; more often the subordinate's legitimate desire to do things his own way, to introduce new methods, etc., appears as an attack upon the older man's authority or peace of mind. The corporation therefore has to combat the danger of bureaucratic ossification and bureaucratic timidity. It must make it attractive and rewarding for the organization as a whole and for every one of its subdivisions to develop men of ability and initiative. It must encourage and reward leadership, offer chances for experience and training. Above all, it must make it clear to each supervisor and manager that the training and development of subordinates is a part of his duties. It must be made to be to the self-interest of executives to look upon their subordinates and potential successors as human assets whose maximum utilization is as important to the institution as is the maximum utilization of natural resources. To have trained a potential successor must become one of the achievements which qualify a man himself for promotion, instead, as it far too often is today, a stumbling block.*

Further, the big-business world does not, like a small business society, have an automatic and objective yardstick for a man's performance and achievement. In the small business society a leader was tested on a comparatively moderate level of responsibility and command by the objective yardstick of success in the market which, while not just, is at least beyond anybody's manipulation and therefore impersonal and objective. In the big-business corporation not one man, save at the very top, can normally be judged in terms of economic success in the market, as the contribution of the individual is too small in terms of the whole to be measurable independently. At the same time, the nature of business makes it both impossible and undesirable to have advancement and success made dependent on professional examinations or on seniority which in other institutions supply impersonal criteria. Hence there is a real danger that a man's ability and achievements be judged exclusively by subjective and personal impressions, which even with the best-intentioned management must lead to favoritism and must demoralize the organization. At the same time the fact that Big Business is not automatically equipped with the objective yardsticks on

* An interesting discussion of this problem is to be found in a paper read under the title "The Selection and Development of Executives in American Industry," by Edward R. Stettinius, Jr., then Chairman of the Finance Committee, United States Steel Corporation, at the Harvard Graduate School of Business Administration on September 17, 1936, in connection with the Harvard Tercentenary. While I feel that Mr. Stettinius' attempt to reduce the art of leadership and leadership-training to a manipulative technique would be likely to do much more harm than good, his discussion of the problem itself—especially his insistence upon human assets as the most valuable possession of any organization—is of fundamental importance.

which the small business society relied, also means that it does not automatically test a man in an independent command, except at the very top, that is, in a position in which failure might be disastrous. The large organization thus has the definite task of finding objective yardsticks for the abilities and achievements of junior executives and of finding means of putting them in independent commands at subordinate levels.

The final and perhaps the most difficult problem of leadership with which industrial society is faced, is that it does not automatically give that balance between specialist and generally educated person which is the essence of leadership. Management of the corporation requires a much greater degree of general comprehension and understanding than management of a small business. This is simply another way of saying that a corporation is an institution and no longer a mere tool. At the same time Big Business not only requires an enormous corps of highly specialized experts but puts a tremendous premium on specialization during a man's formative years. Moreover, the large corporation does not supply the almost automatic antidote to extreme specialization which the small business of yesterday gave. In a small firm or shop even the apprentice was forced by his contacts with his fellow employees and their work to see the business as a whole and to understand the points of view and the problems of other departments; also, the apprentice's advance or promotion would depend on his ability to work in some other place than the one he had been trained in. In Big Business, however, the organization is so vast that contacts outside of a man's specialty are almost impossible. The business seems to be so complicated as to stultify any attempt to see more than the individual's department. Finally, promotion is usually the result of progressive specialization. Hence it is possible in a large corporation to go up almost to the top without ever acquiring an understanding of the whole or an ability to think in terms of the whole. Yet at the same time it is essential for Big Business that its specialists be forced to become "generalists" as early as possible.

A professional army has very much the same problems as the large corporation. It too cannot automatically test a man in an independent command until he has reached such eminence that his failure would endanger the whole. It too needs a large body of specialists who at the same time must be capable of command, of general understanding and of decision. Finally, it too suffers from the natural tendency of its members to look upon an able subordinate as a threat to their own jobs. An army solves these problems by subordinating its entire peace-time organization to the one task of training and selecting leaders through the alternation of periods of formal schooling in a specialty with periods of commands, maneuvers, etc. But the corporation cannot subordinate its organizations to the needs for training. It must perform while it trains; the very means by which it trains its leaders must in themselves further the general purpose of its institutional life, that is, efficient production.

The Problem of Policy

Because the corporation is an institution it must have a basic policy. For it must subordinate individual ambitions and decisions to the needs of the corporation's welfare and survival. That means that it must have a set of principles and a rule of conduct which limit and direct individual actions and behavior. It must be possible for the individual who acts as an organ of the corporation to ascertain without much doubt whether his actions are in accord with the long-term interests of the corporation he serves. It must be possible for all members of the organization to obtain a final and binding decision on policies through a clearly defined procedure. Finally, the corporation, like any institution must have a constitution which clearly establishes authority and responsibility, both for the making of policy and for its execution.

This raises the problem of the proper balance between adherence to principles and adaptability to changing conditions. This is a particularly pressing problem in the large corporation which by definition not only operates in a medium subject to continuous change but is itself the leader of this change and without function except as the initiator of economic and technological progress. On the one hand, there is a real danger that rigid insistence on policy and precedent will stifle the spirit of adventure and initiative on which all business enterprise depends. On the other hand there is a real danger that speculation be mistaken for initiative. This applies especially as a profit arising from a vital improvement in productive methods looks just the same on the books as a profit resulting from a "flutter" in the stock market. Yet, one might be the making of the corporation, while the other might lead to its collapse. The corporation needs thus in the first place the means to distinguish between changes in economic conditions which are fundamental and to which the policy must adjust itself, and changes which are purely transitory and have to be handled on the basis of expediency. Secondly it needs a means to distinguish between apparent and real profit.

Another problem of corporate policy arises out of the necessary reliance on formal systems of accounting and organization which invites bureaucracy. The very fact that economic life is so insecure and changing puts a premium on the known and "safe." The large corporation often does not have the means to stop or even to discover the bureau-

cratic dry rot after it has set in. There are no critical outsiders such as, for instance, the cabinet ministers and par-
liamentary secretaries in England whose background and
approach are completely different from those of the Civil
Service. The top personnel of the corporation is recruited
from within the organization. If the organization has become
bureaucratic, the top people will have lost flexibility too—in
the same way in which bureaucratic dry rot extended through
the French Army of 1939. The premium on expert knowledge
contributes substantially to this danger because it puts emphasis on the "professional view" as does the isolated life which
the average managerial employee of the large corporation
often leads.

These problems can only be solved, if there is a policy
and somebody to make it. This implies first a definition of
the nature and function of policy as something that can be
isolated from the normal routine. Many corporations are like
the man who had never realized that he spoke prose; they
do not know that they have a policy. This ignorance is dangerous. It makes it difficult for them to know what they are doing
and why, and it also may lead them into making a sacred cow
out of a meaningless or obsolete rule by calling it "policy."
The same applies for the policy-making organ: it must be
clear who makes policy, how and on what basis.

This leads to the question of the relation between policy
and production, between policy-makers and administrators.
It also leads to the problem of the relationship between the
two basic—and often conflicting—concerns of policy: the
concern with the survival of the corporation as a smoothly-
functioning administrative unit and the concern with the purpose of the corporation as an efficient producer.

In every institution there is a latent conflict between the
long-term demands of policy and the day-to-day conduct of

business. Cutting across these lines there is always a latent conflict between the administrators who define efficiency in terms of the perpetuation of the administrative machine and the "doers" who define efficiency in terms of the aims and purposes for which the institution exists. These conflicts are not only inevitable, they are necessary; and no institution could function unless all four trends were equally represented. Yet no institution could survive unless these inherently conflicting forces are balanced. Hence, the corporation needs a supreme policy-making organ through which these conflicts are resolved.

The Yardstick

The purpose of the corporation is to be economically efficient: it must therefore be measured by a yardstick of efficiency, which means objectively, impersonally and independently of emotions or desires. At the same time the modern large corporation cannot rely without reservations on the yardstick of success in the market as it was developed under small business conditions. In the first place, this yardstick measures total performance and does not measure the performance of divisions and executives within the corporation; it does not automatically apply a gauge to leadership. Secondly, it does not automatically distinguish between profits resulting from changes in the competitive position of the corporation, and profits due to fortuitous circumstances. In other words, it does not supply an immediate or reliable gauge of efficiency and strength. What is needed, therefore, for the corporation is a yardstick that will eliminate the extraneous fluctuations from the evaluation of competitive achievement, and that will make it possible for the corporation to gauge on an impersonal and objective basis the performance of its executive personnel.

The first rule of the corporation as an institution is survival as an efficient organization of human efforts to the common end of most economical production. To this end it must have a policy which harmonizes the divergent claims of administrative and purposive rationality; which makes possible adaptation to change and rejection of pure expediency; and which makes possible individual local action by providing a yardstick and a framework. The corporation must be capable of finding all the talents and abilities in its organization; of developing them both as specialists, (that is as high-grade human tools) and as "generalists" (that is as educated people capable of judgment and decision) at the same time; of bringing out their best while neutralizing their weaknesses; and of testing their abilities for independent command at a level low enough to make failure harmless. The distribution of power and responsibility, the formulation of general and objective criteria of policy and action, the selection and training of leaders—these are the central questions of corporate organization.

2

DECENTRALIZATION

CAN the corporation satisfy these basic requirements of institutional life and by what means? This question we expect to be able to answer by studying the organization and the administrative policies of General Motors.

In this study General Motors is considered only as an example of the social structure and of the institutional problems of the big-business corporation. No attempt will be made to give a description of General Motors as such, or of its history—let alone of its products and results. However, an elementary knowledge of the main outlines of the organization and of its policies will be useful.

The domestic manufacturing properties of General Motors can be classed in three groups according to their main peacetime products. First in employment and volume of business comes the automobile and truck group: Chevrolet, Buick, Oldsmobile, Pontiac, Cadillac and General Motors Truck. To this group belongs also the Fisher Body Division, which produces the bodies for all automobile divisions and which works in closest contact with them. Most of the Fisher plants though managed separately by the Body Division, are physically combined with the assembly plants of the automobile producers.

The second group consists of the manufacturers of automobile accessories who produce most of the accessory needs of the automobile plants. A good many of the accessory producers sell also outside of General Motors. In addition to the spare parts and replacement business which is very important for practically all accessory divisions, some of them, notably the producers of spark plugs, roller bearings, ball bearings and electrical motors, sell directly to other industrial producers who in some cases account for more than fifty per cent of total sales. To this group also belongs Frigidaire—both historically and according to its manufacturing and engineering problems—which sells exclusively to the public.

The third group of manufacturing properties consists of three Diesel engine producers in Cleveland, Detroit and La-Grange, Illinois, whose products comprise small Diesel engines for trucks, marine Diesel engines, and the huge Diesel-electric locomotives which pull America's stream-lined trains. The Allison engine division producing aircraft engines also belongs in this group of non-automotive engine producers.

During the war General Motors added to these three main foci of activities a number of aircraft producing plants located on the Eastern seaboard; these plants which were under one management and organized in the Eastern Aircraft Division presented a special reconversion problem.

These three groups of manufacturing properties are organized in about thirty divisions ranging in size from Chevrolet and Fisher Body, which would be among the largest American businesses by themselves, to small one-plant appliance divisions, employing in peacetime less than a thousand men. Each of these divisions has its own divisional manager who is served by almost as complete a staff as if he were heading an independent business: production manager, chief engineer, sales manager, comptroller, personnel manager, etc.; in other words, each division is organized as an autonomous unit. The three largest of these divisions: Chevrolet, Fisher Body and Buick, are represented in the top management by their own divisional managers. The other divisions are organized in groups according to their products, each under a group executive who, as a vice-president of General Motors, acts as representative of his group in the central management of the corporation and as adviser and representative of central management for the divisional managers of his group.

Side by side with this organization according to products there is, as a part of central management, a set of functional service staffs: manufacturing, engineering, sales, research, personnel, finance, public relations, law, etc., each under its own vice-president. These staff organizations advise both central management and the divisional managers, act as liaison between the divisions and formulate corporation policies.

The "line organization"—the manufacturing divisions— is headed by the President and his two Executive Vice-Presidents; the "staff work" is headed by the Chairman of the Board who is the Chief Executive Officer of General Motors, and by the Vice-Chairman of the Board. These five officials form a team. They work through and with two closely co-ordinated committees, one on policy, one on administration. In addition to top management these committees contain the senior administrative and staff officers of the company, former officers now on the Board of Directors, and representatives of the major stockholders.

These two committees are the central organ of co-ordination, decision and control, and may well be called the government of General Motors. They pass on all major decisions in the fields of policy and administration. They hear periodic reports on conditions, problems and achievements in all branches of the business. And they are the court of last appeal should there be serious disagreements on policy within the organization. Hence all members of these committees— whether departmental executives in charge of service staffs or divisions, or members of top management—are almost automatically informed at all times about the work of all divisions, about all important problems and decisions in all fields, and also about the great line and the over-all policies of the company. These functions, integration of "staff" and "line," combination of a variety of experiences and special backgrounds into one policy, presentation of the over-all picture to all the senior men, may well be more important in the normal course of affairs than the decision-making power of the committees.

Each of these two top committees meets regularly to discuss and to decide. The actual executive work is, however, done by a number of specialized sub-committees, each in charge of a field such as engineering, labor, finance, public relations, distribution, etc. These sub-committees are very much smaller. They are built around a number of men from the field in question. The vice-president in charge of the appropriate service staff usually acts as the chairman. The membership includes experts in the field both from central management and from the divisions. But on each sub-committee there sit also several members of the top-management team and senior executives from other fields to balance the sectional viewpoint of the experts, to bring in a broader background of experience, and to relate the work of the sub-committee to the corporation as a whole. These sub-committees, in monthly meetings, actually work out the recommendations and presentations on which the two top committees act.*

---

* I have not come across much evidence that theories of governmental organization or historical examples had any considerable influence on the development of General Motors' managerial organization. The impetus seems to have been supplied mainly by experience and needs. Yet, there is a remarkably close parallel between General Motors' scheme of organization, and that of the two institutions most renowned for administrative efficiency: that of the Catholic Church and that of the modern army as first developed by the Prussian General Staff between 1800 and 1870 and later adopted everywhere. I tend to think that this scheme represents one of the basic solutions to the problem of institutional organization for survival and efficiency—the other one being the system of checks and balances between organs constructed upon contrasting

Neither this sketch nor an organization chart can, of course, show the outsider how the organization actually functions. But it should give some impression of the administrative and organizational problems that have to be solved in order to make it run efficiently. There is the sheer size of the business —250,000 workers in peacetime, twice that number during the war. There is a problem of diversity: not only do the finished products—over two hundred in peacetime—range from a Diesel-electric locomotive costing $500,000 to a bolt costing a fraction of a cent; the production units required range from gigantic plants with 40,000 employees to machine shops. There is a problem in autonomy: the five hundred men of ability, experience and ambition who are needed in major executive jobs in order to turn out all these different finished products of General Motors could not possibly be organized and managed from the top. There is a also a problem of unity: with the bulk of the company's products focused on one final utility, the automobile, and therefore directed towards the same market, the divisions could not be left to their own devices but must be one in spirit and in policy. Divisional management must be both autonomous and directed; central management must at the same time give effective, unifying leadership and be confined to regulation and advice.

General Motors could not function as a holding company with the divisions organized like independent companies under loose financial control. Central management not only has to know even minor details of divisional management but the top officials have to exercise the power, the prestige and the influence of real bosses. On the other hand General Motors could not function as a centralized organization in which all decisions are made on the top, and in which the divisional

---

principles of rule, for instance the one-man executive, committee-judiciary and many-men legislature of the American Constitution.

managers are but little more than plant superintendents. Divisional managers too must have the authority and standing of real bosses.

Hence General Motors has become *an essay in federalism* —on the whole, an exceedingly successful one. It attempts to combine the greatest corporate unity with the greatest divisional autonomy and responsibility; and like every true federation, it aims at realizing unity through local self-government and vice versa. This is the aim of General Motors' policy of decentralization.

Decentralization, as the term is usually understood, means division of labor and is nothing new. In fact, it is one of the prerequisites of any management whether that of a business or of an army. But in General Motors usage, decentralization is much more than that. In over twenty years of work, first from 1923 to 1937 as President, since then as Chairman of the Corporation, Mr. Alfred P. Sloan, Jr., has developed the concept of decentralization into a philosophy of industrial management and into a system of local self-government. It is not a mere technique of management but an outline of a social order. Decentralization in General Motors is not confined to the relations between divisional managers and central management but is to extend in theory to all managerial positions including that of foreman; it is not confined in its operation within the company but extends to the relations to its partners in business, particularly the automobile dealers; and for Mr. Sloan and his associates the application and further extension of decentralization are the answer to most of the problems of modern industrial society.

The Aims of Decentralization

Because General Motors considers decentralization a basic and universally valid concept of order, I asked several General Motors executives—particularly men well below the top —what in their opinion decentralization seeks to achieve. The following is a summary of the views of a good many different people. One man gave an unusually full statement of what he believed to be the aims and achievements of the policy of decentralization that was of particular interest because he himself had joined General Motors only two years earlier after a distinguished career in another big business organized on radically different lines; his statement—completely unrehearsed as my question was sprung at him in the course of an informal chat—has therefore been regarded as particularly valuable.

We shall have occasion later to discuss the question how much of its program decentralization actually realizes; here are the advantages claimed for it:

(1) The speed with which a decision can be made, the lack of any confusion as to who makes it and the knowledge of the policies on which the decision is based by everybody concerned.

(2) The absence of any conflict between the interests of the divisions and those of General Motors.

(3) The sense of fairness in dealing among executives, the certainty that a good job will be appreciated, the confidence and feeling of security that comes when personality-issues, intrigues and factionalism are kept under control.

(4) The democracy of management and its informality. Nobody throws his weight around, yet there is never any doubt where the real authority lies. Everybody is free to criti-

cize, to talk and to suggest; yet once the decision is taken, nobody tries to sabotage it.

(5) The absence of a gap in the executive group between the "privileged few" and the "great many." "Mr. Wilson (the President) could not arrogate to himself any right he does not accord to his associates."

(6) There is a very large management group. Thus there is always a supply of good and experienced leaders, able to take top responsibility.

(7) Decentralization means that weak divisions and weak managers cannot ride for any length of time on the coat tails of successful divisions, or trade on their own past reputation. "At the company I came from [this from the informant mentioned above] nobody ever knew whether the foundry was run efficiently or not, whether our foundry manager was a good or a bad manager; the foundry costs were centrally merged in the general costs. In General Motors, this foundry would be a division, so that the costs and the results of foundry operations would at once be visible to everybody."

(8) Decentralization means the absence of "edict management" in which nobody quite knows why he does what he is ordered to do. Its place is taken by discussion and by policies which are public and which are arrived at as a result of the experiences of all the people concerned. "Perhaps my greatest surprise when I joined General Motors [so again the above-mentioned informant] came when I attended my first 'Sloan meeting' [see below] and saw the extent to which even minor executives are informed of the reasons for company policies, and are encouraged to speak their mind freely and to express their opinions, however much they disagree with central management. In . . . . [the company where my informant had spent twenty years and where he had risen from apprentice to chief engineer] even senior executives

were never told the reason for any central management decision."

It is obvious from this summary—as indeed it was obvious in my talks—that the executives of General Motors do not only consider decentralization to be the correct concept for the organization of a big business but that they feel that, at least on the level of top management, the concept has been realized and its aims achieved.

Central and Divisional Management

Decentralization, as said above, is not considered as confined to top management but a principle for the organization of all managerial relationships. It was developed, however, out of the problems of co-ordinating central and divisional management into one whole. It has been tested most thoroughly on the top level of General Motors; and it has been most generally accepted and most successful on this level. Hence we shall study the meaning and the effects of the policy of decentralization by analyzing the relationships between central and divisional managements.

Central management has twofold functions under a system of decentralization. It is at the same time the servant of the divisional managers, helping them to be more efficient and more successful in their autonomy, and the boss of the corporation. And in this role it has to weld several hundred aggressive, highly individual and very independent divisional top executives into one team. These two jobs are apparently contradictory but actually interdependent. Their solution is attempted in various ways: (a) through the power of central management to set the goals for each division and for the whole corporation; (b) through its power to define the limits of authority of the divisional manager and through the power to appoint and remove divisional managers; (c) through its constant check on divisional problems and progress; (d) through relieving the divisional manager of all concern with problems that are not strictly part of the process of production and selling; (e) and finally through offering him the best obtainable advice and help through the service staffs of central management.

(a) The manufacturing program of the various divisions has to be approved by central management, particularly as far as the car divisions are concerned; central management sets the price range within which Chevrolet, Buick, etc. operate. Beyond this range they cannot go without specific authorization. But no attempt is made to prevent Oldsmobile, for instance, from trying to displace the low-priced Buick car. No attempt is made to tell Chevrolet what prices to pay the Fisher Body Division for its bodies. No attempt is made to force any of the car divisions to buy its accessories, such as lamps, from one of the General Motors divisions if the manager of a car division can show that he can get better value elsewhere.

Similarly in respect to the Diesel divisions, it is central management that will have to decide whether the overlapping production programs of two of these divisions—the result of historical developments antedating their acquisition by General Motors—are to be maintained or whether each division is to specialize on one type of engine.

Central management not only delimits the divisions against each other, it fits them into a general pattern as part of the unified corporation. It establishes the general over-all aim and allots to each division its role on the team. It establishes a total production goal on the basis of an analysis of the economic situation and assigns to each division its minimum quota. It determines how much capital to allot to each division.

Above all, central management thinks ahead for the whole Corporation. It is thus differentiated from divisional management not only in power and function but in time. A good divisional manager is fully as much concerned with the future as with the present; indeed one way to distinguish a divisional manager from divisional employees—some of whom, such as the managers of a few large plants owned by the big divisions, have many more people working for them than the manager of a small division—is by the divisional manager's responsibility for the long-term future of the business he runs. But it is not his responsibility to decide in what direction his division should develop; that is the responsibility of central management however much it may rely on the advice of divisional management. It is also the responsibility of central management to foresee problems and to work out solutions in advance. Central management furthermore works out major policy decisions applicable to problems common to all divisions. Finally, it decides on expansion into new lines—for instance on the expansion into the Diesel field, on the acquisition of new properties and the establishment of new divisions. *Of all the functions of central management, this responsibility to think ahead is perhaps the most important as it more than anything else makes General Motors a unified institution with but one purpose.*

(b) Central management determines the limits within which the divisional manager operates. Within General Motors this is usually expressed by saying that central management makes policy decisions, while the divisional manager is in charge of administration. This is, of course, a misunderstanding. Every executive down to the lowliest assistant foreman makes policy decisions; and every executive, up to the Chairman of the Board, has administrative duties. But central management determines both the areas of decision for the divisional manager, and the general rules to which his decisions have to adhere. To phrase it in terms of constitutional law, policy decisions of a divisional manager must rest on an explicit or implicit delegation of policy-making power and must conform to implicit or explicit commands or be *ultra vires*.

And behind this, as an ultimate recourse, there is the absolute power of central management to remove a divisional manager and to appoint a new man in his stead. Obviously it is a rare and grave decision to dismiss the manager of a division, and it is regarded as most important by central management that it should be taken not on the basis of a personal impression regarding the man's ability and achievement, but on the basis of objective records. But this is voluntary self-restraint on the part of central management which does not affect its unquestioned final power of removal.

(c) More in evidence in every day business conduct is the control through contact which central management exercises over divisional managers. Largely this is informal and a question of advice, discussion or mutual respect built up over years of collaboration. The vice-president in charge of a group of divisions, for instance, has a very real power; but it is rarely, if ever, exercised in the form of orders. Rather it makes itself felt through suggestions made in discussing problems or achievements of the division, in discussing central-management decisions, or as a result of the respect the divisional manager has for a man who, as is usually the case, has successfully been a divisional manager himself. The same kind of informal but very real control is exercised by the sub-committees of the Policy and Administration Committees with whom managers discuss their problems, plans and policies, and, as will be discussed later, by the service staffs.

However there is a formal safeguard of central-management control, a formal veto power on all capital investments beyond a certain limit and on the hiring of executive personnel beyond a certain salary. This veto power is rarely exercised as a divisional manager is unlikely to make such a proposal without the support of his group-executive and of the appropriate service-staff. But it has the important result that practically every major policy decision of the divisions has to be discussed extensively with central management.

Equally important is central management's role in helping the divisional manager to be as effective as possible.

(d) To this end the divisional manager is relieved of all worry over financial matters. As president of an independent company, he would have to spend a great deal of his time in obtaining the capital necessary for expansion. This worry is taken off his shoulders completely. It is the job of central management to obtain the capital for him for any program that has been decided upon as desirable. The same holds for legal matters. Also, General Motors has a uniform accounting system supervised and managed centrally. Finally, most union contracts and all negotiations in labor matters are handled centrally by a staff of the Corporation under a vice-president; this is, however, not the result of a decision to relieve the divisional manager of a worry only incidental to the business such as underlies the centralized handling of financial, legal and accounting matters, but is the result of the demand of the United Automobile Workers Union for a uniform contract for the company; and the wisdom of such a centralized labor policy is hotly debated within the Corporation.

(e) Finally, the divisional managers are served through the service staffs of central management. Their first function is to advise the divisional manager whenever he feels in need of such advice. It is, for instance, quite customary for a newly appointed divisional manager to come to the Detroit office to obtain advice on the distribution of the bonus (see below) within his division. During the war the manufacturing staff at Central Office worked out the basic manufacturing processes for many war products upon the request of the divisions; it is typical however of the way these staff agencies work that the final details of production and improvements in working methods were left entirely to the division.

Another important function of the staff agencies is to act as liaison between the various divisions, and particularly as centers of information on new or improved methods. If, for instance, one division has worked out a new way of treating cast aluminum which cuts down costs by five per cent, the other divisions interested in this or similar problems will at once be informed by the service staff. In this way, the service staffs attempt to make sure that all over General Motors the most advanced methods are used. In the same way, information about new problems that have arisen in one division and about difficulties to be encountered with a new product, a new method or a new labor policy is collected and transmitted to all the other divisions to save time and avoid costly errors. Similarly, the staff experts make available to the divisions the most up-to-date methods developed outside of General Motors, whether in research, in merchandising, in the handling of public relations, etc. This service function of central management alone probably is worth considerably more to the divisions than the one-half of one per cent of turnover that is charged by General Motors for the upkeep of the entire central management.

It should be emphasized that the staff agencies in their relations with the divisions rely on suggestions and advice, and that they have no direct authority whatsoever over the divisional manager and his policies. Of course they might appeal to top management in a last attempt to force an obstructionist divisional manager into line; this, however, is a theoretical rather than a practical recourse. In the normal course of events the service staffs have to "sell themselves" to the divisional manager, and have to rely on their ability to convince the divisional management and on their reputation and achievements. No divisional manager is under compulsion to consult the service staff or to take their advice. Yet the relationship between service staffs and divisional managers is on the whole quite frictionless.

Just as the service staffs apprise the divisional management of all important developments outside of his own division, they inform central management of all important developments within the divisions. To the service staffs—though not exclusively to them—central management owes its knowledge of the details of production, engineering, distribution and personnel management throughout the business, which is one of the most important factors in the teamwork between the policy-makers at the top and the administrators in the division.

Finally, it is the job of the service staff to formulate future policies in closest collaboration with both divisional managers and central management. The staff agencies themselves cannot lay down policies; they can only recommend. They must convince both the central management dealing with broad problems of corporation policy and the divisional managers with their concrete tasks, before any of their recommendations will be accepted as general Corporation policy.

Like any formal analysis of a functioning organization this description fails to convey what is really the most important thing: the way in which the organs of central management work. It gives only an outline of the frame within which central management operates, and not the picture itself. When we turn to the *divisional manager,* we cannot give even the frame. The nearest description of his status and operations might be to say that within the limits of policy and decision set for him by central management, he operates on his own as the boss of his outfit. He is in complete charge of production and sales. He hires, fires and promotes; and it is up to him to decide how many men he needs, with what qualifications and in what salary range—except for top executives whose employment is subject to a central-management veto. The divisional manager decides the factory layout, the technical methods and equipment used. He works out the capital requirements of his division and plans for expansion and for new plants—though central management must approve of major investments. The divisional manager is in charge of advertising and public relations for his division. He buys his supplies independently from suppliers of his own choice. He determines the distribution of production within the several plants under his jurisdiction, decides which lines to push and decides on the methods of sale and distribution. He makes contracts with dealers and gives or cancels their franchises. In everything pertaining to operations he is as much the real head as if his division were indeed an independent business. According to the estimate of several divisional managers—corroborated by members of the central management—ninety-five per cent of all decisions fall within his jurisdiction.

But this description, while correct, fails to convey one intangible though very significant fact: the atmosphere of a team of which the divisional manager is a member. There is no "General Motors atmosphere" and very definitely no "General Motors type." In fact I am greatly struck by the difference of atmosphere between divisions, and by the variety of personality and background between individual divisional managers. This variety is not only permitted, it is definitely encouraged by central management; for it is held that every man will do his best job when he does it his own way, and that each division will do its best job when it feels a pride in its tradition, manners and social climate. Hence central management refrains as much as possible from telling a division how to do its job; it only lays down what to do. Yet the divisional manager, though left alone as long as he does a good job, is conscious of his place on a team.

This is largely the result of two broad policies which will be discussed later in some detail: the system of impersonal yardsticks by which the performance of divisional managers is measured objectively in terms of their contribution to the team, and the interchange of factual and personal knowledge by which the divisional managers are kept informed of their place in the team, and of the work of the team. But the dual position of the divisional manager as being at one and the same time the autonomous boss of his division and a member of a unified team shows best in the administration of the General Motors Bonus Plan—which in itself is an important reason why this dualism works without too much tension.

General Motors sets aside each year a considerable part of its net profit for bonuses to executive employees, to be paid in General Motors shares (during the last years a cash alternative has been offered for part of the bonus to enable the recipients to pay wartime income taxes on the bonus without having to sell General Motors stock; this is, however, considered a temporary expedient). Top management decides how much bonus each divisional manager is to receive as his own personal compensation. It also decides the total to be allotted to each division for distribution among the employees below the rank of divisional manager. While guided by a formula expressing both the total results of the corporation and an appraisal of the results of the division, central management is independent in these decisions. Who is eligible for participation in the bonus is also decided centrally for all divisions; participation is usually confined to men above the income level of a general foreman. Finally there is a definite and strongly recommended pattern of bonus distribution. The more important a man's position the greater should be his stake in the profit; while bonuses in the lower ranks of management should be a relatively unimportant "extra," bonuses of higher executives should be a major source of income though very elastic.

But within these general rules and recommendations the divisional manager decides how the bonus is to be distributed among his subordinates. He may single out one department for a special award or penalize another. He may reward or penalize individuals. To safeguard against arbitrary or partisan decisions he has to obtain the approval of central management before he can make radical departures from precedent, and has to explain his reasons. Once approved, however, his decision is final.

For General Motors executives, particularly for the senior men, the bonus is in normal years a very important part of their income. Hence the power of the divisional manager to decide on its distribution makes him the boss in a very real sense though the general rules and the veto power of central management over the plans of the divisional manager make it difficult for him to be arbitrary or spiteful or to play favorites. At the same time the stake the divisional manager himself has in a bonus which represents both the results of his own division and the results of the whole business, tends to give him a strong incentive to do his best in running his division and to play a co-operative part on the team that is General Motors.

The bonus enables the divisional manager to be both independent and a member of the group. Under normal business and tax conditions the divisional manager even of a small division should become in a few years a moderately wealthy man, if he keeps his bonus stock as he is strongly urged to do. Thus he will soon be financially independent. He need not hesitate to express his own opinion, to object to corporation policy, or to run his own division his own way; for he does not have to keep his job at all costs, nor does he regard himself as in any way inferior to the men in central management; they may be much wealthier than he is but the difference is one of degree rather than one of kind. At the same time his prosperity is directly bound up with the prosperity of General Motors, the shares of which are usually his major asset. It is not a decisive factor in the working of the system of decentralized management that the executives of the company are the largest individual (that is non-corporate) shareholders as a result of the bonus plan, and that General Motors shares are the major assets of most of its executives; but it is important.

A Two-way Flow

Division of powers and of functions, unity in action—this definition of a federal union would be a fairly accurate description of the aim of General Motors' policy of decentralization. Such a union cannot rest on blind obedience to orders. It must be based on an understanding of each other's problems, policies, approaches, mutually between central management and divisional managers. Every one must not only know what is expected of him but also how his neighbor will act and why. It is a problem which all large organizations have to solve. Concretely, General Motors could not function if every decision had to be approved by a few overworked men in New York or Detroit. At the same time, it could not function if these men at the helm did not know of every major move within the business. Similarly, it could not function if the divisional managers had to determine basic policy at every step; and it could not function if they did not know and understand policy decisions and the reasons behind them. The first requirement of General Motors' management is, therefore, that as many of its executive employees as possible understand the policies, the problems and the program of the company and of its divisions. Both information and decision must flow continually in two directions: from central management to the divisions, from the divisions to central management.

We have already mentioned some of the devices used. The vice-president in charge of a group of divisions acts as a constant liaison on policy and performance between head office and division. The service staffs provide liaison in the technical fields not only between central management and divisions but between the divisions themselves. The sub-committees through which top management works have members from the divisions and call in divisional executives all the time to advise and be advised. In addition, there are special meetings to create common understanding, which are being held twice a year in Detroit under the chairmanship of Mr. Sloan, and at which important or acute problems are discussed. At these meetings the results of the various divisions are also shown and reasons for success and failure are discussed. Suggestions from the divisions or from central management are brought up for debate and unplanned but effective personal contacts are established between central management and divisional personnel. About two to three hundred people attend these meetings regularly; an equal number is invited in rotation. Thus practically every senior employee—beginning perhaps at the level of plant superintendent—has an opportunity to see the business as a whole, to see his place in it and to familiarize himself with the basic policies and the program of the company.

These meetings have been held for more than ten years and have been singularly successful. However, the group was felt to be too large to establish the personal contact between central office and divisional personnel that is necessary for the general understanding of policies and problems on which General Motors depends. Therefore the "Sloan meetings" in Detroit are now being supplemented by smaller meetings in the various centers of production in which members of the central management meet for several days with local executives of the divisions. The attendants at these meetings include all the people who are invited to the "Sloan meetings" and a number of lesser employees from the local plants and offices. Similar meetings are being held with dealers.

By these means managerial employees of the corporation are kept informed on policies and problems: they are also constantly brought into the determination of policies. No important policy decision is made without consulting the divisional executives affected by it. It is the right as well as the duty of every managerial employee to criticize a central management decision which he considers mistaken or ill-advised. In fact, the one definition I could obtain who is considered an executive in General Motors was: "A man who would be expected to protest officially against a policy decision to which he objects." Such criticism is not only not penalized; it is encouraged as a sign of initiative and of an active interest in the business. It is always taken seriously and given real consideration.

Central management does not of course base its decisions on the votes of the divisional personnel. It may completely disregard the opinions of divisional management. But in turning down a divisional executive it will attempt to explain to him its reasons. It is a standing rule that central management is to rely on persuasion and on rational proof rather than on an order. In debatable matters central management often prefers to wait until the divisional managers have themselves come and requested a policy decision rather than dictate from the top.

An example may illustrate the nature of this relationship. Several years ago, it was laid down as a general policy that all foremen should be on a salary basis rather than on hourly pay, and should enjoy seniority in layoffs over all hourly workers. During the war the number of foremen doubled. The new foremen were given the same status as the old foremen, lest they feel deprived of the relative security of seniority and thus in a worse position than the hourly workers in the event of a postwar depression. This decision was seriously attacked by several divisional managers who felt that it demoralized the old foremen who should be distinguished in some way as the permanent supervisory force of the company. The divisional managers brought their argument before the central management which at once agreed to reconsider the whole matter.

On the other hand central management does not hesitate to interfere directly and even ruthlessly whenever the interests or policies of the business are at stake. There is perhaps no greater contrast than that between the consideration shown to a divisional manager in all matters pertaining to the management of his division, and the co-operation expected of him in all matters where his conduct and policies directly affect the company as a whole. It is precisely here that the General

Motors concept of central management functions pays its highest dividends. Because policy matters are usually discussed well in advance of the time when they become pressing, they can be handled leisurely and discussed freely and carefully. This, it is claimed, makes it possible to give all concerned a chance to think things through and to speak their minds without causing dangerous delay. Above all it makes it possible for central management to acquaint itself with the views of divisional management and vice versa. As a result when the time comes to put the policy into action everybody should know what he is supposed to do and why; every divisional manager should not only know where general policy begins and his autonomy stops but he should also accept the general policy as something he has helped formulate. Thus the question whose responsibility a certain decision is, will arise rarely, if ever.

Freedom and Order

The impression that emerges from an analysis of the aims of General Motors' policy of organization is one of great individual liberty in which every man—at least among the three to five hundred first- and second-line executives—is to be allowed as much responsibility as he is willing to assume. There is little emphasis on title, rank or formal procedure. Indeed, the one thing that is most stressed by all executives is the "informality" that exists in the relationships among the members of this group and in the division of their work. This raises the question how General Motors avoids the dangers which according to age-old experience threaten every federal and especially every committee form of government: the danger of a deadlock between co-ordinated organs, the danger of a break-up of the organization in factionalism, intrigues and fights for power. It has always been a basic axiom of political theory that freedom such as General Motors accords to the members of its top management group, is only possible within a clearly defined order with a strict division of authority and responsibility. General Motors, however, seems to lack largely what might be called a clear division of powers. Yet decisions must obviously be arrived at without too much delay or uncertainty as to who is entitled to make them, so as to enable the corporation to function in a highly competitive market. The question thus arises what it is that makes this "informality" possible. Can it be based solely on good will and on good intentions? Or does it require a strict frame of objective policy as a condition of individual freedom? This, needless to say, is not a new but a very old question of politics—known in this country perhaps best as it appears in the conflict between Jeffersonian and Hamiltonian ideas of politics.

There is a tendency within General Motors to explain its functioning as owing to human individual good will rather than to institutional structure. There is a good deal to back up such an explanation. There can be no doubt that the informality, the reliance on information and persuasion, and the absence of "edict management" reflect accurately the personality of the man who developed General Motors to its present position—Alfred P. Sloan, Jr., for more than twenty years its active head. It is also certain that without Mr. Sloan's personality the system could never have grown up and established itself. Yet the tendency which underlies this "personality" explanation, to seek the basis of a political order in the personality of the ruler or in the good will of the citizens, is actually a very dangerous one. That it is current within General Motors is a potential weakness as it implies a lack of understanding by the organization of the factors from

which it derives its strength. If it were true that the General
Motors' system rested on individual good will, it could hardly
survive the life span of one man. It would also have validity
only for an organization headed by one particular type of
personality and could not be regarded as a general model of
industrial organization, which is precisely what General
Motors aspires to be. Finally—and this is probably the most
dangerous point for General Motors itself—such a belief
might lead to a false sentimentalism, which evaluates executives according to the lip-service they pay to humanitarian
principles, rather than according to their achievements.

Actually, General Motors' decentralization does not rest on
the good will of the men in top management positions. It
could, if necessary, function without the personal qualities
which Mr. Sloan has shown in his long administration. Indeed it has been functioning with senior executives whose
personalities were the very opposite of his, and who had
nothing of the informality and of the respect for their fellow
workers which would seem to be required. There must thus
be an objective, impersonal frame of reference to make possible if not mandatory the freedom of decentralized management. This objective frame is given in the use of modern
methods of cost accounting and market analysis as an impersonal yardstick to measure achievement of both policy-makers
and production men.

This objective yardstick is comprised of two sets of measurements which apply equally to divisional management and
its subordinates and to central management and its policy
decisions: (1) Base pricing which gives an objective measure
of the efficiency of the Corporation and of its subdivisions as
a producer; (2) Competitive market standing which shows
automatically and immediately the efficiency of the Corporation as a seller. Together these two gauges are supposed to

show over-all efficiency and supply an immediate and objective check on decisions and policies.

The function of the system of base pricing is to measure the productive efficiency of all units of the business and also to eliminate from the measurement of productive costs all extraneous and transient factors, particularly those introduced by the fluctuations of the business cycle. Its core is that careful analysis of all the cost factors that enter into production at various rates of capacity which is the basis of modern accounting. This makes it possible to determine at one glance whether a certain division—or a department within a division—is producing with greater or lesser efficiency than the norm, and why. It also shows whether a good result is attributable to an increase in efficiency or to an improvement in methods, or whether it is the result of purely accidental factors for which management cannot claim credit. Above all, it makes it impossible to be deceived by a high profit in boom years if such profit is actually purchased at the expense of productive efficiency, that is at the risk of a permanent impairment of the company's strength. Conversely, it prevents a divisional manager from being blamed for the disappointing returns of a depression year when actually the result was caused by factors over which he had no control. Thus, a divisional manager will be held accountable for a deterioration of productive efficiency even when it is concealed by an increase in total profits; and he will get the credit for any strengthening of managerial efficiency, even when as the result of bad business conditions, his division operates at a loss. The cost analysis of base pricing thus gives an objective standard of manufacturing efficiency.

The instrument of base pricing also furnishes a yardstick for policy decisions—both before they are taken and afterwards. It shows the factors of productive efficiency that are likely to be affected by a policy decision, thus substituting facts for personal differences of opinion in policy arguments. It shows how costs will be affected by policy decisions deemed necessary or advisable not for reasons of productive efficiency but for such reasons as labor policy, merchandising, public relations, etc.

Base pricing also shows the use made of General Motors' capital. It measures the rate of return on capital invested and the factors: rate of capacity at which the plants operate, lifetime of the productive equipment, etc., on which this rate depends. The assumptions under which any given investment is made can thus be isolated and checked against actual economic developments all the time. It thus furnishes a basis for policy decisions on expansion and measures the advisability of proposed new capital investments.

It is indicative of the concept of management that is embodied in General Motors organization that the cost analysis underlying base pricing is made by the divisions—just as it is customary in a good many divisions to have the department heads such as superintendents and foremen make the cost analysis for their jobs. The necessary check is supplied by a comparison of the cost analysis of each division with those of other divisions within the company making comparable products or using comparable methods—one reason for the company's insistence on uniform accounting practices throughout all divisions.

Efficient production is only one element in the success of a business in a free-enterprise economy, and has to be complemented by ability to sell one's products in the market. Hence, in General Motors an objective analysis of the market and of the competitive standing of the products is used as the second measurement. The consumer's decisions and preferences are combined with the facts of the engineer to give an impersonal basis for decisions and for the evaluation of performance. Again the problem is how to eliminate purely extraneous fluctuations in measuring performance. This is done for the car-producing divisions by measuring their achievement and competitive standing not in terms of total sales but according to the ratio of their sales to total automobile sales in their price range. A car division which would show a loss in percentage of its potential market would be considered as losing ground even though—as a result of prosperous business conditions—it might roll up high absolute sales figures. On the other hand, it is generally understood that the management of Cadillac has been doing an outstanding job over the last fifteen years, even though the dollar volume of sales has gone down sharply. The share of the division in the total sales of high-priced cars has risen; the fall in absolute sales volume is thus not chargeable to Cadillac but to a shrinkage of the market for higher priced cars over which the Cadillac management has had no control and for which it can not be blamed.

Since the accessory divisions produce largely for use within General Motors their efficiency could not be measured in terms of their competitive standing on the consumer's market. Hence they are measured by a different—and perhaps even a more severe—standard, their ability to supply the car divisions at lower cost than any outsider. As mentioned above, no car division is under compulsion to buy from the accessory divisions, or under compulsion to pay the prices demanded by them. To obtain the custom of the car divisions, each accessory division must be able to meet the lowest prices of outside accessory manufacturers and to satisfy the quality and styling requirements of the car divisions. Most of them are therefore subjected to the test of competition as much as the car divisions. And while individual car buyers will often decide on the basis of habit or advertising appeal, that is on economically non-rational grounds, the accessory producers have to satisfy a buyer who is interested only in tangible and provable economic factors.

The yardstick of market performance is based on the assumption that consumers' buying preferences and even their prejudices are as much objective facts for the producer as are the facts and figures of engineering and accounting which underlie base pricing. It is as necessary to analyze the consumer's preferences as it is to analyze cost factors. Without knowledge of the elements which make up the consumer's decision, it would be impossible to find the causes of faulty selling performance or to plan rationally for improvements in the competitive position of a division, or of the business as a whole. Hence, General Motors has built up a comprehensive consumer research organization.

The combination of these two elements of objective analysis, base pricing and competitive market standing, has made possible a considerable degree of production planning. Annually each division submits estimated schedules for the next year in which it gives tentative figures for sales, costs and expected capital requirements on the assumption of a good, an average, and a bad year for the industry as a whole. It also indicates which of these three estimates it considers most likely on the basis of its knowledge of business conditions, trends in the used-car market, etc. By correlating the estimates of the various divisions, central management obtains a fairly representative picture of conditions in the industry as a whole. By closely checking this composite judgment of the producing and selling personnel against the analysis of the consumer research staff and of the company's economists, a result is obtained which should not only be fairly reliable but which also is comprehensible to the executives, thus setting an objective frame for the work of the members both of central and of divisional management.

Through measuring the efficiency and achievement of both policy decision and administration against the objective criteria of cost and efficiency, of return on the invested capital, and of competitive standing in the market, General Motors aims at the elimination of personal and subjective elements in the relationship between boss and subordinate, central management and divisional management. The questions, how efficient is a man, how successful is he, and how important is he to the company, do not have to be decided on the basis of subjective preference. In fact, they should not have to be decided at all; they should be answered clearly by the objective yardstick that records efficiency and achievement immediately and automatically. The President of the company does not have to tell a divisional manager that he is not satisfied with him; the divisional manager knows it anyhow by looking at the figures based on his own cost and market analysis. Similarly, the President does not have to justify a promotion to the colleagues of the promoted man; he has the man's record which is known within the company. Also the objective yardstick should limit the personal element in policy decisions. If a man's opinion or suggestion are overruled it should be not because of the higher rank of the boss, but because the facts are against him. That would make it possible for superiors freely to admit mistakes to their subordinates—perhaps the most important thing in human relations. In fine, this objective yardstick should not only make possible informal and friendly personal relations, a spirit of teamwork and a free and frank discussion. It should also

—at least, that is what the people in General Motors claim— make the organization of management as a team on a federal basis natural and almost inevitable by erecting strong barriers of fact against action based on nothing but seniority and rank.

HOW WELL DOES IT WORK?

OUR analytical description of decentralization gives the impression of a carefully worked-out system. This impression is by and large correct—for the system as it is today. But this analysis also seems to imply—as does every systematic description—that today's structure has been planned this way. This implication is dangerously misleading. Indeed decentralization would be worthless and unworkable, if not outright destructive, had it been imposed as a theoretically-devised plan of corporate organization. Not only would such a plan have been rigid, doctrinaire and incapable of growth and development, it would have antagonized the people who were to work with it and under it as an artifact spun out of thin air, unrelated to actual experience and actual problems, and imposed on them by executive fiat. Decentralization, in other words, would have been regarded as a form of "enlightened despotism." The important fact about "enlightened despotism"—also the one fact "enlightened despots" always forget —is that, while it appears as enlightenment to those in power, it is despotism pure and simple to those under it. Another and potentially even more serious result of a theoretical over-all plan would have been that every practical problem demanding a solution would have appeared as a challenge to the plan and as an attack on its basic principles—simply because no plan, however good, can foresee practical problems of the future and can solve them in advance. Finally, a theoretical system is always more concerned with the question whether the solution to a concrete situation is in harmony with the principles of the plan, than whether it is appropriate to the situation. A theoretical plan becomes an end in itself; and concrete administrative action—the first job of any system of government—becomes impossible.

This is not to say that decentralization has been evolved "pragmatically," that is, without reference to an underlying concept. Certainly, when General Motors first began to be organized as a unified body about thirty years ago, its leaders had concepts of management and of corporate organization, aims they were striving for, beliefs, particularly how things ought not to be done. The general idea that a corporation must have a policy seems to have been accepted by top management during the first World War or shortly thereafter. The general concept of decentralization as applied to the relations between central management and divisional managers, and the general idea of objective yardsticks, date probably back to the early twenties. But these were general principles of organization and procedure—principles how to do and not to do things, rather than what to do or not to do. The corporate organization itself, the concrete organs, the concrete policies, the concrete decisions were developed gradually and in dealing with concrete situations and concrete personalities.

Most of the demands for "planning" made today are based on the false assertion that "muddling through" and aimless floundering are the only alternatives to over-all, theoretical, for-the-future planning. That General Motors owes its strength precisely to that use of principles and concepts as guides for concrete, unplanned and unforseseen action of which the "planner" knows nothing, is thus of general importance. The most successful attempt to provide a basis for the political organization of the future, the American Constitution, used the same method. The Constitution is not a "plan" of Government, laying down what ought to be done. Neither is it "pragmatic." It establishes a few, simple organs of Government with enormous powers of which only the limits are given. It establishes an objective yardstick in the law. It provides a few, very simple principles of decision in broad language; most of them, it is noteworthy, lay down how not to act, with the significant exception of the provisions for the revision of the Constitution which establish a positive procedure. But the actual organization and system of Government were wisely left to concrete experience—a wisdom on which the success of the Constitution rests in large part.

Because General Motors' system of organization was evolved historically, the actual organizational reality necessarily abounds with exceptions to the general organizational concept. In the case of almost every division there are special historical reasons why this or that general rule is not observed: a special problem of production, a valuable but cantankerous sales manager, long since honorably retired, who did things his own way, or a particularly good or particularly bad atmosphere of labor relations, etc. Where the logician and system-maker would expect logical consistency, there are large gaps. This or that problem that theoretically should have been answered one way or another, simply has never come up and has not been answered at all. In other words, General Motors is a functioning and moving organization of human beings and not a static blueprint.

But it is not only impossible for the reality of General Motors to be a reproduction of the decentralized federal union of its concept, it would also be highly undesirable. The purpose of such a concept is never to serve as a rigid rule. Rather it is to be used like a compass bearing taken across rugged mountains. The actual trail will follow the natural contours of the terrain; but the bearing will give the deviation from the true course at every step and will thus ultimately lead to the objective, however great the detour and however much the objective has been lost sight of on the way.

This is true of all human organizations. Being human they can never aspire to perfection and must thus make imperfection workable. Being human they also have to reckon with the very considerable differences of temperament, ability and rhythm between individuals. A system of organization that is thirty per cent effective, will be more efficient and stronger than one that pretends to ideal efficiency. In fact it can be said that for a decentralized management to be efficient, it must contain at least a sprinkling of executives who pay very little attention to the rules of decentralization and are inclined towards a rather autocratic, "do-this-or-be-damned" attitude. For every institution will sooner or later run up against a situation which cannot be solved on the basis of factual analysis and policy, on which agreement cannot be reached, and for which there are no precedents. Such Gordian Knots can only be cut; and unless there is somebody in the organization who would rather cut than unravel knots, the decision will be avoided altogether in the name of reasonableness. High-handed, arbitrary, even dictatorial behavior may thus be not only no contradiction to decentralization, but a prerequisite for its functioning, provided only that such behavior is seen and understood by everybody—including the dictatorial executive himself—as an exception and as a deviation from the norm.

What we are asking when we raise the question whether General Motors has realized its own concept of management, is not whether the company in its actual workings conforms to a blueprint but whether it uses decentralization as its over-all "true course," as the norm for actual behavior—

never realized entirely but always inferred—and as the basis for the approach to, and the solution of, new problems.

The Conversion to War

To find out how much realization there is of the concept of decentralized management, we shall study General Motors' conversion from peace to war production. Here was a brand-new problem of terrifying proportions. There were no precedents; indeed its successful solution depended upon the ability of the company's executives to disregard most of the lessons they had spent a lifetime to learn. Was this successful conversion based on the principles and organs of decentralization? Or did General Motors in the pinch have to give up its concepts?

In 1941 the automobile business had the biggest year in its history and all divisions worked full time on satisfying record consumer demands. Central management, however, was no longer concerned with the problem of peacetime production. As it is the function of central management to think ahead, the two top committees of General Motors began early in 1941 to worry about the peak armaments load which the corporation might be expected to carry two or three years later. First, central management decided that General Motors as the largest and most experienced producer of mechanical goods should go after the difficult and critical rather than the routine jobs. Then the problems were narrowed down to three: the determination of the speed with which war orders would come and the probable date of their peak; shortages of labor; and transportation bottlenecks.

A considerable time before Pearl Harbor central management had decided that labor supplies would be the critical and controlling factor in the war program, and that the extent to which General Motors could produce for the war effort would depend on its ability to avoid labor shortages. Hence in the spring of 1941 central management made case studies of the future labor situation in each of the geographic areas in which the company operates. The magnitude of this task can be seen from the fact that General Motors operates important plants in twenty industrial districts distributed over ten states; in some of these areas its plants are the major employers, while in others General Motors is only one of a number of employers, so that the labor needs of other companies had to be taken into account as well. By the fall of 1941 the employment limits had been worked out for each major plant-city, and it was possible to plan to throw the maximum expansion into the areas where industrial workers would be obtainable most easily. On this basis alone the divisions were allocated the maximum war business they could accept; neither finance, plant equipment, available floor-space, nor type of production usually handled by the plant were considered decisive wherever labor could be obtained. This policy in all its details was completed three weeks after Pearl Harbor, that is, even before the Government was ready to give out armament orders. And though the armaments program underwent great changes, actual experience proved these forecasts of possible maximum production in each area to be correct within a margin of ten per cent.

As a result of this planning, divisional managers knew from the start precisely how far they could commit the company and how much work they could and should accept. From the start, the divisional managers knew that they had to plan on a war production job scheduled to average twice the annual peacetime peak load. This made it possible for them to plan for maximum expansion at a time when many other corporations were still thinking and working in terms of much lower goals. Therefore, much of the job of building plants, of designing and buying new equipment, could be done at a time when there were as yet no major shortages of building materials and machines. Finally, General Motors never had a serious labor supply or housing problem, and never had to go to the Government for housing or transportation. Nothing is considered by General Motors management as much a proof of the soundness of its organization as the fact that it succeeded in foreseeing and forestalling wartime labor and transportation shortages.

Besides setting the maximum beyond which no divisional manager could accept orders without special approval by the Administration Committee, central management also set the minimum by laying down that every manager had within the shortest possible time to expand to the limits established for him. Central management supervised the war job of the divisions to the extent that any falling behind in delivery schedule had to be reported and explained; in serious cases of nonfulfillment of contractual obligations or promises, central management would actually step in. Otherwise, the divisional manager was entirely on his own. He alone decided what to produce, where and how. He priced his products for the Government, worked out delivery schedules, and was responsible for the methods of production. He decided what new plants and new equipment he would need and how the load of war work should be distributed between the plants. To help him in all this, he had the assistance of the service staffs of the company which acted as a clearinghouse for new methods of production, as agents in the search for scarce supplies and in the discovery of subcontractors, etc. In addition, central management handled the legal side of all contracts for the divisions, and all matters of finance. A new service staff of central management was set up to assist the divisional managers in handling war orders. The divisional manager reported to this war staff in Detroit all orders which he had accepted as well as those which he did not feel capable of handling himself. Thus, competition between the divisions for the same order was eliminated as was also the danger that an urgent war job would not be done because it was not offered to the division best equipped to handle it.

In obtaining orders, however, the services of central management went far beyond advising and informing. In going after war business and in the attempt to make the facilities and experiences of General Motors most useful to the war effort, General Motors management worked as one team rather than on the basis of a nicely balanced division of powers. It was here that the policy of keeping the largest possible number of executives fully informed on corporation policies and practices paid the highest dividends by enabling both central management and divisional managers to act according to the requirements of the situation, rather than according to a formal organization chart.

A very large part of the war orders was accepted by the divisional managers on their own, often without any consultation with central management. If they felt that their plants were able to turn out a certain new product, they went ahead. In a good many cases individual divisions were approached directly by the armed forces. In other cases divisional managers with their own staffs, worked out the lines of production which they were best equipped to handle, and made the bids for war orders on this basis. Others went to Washington to find out which products would be most urgently needed or which presented the most difficulties in production; and they accepted war orders on that basis.

The degree to which divisional managers were left alone as long as they did a satisfactory job is shown by the fact that one of them agreed to the cancellation of the largest war contract General Motors held at that time and to its replacement by a contract for an entirely new product, without even informing central management before he signed. Months of preparation had been spent on the old contract; and in pre liminary talks some of the most powerful men in central management had decided that the new product was one which General Motors could not produce satisfactorily. Yet, when the divisional manager decided to go against the almost unanimous opinion of central management rather than turn down the armed forces, his decision was final.

On the other hand, central management in many cases would suggest to a divisional manager that he accept certain work. At one stage, the Army urgently needed medium tanks. Central management studied the production problem and came to the conclusion that the one thing absolutely necessary for tank production is adequate floor-space. The one division with surplus floor-space did not, however, possess the equipment and the engineers for such heavy work both of which central management found in another division. The two divisions were then brought together to work out a scheme under which the floor-space of one and the experience and equipment of the other were merged—under one divisional management, however.

In one case central management actually accepted an order. This happened when the Navy asked General Motors to go into the production of carrier-borne aircraft under conditions of engineering and manufacturing so new and difficult as to make it impossible for any existing division to handle the job. Central management therefore created a new division by bringing together under one new management a number of plants on the Eastern seaboard that had previously belonged to several divisions. However, once this new division was started it was left entirely to the new divisional manager to do the job, to organize his plants, men and machines. It was also left to him to work out modifications of the contract and to accept new orders for new models.

Similar methods were applied to the planning for reconversion to peacetime work. The division between policy-making central management and executive divisional management made it possible for General Motors to plan for peace without in any way neglecting full war production, just as in 1941 it could prepare for war production without neglecting a record peacetime business. As soon as the main job of conversion to war had been done—around the middle of 1943—central management could begin to plan for peacetime conversion. Central management decided that General Motors should expand its capacity in the immediate postwar years, even though the postwar buying boom in automobiles might be short-lived. Central management also worked out the forecasts for postwar automobile production on which the over-all policies of the company were to be based. Finally central management decided on an expansion program of five hundred million dollars for the immediate postwar period. After that decision which was taken in close consultation with divisional executives but independently of them, divisional managers were called in and were informed fully of the reasons for the decision and of the arguments behind them. They were also asked to voice whatever objections to the decisions they might have, which were thrashed out in a series of meetings. Divisions were then asked to prepare their own plans for the actual job that had been set for them within the frame of the total expansion program. And while their plans in every single case were reviewed carefully by the central committees of the company, it was left up to the divisions to decide how to do the actual job.

Nobody inside General Motors would pretend that the organization of the war effort corresponded in detail to the systematic blueprint given in the last section. Instead of the neat, functional division between central management and divisional managers of the theory of decentralization we have in practice a series of huddles and scrimmages in which functions and tasks are divided according to the accidents of the concrete situation, or the individual ability, aggressiveness and drive of the people concerned. There are obviously areas in which the nature of the war job made impossible that divisional autonomy which decentralization prescribes. If there is only one customer, the Government, orders and distribution will tend to be centralized. When a strike becomes a threat to national security, labor policy will tend to be taken over more and more by central management if only because the responsibility is too heavy for the divisional manager. And since General Motors imposed on itself a voluntary profit-limitation on war orders—similar to that later made compulsory by law—pricing and its corollary, re-negotiation of government contracts after their completion, became largely central-management matters.

The nature of the war job also made it impossible to realize that corporate unity on which decentralization rests. Instead of the 250 closely related or complementary products of peacetime, General Motors made more than 3000 largely unrelated war goods. There could be no production policy, no "range" planned and imposed by central management. The most that could be done was to prevent divisions from competing against each other, and to promote subcontracting between them wherever possible. Otherwise physical and accidental factors—available labor, floor-space, army needs, willingness of a particular manager to accept an order or expiration of a contract just when facilities for the production of a new product were badly needed—largely determined production policy.

And yet, it is also clear that underlying this apparent confusion there was a strong pattern around which action tended to organize. There was probably no one move in the conversion from peace to war which followed exactly the theoretical rules of decentralized management. But there were also very few, as our sketch shows, which did not obtain their tenor, their direction and their effectiveness from the principles of decentralization. It was precisely because General Motors had such a definite concept that it did not have to be pedantic about its realization but could let each man work his own best way, let each situation resolve itself according to its own logic. In other words, while no one rule of decentralization was fully or literally observed and realized, the pattern was always there. And while the success of General Motors conversion to war is not traceable to any one rule of decentralization, the company could not have done what it did in the way it did it, without the pattern, the concept, the principles of decentralization.

It should be emphasized that, so far, we have been concerned only with decentralization in its original and narrowest application as the basis for the relations between central management and divisional managers; and our conclusions apply exclusively to this one, rather special application. In the next two sections as well as in a later chapter we shall discuss the application of the principle of decentralization to other spheres of industrial order: to the relations between the producer and the distributors of his product, to the relations between managerial personnel within the divisions, and to labor relations; and we may well find a very different situation then. But within these limits, that is as a concept of industrial order on the level of management, our conclusion would be that General Motors realizes its concept of decentralization sufficiently to obtain from it an over-all pattern of behavior and a basis for the successful solution of the most difficult concrete problems of economic life.

Unsolved Problems

How successful decentralization is we have just seen. But how *valid* is it? Does it actually give an answer to the problems of institutional order: the supply and development of leaders; the orderly succession in top management without dependence on geniuses or wars of succession; the formulation of a policy flexible enough to cope with concrete problems, fixed enough to serve as a guide; the development of objective, impersonal yardsticks of policy and performance?

Our analysis maintains that decentralization gives General Motors a clear policy and a definite organ for policy decisions. Yet the rules apparently never become an end in themselves so that policy remains the servant of corporate purpose instead of degenerating into its master. The policies of General Motors aim at eliminating arbitrary whims and dictatorial dicta in management relations and at substituting instead a spirit of team work without, however, ever abandoning order and authority. They tend to put all authority under the objective control of an impersonal law—the objective yardsticks—but thereby should make authority only stronger and more legitimate. This should result in a genuine federation in which authority is based on function instead of on rank, and in which decisions are based on the impersonal criterion of a supreme law rather than on power. This also should create the conditions under which a genuine *esprit de corps* can develop which leads executives to accept the good of the corporation as their own good and goal, and which works that change in a man that makes him bring more out of himself than he really has.

Above all the General Motors policies successfully establish a functioning corporate government. As the top management of the corporation consists of five men of almost equal authority, there should be a continuity; succession should be a process of gradual co-option of the ranking executives rather than an abrupt change of command and of policy. The same holds true by and large of other managerial positions. There are always enough people available who are familiar with the work. Their records are clear enough and based on a yardstick of achievement so that selection can be an impersonal and rational process rather than a civil war. The teamwork organization of management, the assistance rendered by the service staffs, and the constant check against base price, market quota and consumer's opinion, make it possible for ordinary human beings to run this enormous machine.

All of this must be read with the reservation in mind that actual performance is only an approximation to theoretical potential. Yet even if decentralization were completely realized, it still would fail to solve two big problems and to satisfy two basic needs of the corporation as an institution: (a) the conversion of the specialist needed at the lower levels into the leader with a general outlook and education needed at the top; (b) the breaking of the isolation in which the top executives of any big organization live inevitably, and which endangers the survival and efficiency of an institution which, like the corporation, has to live and to function in society. Both are problems of creating and training those rarest of all human qualities, imagination and understanding. And decentralization, being concerned with organization, cannot, by its very nature, provide something as unorganizable as imagination or understanding.

As for the problem of leadership-education, there are apparently a good many different ways in which it might be attacked. In the first place—and that is the approach of some of the senior men—it might be argued that people should never be allowed to become specialists confined to the knowledge of one field. At least, the man with leadership ability should be separated at a very early stage from the man with special skill and talent. While the latter should be allowed and even encouraged to specialize in his skill or in one type of research, the former should be systematically trained to understand and comprehend the whole rather than one particular part. Thus, right from the start—beginning with the foreman—men of executive ability should be transferred systematically from manufacturing departments to sales or personnel departments, from work as a draftsman to work as a foreman, etc. They should not be given any executive position, not even a junior one, until they have worked in a good many departments of the business—a plan actually followed in one of the major accessory divisions of General Motors. That process of all-around training should continue right through, partly by planning vacations so that the substitutes of a man on leave would always be taken from another department, partly by an intelligent system of promotion under which a man would be advanced according to the type of experience he needs rather than to the type of experience he has had.

Following a similar line there are more ambitious proposals to use certain staff services of the corporation especially for the general over-all education of promising young men. There are several services which, by the very nature of their work, always have to see the business as a whole, and which must deal, at least in an elementary fashion, with all its aspects. Thus even a subordinate in these staffs obtains a view of the whole and a general acquaintance with all its main phases. This applies particularly to Public Relations, Customer Research and Labor Relations, all of which, while themselves special fields employing special techniques, focus on General Motors rather than on one division or one department. Hence the proposal to use these—and perhaps similar service staffs—as a training school; instead of recruiting their own permanent personnel from the outside, those staffs would accept able young men from the divisions for a few years' service in rotation.

A different approach is favored by other executives who maintain that specialization in the beginning is not only necessary but wholesome, and that the young and inexperienced employee does not possess the maturity necessary for a general education. What is needed according to this view is a liberal education at a comparatively advanced level and mature age. Representative of this approach is the suggestion of one of the senior men in General Motors' personnel management to run at General Motors Institute (a large engineering and adult-education school maintained by the company in Flint, Michigan) a one- or two-year program for promising junior executives between twenty-five and thirty-five years of age, similar to the Niemann fellowships for journalists at Harvard University. During this fellowship-period the employee would receive the same salary as in his last job. He would be free to choose his subjects and he would be offered the chance to work under the best men from major universities and from industry, who would be invited for a year or two to join the faculty of General Motors Institute as visiting professors. This idea seems to be widely supported—though there is apparently a split between those who, following the Niemann plan, advocate that emphasis during this period should not be on engineering, manufacturing or other technical subjects, but on government, history, economics, philosophy and perhaps even on the arts, that is, on the basic subjects of a liberal education, and those who favor a postgraduate course in business management and production.

It should be clear from this list of some of the ideas which are being discussed within General Motors that the question of specialist versus generally educated person is not a problem that is unique to the big-business corporation. It is part of the debate on vocational versus liberal education that has been agitating the educational world for a long time. It may well be easier to solve this basic problem of modern education within an institution like General Motors than in formal education.

The second problem, that of breaking the invisible isolation of the corporation executive, is much more difficult. The executive of a big business affects society by every one of his moves and is affected by it. Yet he inevitably lives in an artificial environment and almost as isolated as if he were in a monastery. This isolation is necessary. The executive of a big corporation—like the executive of any big organization— is too busy to see people except on business. Problems have to be presented to him in a form which allows him to act, that is, stripped of everything not pertaining to the business of the moment. His contacts outside of business tend to be limited to people of the same set, if not to people working for the same organization. The demand that there be no competing outside interest and loyalty applies to the corporation executive as it does to the army officer. Hence executive life not only breeds a parochialism of the imagination comparable to the "military mind" but places a considerable premium on it.

In our present-day society this isolation is emphasized far

beyond the necessary. It is, for instance, made practically impossible for the corporation executive to find out anything about the ideas, concerns, approach and mentality of labor in his frequent contacts with union leaders—or for union leaders to find out anything about management and managers. For those two never meet except as antagonists trying to defeat each other: social and legal conventions—certain provisions of the Wagner Act, for instance—decree that their contacts be confined to the extraordinary: the conflict situation, rather than to the normal day-to-day relationships. Similarly, social convention has decreed a relationship between corporation executives and government which makes it most difficult for both to get to understand each other and to acquire the imagination to see each other's motives, approaches and actions. Even though the great majority of businessmen working in Washington for the war effort hated their government jobs as much as most of the other "temporary bureaucrats," they seem to be almost unanimous in their conclusion that their war service has given them a new understanding of government and politics; and there seems to be substantial agreement among these men that a period of work in and for the government should be part of the regular education of the young business executive. But while the isolation of the executive of the large corporation can be lessened, a certain— and considerable—amount of mental parochialism is essential for the discharge of his duties.

Yet this parochialism of the executive imagination is also very dangerous for the corporation. A corporation lives in society. Yet, the isolated executive cannot know—because he cannot imagine—what the effect of his action will be. He can know only the arguments that are relevant to his job and to his environment. Nobody can see except from his own point of view; and the executive's angle of vision must be a narrow one for him to be effective. The fact that other people in other positions have another point of view may not only escape the corporation executive. It may even be incomprehensible to him. He may know that every action of the society outside affects the corporation and its very survival as an efficient producer: the action and reaction of consumers, of labor, of voters, etc. But the isolated executive has no means of understanding why the outside world acts nor of foretelling how it will act.* Surveys, straw votes and other techniques are not the answer; for what is needed is not "facts" but an ability to see the facts as others see them.

The parochialism of the military imagination inspired Clemenceau's epigram that war is too important to be entrusted to the generals. Yet neither Clemenceau nor anybody else has been able to fight a war without entrusting it to the generals, that is to trained military executives. Industrial production is also too important to be entrusted to men of parochial imagination, and yet has to be entrusted to men inevitably liable to it, namely the trained industrial executive. It is idle to suggest, as does Clemenceau's epigram, that the question can be solved by a change of executives or of the rules under which they are being selected. Whoever works in a big organization, especially at or near the top, will inevitably be bounded by it wherever he comes from. Hence the question is how can the corporation give its management the imagination, the understanding of the outside point of view, of the public's (consumers, workers, voters, government) imagination and of the limits thereof.**

---

* A very good example of this is the inability of most American industrial executives to understand that Franklin D. Roosevelt would be re-elected in the presidential elections of 1936, 1940 and 1944 or why; another one, the inability of Henry Ford to conceive that "his" workers could possibly vote for a union.

** Needless to say, all this applies to any large-scale organization. We have mentioned the problem of the "military mind." But when Congress in 1943

This problem is not caused by bigness; it exists in every organization. But in a large organization it has to be solved by special means whereas it takes care of itself—by and large —in a small business. Just as the specialist in a small business can not help knowing what goes on in other departments, the executive in a small business can not help knowing what goes on outside his business. In addition the small, and even the medium-sized, business has in the Board of Directors an organ which, if properly organized, can supply the executive with an understanding of the reasoning, points of view and reactions of outside groups particularly important to the business, such as stockholders, bankers, community leaders and major customers.

In the large corporation, the automatic contact with the outside world is lacking almost entirely and by necessity. The Board of Directors cannot function as it does in a small business. The control of a large corporation is such a complex job and requires such constant attention that the outside Board member, who has his own affairs to look after, can know very little about the business—too little on the whole to be useful as an outsider. And the full-time Board member is simply another executive of the corporation. There have been many proposals of late to "restore" the lost function of the Board of Directors by adding to it members representing the government, the public, labor, and the consumer. In some cases such moves would have merit; representatives of the main shippers on the board of a railway, of the community on that of a public utility, of the medical profession on that of a pharmaceutical house, should have a good deal to contribute. But on the whole the solution does not seem to lie

---

revolted against the "professors" in the government's economic control agencies such as the Office of Price Control, it really revolted against the predominance of the "academic mind" and its inability to imagine and understand economic problems as business and the public see them.

in reforming the Board of Directors. In the first place, imagination is needed far more constantly, far more systematically and far more generally throughout the business than could be supplied by a Board small enough to be workable. Secondly, the imagination has to be supplied in connection with concrete problems and concrete situations to be usable; otherwise it is just pious phrasemaking. And an outside director in a large corporation cannot know enough to be specific; he must remain a figurehead.* Hence General Motors' decision not to clutter up the Board of Directors with outside members but to restrict it by and large to top executives of the company, former top executives now retired and top executives of the Du Pont Company which owns a controlling interest in General Motors, is probably wise. But, of course, while this makes the Board of Directors usable as part of the executive organization, it does nothing to break the isolation of the executives.

To say that General Motors has worked out ways to solve this problem would be a gross exaggeration. Even to say that its management as a whole realizes the importance of finding a solution would be to claim too much. Awareness of the problem, even of its existence, is by no means general; and it is, of course, least understood where the isolation is the greatest, that is among the executives primarily engaged in technical or production jobs. Yet, the corporation has found workable solutions in specific areas where the danger of isolation was particularly obvious and concrete. And it is now engaged in evolving a long-term program of bringing

---

* The complete futility of the labor members which were appointed to the Boards of Directors under the corporation law of Republican Germany shows very clearly that in the modern large corporation, board membership by itself is pretty useless both for the corporation and for the group represented unless it is coupled with a detailed knowledge of the business which the outside board member simply cannot possess.

an understanding of the viewpoint, reaction and approach of the outside world to the executives.

There are three fields in which General Motors has developed specific instruments to break the imaginative isolation of the corporation executive: customer relations, dealer relations and—still very much in its infancy—community relations in its plant cities.

The oldest and most generally accepted of these is customer relations as organized in the Customer Research Staff. What makes it so effective is that the concrete importance of its findings is clear to everybody. The customer's reasons, reactions and viewpoints determine whether he will buy a General Motors car. Normally it is very difficult to convince people that things and factors are relevant to others when they are irrelevant to them; and Customer Research has had plenty of difficulties with its basic contention that the public's beliefs, habits, idiosyncracies or even fallacies are as much a "fact" as the engineer's figures. But because it is so obvious that the engineer's job and the prosperity of his business depend fully as much on the public's acceptance of the engineer's product as on the engineer's being right, Customer Research makes immediate sense—though its general acceptance today is due as much to the quality of its work as to the soundness of the concept. Customer Research is an organ which intentionally, systematically and continuously supplies the customer's point of view to management, and which enables the designer, engineer, production man and salesman to see himself and his work as others see it.

A similar end is aimed at with very different means in the organization which tries to give the executive an understanding of the dealer's point of view and concerns. This organization, which will be discussed in detail in the next section, consists of two independent bodies: a Dealer Relations

Council composed of representative dealers who meet regularly with the company's top executives; and the Motors Holding Division, a division of General Motors, which is actually itself in the dealership business on a large scale, grubstaking several hundred dealers all over the country. Through these two bodies—the one working mainly with central management, the other mainly with the sales executives of the divisions—the company receives all the time, a knowledge, if not an understanding, of the dealer's position, concerns, problems, points of view and prejudices.

The gains resulting from an understanding of the views and reactions of the community in which a plant is situated and in which its employees live, are in the long run as important as the gains to be derived from understanding either consumers or dealers. But they are not as immediate and concrete. Also, community relations have to be organized on a community basis, that is around divisional or plant managers which always takes more time than setting up a staff in the central office. Hence so far community relations have been organized really successfully only in one of the many major industrial centers in which General Motors operates—Dayton, Ohio. This is generally admitted to be but the beginning of a determined attempt to give divisional and plant managers an understanding of the community they operate in—and at the same time to give the community an understanding of the problems, approaches, concerns and views of the division or plant.

The plant-city committee in Dayton represents all the important industries in the city. But in concept and organization, it is a projection of the "Sloan meetings" in Detroit. In addition to the top men of the local plants, the Dayton plant-city committee comprises local leaders from all walks of life: city officials, religious and educational leaders, union officials, businessmen, newspaper editors, etc. It discusses industrial problems and decisions which affect the life of the community or community problems which affect the plants, such as housing, employment, traffic regulations, city planning, location of industries, labor supply and wages.

Contrasted with these attempts to solve specific problems of the imagination in specific areas by specific techniques, there is the proposal for an over-all and general program of public relations to supply an understanding of the outside to the General Motors executives. This proposal is a logical result of the evolution of General Motors' concept of public relations.

To the general public "public relations" means publicity —essentially an extension of advertising from advertising a product to advertising its producer. And the term "public relations" has thus acquired a rather unfavorable connotation of ballyhoo, press agentry, propaganda and white-washing. Undoubtedly General Motors also uses its public relations department for these things; but it has been slowly realized that the emphasis should be on acquainting the broad public with the problems of General Motors rather than on convincing it of the company's virtues and achievements. This approach logically led to the realization that to reach the public with its problems, General Motors must understand the public's problems first.

Every major decision of a great corporation affects the public somehow, as workers, consumers, citizens; hence the public will react consciously or subconsciously to every move the company makes. On this reaction depends, however, the effectiveness of the company's decision to no small extent— simply another way of saying that any corporation lives in society. Hence the effectiveness of the executive's decision depends not only on his understanding the problems of his business and the mentality of his associates but on his understanding the public attitude to his problems—both, what the public believes, and why. He may disagree with the public; but he must first understand why it holds views that seem so radically and foolishly wrong to him. Hence the program of public relations is to give both central office and divisional executives a knowledge of public attitudes and beliefs and an understanding of the reasons behind them.

So far, plans are being made for work in the areas of labor relations, plant-city relations and general public relations. The program is still in an early stage; and techniques have yet to be worked out and organizations to be set up. Also, it is perhaps not generally understood within General Motors' management that the main purpose of such a program is not tell the public but to listen to it—just as Customer Research did not start out to educate the public but to educate the corporation. If successful, the program would go a long way towards eliminating the dangers inherent in the inevitable isolation of the executive in a large organization.

Our conclusion would thus be that in decentralization General Motors possesses a concept adequate to the solution of its own chief institutional problems—with the exception of those problems of understanding and imagination which require special solutions. We should, however, mention one major reservation: it is highly questionable whether decentralization could be used successfully even for relations such as those between the divisional managers and central management in General Motors, were the present trend towards governmental centralization to continue. We have seen that the insistence of the United Automobile Workers Union on one labor contract for the whole of General Motors has made necessary a centralization of labor relations. There may be even further enforced centralization in this field with the labor contract negotiated on an industry-wide basis which would make impossible whatever local autonomy in labor matters there still is. We have mentioned that the inevitable effects of the war: concentration of all orders in the hands of the government, centralization of raw materials, price and labor controls in Washington, severely limited the scope of decentralization. Decentralization, which aims at the maximum autonomy and self-government of the local producing unit, could not operate were consumption, credit, raw materials and labor organized on a centralized basis, whether the controls be governmental, a cartel, or "one big union."

THE SMALL BUSINESS PARTNER

IN MANY respects the automobile dealer is the prototype of the independent small business man. His business is usually large enough to lift him out of the "tradesman" class. Few automobile dealers operate on a capital investment of less than $15,000; and in many a small town the leading automobile dealer is the largest independent businessman. Yet very few dealerships go beyond the range of small or medium-sized business—at least in terms of capital investment if not always in terms of profits.

The dealer's functions cover a broad range. He sells one commodity: new cars. He also sells another commodity, partly competing with, partly complementary to, new cars: used cars. In connection with these two interrelated merchandising businesses he runs an agency for a finance company and one for an automobile insurance company. Finally, he often—particularly in smaller places—combines his merchandising business with a repair shop which offers mechanical services to the public. There can thus hardly be any phase or any problem of small-business operations which is not encountered regularly in automobile dealerships.

At the same time the automobile dealer is a very unrepresentative small businessman in one respect, the extent and severity of the potential conflicts between his interests and those of his big-business partner, the automobile manufacturer. The dealer is tied to the manufacturer. Unlike the grocer he cannot sell competing brands of the same products but is confined to one make. Yet he has absolutely no control over cost and very little over the price of the product or over the manner in which it is offered for sale. The dealer invests his own capital and stakes his own economic future on the manufacturer's product and on its ability to attract the public.

The dependence of the dealer is heightened by the fact that to the dealer his right to sell a particular brand of cars is necessarily his main business asset. He talks of the agreement which gives him this right as his "franchise"—-a term which carries with it the implication of a vested right which can be taken away only under "due process" and "just compensation." To the automobile company the agreement can, however, never be anything but a "selling agreement" (which is what it is legally) that is, a grant of agency, freely made for a limited period, revocable under conditions laid down by the manufacturer, and renewable only at the manufacturer's pleasure. To the dealer, the "franchise" is capital, "his" capital; but the manufacturer cannot admit that the dealer has any right to the "selling agreement" nor can he allow the dealer to sell or transfer this agreement as if it were his property. In other words, to stay in business the dealer must succeed in holding on to his "franchise" while the manufacturer in order to stay in business must be able to cancel his "selling agreement."

This situation in itself, while explosive, would not be unusual. What gives it its unique character is the fact that— to put it sweepingly—the car manufacturer and the dealer, while tied to each other, are not necessarily in the same business and may occasionally even regard themselves as engaged in competing businesses. The immediate interest of the car manufacturer, his business and the source of his profits, are new-car sales. But the dealer, however unwillingly, is primarily a seller of used cars. In the last prewar years he had to sell an average of two-and-a-half used cars in order to be able to sell one new car. Conditions are different now, in the immediate postwar period, with the automotive reserves of the nation exhausted. But after a transition period we can expect the new-car market to become again predominantly a replacement market as it had been from 1930 to 1941. A considerable expansion in total automobile ownership would result only from major changes in highway construction and city layout. Unless the total number of cars in use increases sharply the automobile dealer's business in new cars will again depend on his success in selling used cars.

This may lead to a situation—by no means uncommon in normal times—where, in order to sell a new car, the dealer has to take a loss on the used car he receives in part payment; he will allow for it more than he can sell it for. In order to sell this used car he will again take a loss on the car traded in against it and so forth. On that part of his business which accounts for about seventy per cent of his turnover—the used-car business—the dealer must take a loss in order to maintain the quantitatively less important new-car business. This means that the dealer's profit depends on his ability to keep the losses on seventy per cent of his sales below the profit he makes on thirty per cent of his business in the form of a commission on new car sales.* How slender this margin is, is shown by the experience of General Motors dealers, who, in a reasonably good prewar year, lost eighty-seven cents out of every dollar received as gross profit on new-car sales in selling used cars.

This way of drawing the picture presents the accounting

---

* This assumes that his overhead costs are carried by the income from his service department, the commission he receives as financing and insurance agent, etc. It also assumes that the dealer does not add a hidden charge to the new-car price—the practice known as "packing." But while in actual practice these assumptions are rarely completely realized, the necessary qualifications would not alter the basic picture.

convention rather than the economic reality of the automobile business. Yet it is true that the main factor in dealer profits is the ratio of used-car losses to new-car profits. This in turn means that the dealer's main chance for higher profits lies in lowering used-car losses, his main danger in an increase in these losses. This applies particularly as the number of used cars that had to be sold to sell a new car had been steadily increasing right up to the war. The dealer will lose if the number of new cars put on the market increases beyond the capacity of the used-car market to absorb the proportionate number of trade-ins; for that, at once, increases the loss on used-car deals. He will gain if the number of new cars available is just a little less than the corresponding used-car market capacity; for that will push up the prices at which he can sell a used car and keep down the price at which he can buy it. In other words the dealer is much more interested in the margin of profit or loss than in the absolute number of new-car sales. This explains the paradoxical fact that many dealers made more money than they ever made before during the war years when there were no new cars, but also no losses on used-car sales.

The profit of the manufacturer, however—at least the immediate profit—depends exclusively upon new-car sales. The more he sells the higher his profit. In terms of immediate results—and this is the criterion by which sales managers usually go and on which they themselves are usually judged and paid—the dealer's loss is the manufacturer's gain. The higher the allowance which the dealer makes for "trade-ins," the more new cars he will be able to sell. There is thus a real conflict between the immediate interest of the dealer and the immediate interest of the manufacturer. And it is in relation to this conflict that the franchise assumes importance.

For it enables the manufacturer to impose his interest on the dealer.

From the point of the dealer it is his right to sell new cars which is the foundation of his business. Without it his capital equipment is not of much value. Above all, the dealer's work and effort, the intangible but most important asset of the "good will of the going concern," is not embodied in something he can take with him, sell or bequeath, but in a better market and a better reputation for his product, that is in something that goes with the franchise. Loss of the franchise is a severe loss; maintenance of the franchise a first consideration. From the manufacturer's point of view the franchise is only a selling agreement which gives the dealer no title. The franchises of the dealers of some of the largest-selling cars can even today be canceled on short notice and without stated cause.

The manufacturer's view of the franchise is amply justified. The right to sell one's product exclusively is a unilateral grant of privilege and must be revocable. But the ambiguity in the economic meaning of the franchise puts the dealer into the power of the manufacturer who possesses a strong advantage in the threat of canceling the franchise. In a situation where there is a latent conflict as there is in the dealer-manufacturer relation, such a one-sided distribution of power must, unless counterbalanced, lead to an abuse of power. Even if the sales manager wants to be fair, he will find it difficult to resist the temptation to use the threat of cancellation to prod the dealer into that high-pressure selling of new cars which leads immediately to higher losses on used-car deals.

It will be said that this is a description of what might happen in extreme cases rather than one of actual conditions. But not so many years ago—in the mid-thirties for instance

—it happened only too often, at least in years of lagging new-car sales.

Such a conflict is dangerous socially as is every conflict between big and small business in the modern industrial society. But it is also very bad business for the manufacturer. A good and loyal dealer organization is as important for the success of an automobile company as a good product; and good dealers are hard to get. In its attempts to eliminate the latent conflict between manufacturer and dealer General Motors was certainly conscious of the broader, social implications of the situation. But above all the problem of fair and satisfactory dealer-relations is a problem of the efficient functioning, success and survival of the company itself—as much as the problem of leadership-training for instance. The dealer-policies of General Motors thus aim at making the company a better organized, more successful and stabler producer. They also aim at making General Motors a better citizen; but that is a secondary rather than the primary purpose.

Dealer Policies

The dealer-policies of General Motors fall into three categories: (1) Strengthening of the dealer's hold on the franchise including the erection of safeguards against excessive pressure on the dealer by the company's sales staffs; (2) Strengthening of the dealer's economic position through increasing his efficiency and helping him to keep down used-car losses; (3) Finally—the arch stone of dealer-manufacturer relations—the resolution of the latent conflict over immediate profits in the common long-term interest of dealer and manufacturer in a healthy automobile market, The short-term conflict still exists potentially; but wherever it threatens to become actual it can be settled in the best long-term interest of both parties.

Into the first category fall the changes in the General Motors dealer contract which eliminate arbitrary or sudden cancellations of the franchise. During its duration—the current contract is for two years from the delivery of the first postwar cars—the franchise can be canceled only for cause and at three month's notice. The actions or omissions on the dealer's part which constitute cause for cancellation are expressly enumerated in the agreement. Before the franchise can be canceled, the manufacturer, in the person of his regional or zone sales manager, will give the dealer a fair warning. Cancellation is not left to the regional or zone sales manager. However strong the case against the dealer, the internal rules of the company provide that it must always be submitted to the general sales manager of the division for which the dealer works—both to insure uniformity and to eliminate the influence of personal animosities. In addition the company is bound to repurchase a dealer's stock and to share in the expenses of his lease in the event of a cancellation of his franchise.

While the dealer is thus protected during the period of his contract he has no legal claim to a renewal of his franchise; nor can the manufacturer give him such a right without losing control over the distribution of his products. This is clearly understood by the dealer. Also, the question of renewal seems to be a much less pressing one than that of cancellation—perhaps because renewal-negotiations can be carried on in cool blood and over a longer period, whereas cancellations used to be made under the nervous strain of a selling campaign. But while most franchises will be renewed as a matter of course, it is in the interest of both dealer and manufacturer to lay down definite rules and to exclude arbitrary and high-handed methods.

Thus another internal General Motors rule: every decision not to renew a franchise must be passed on by the general sales manager of the division. It must be based upon a recommendation of the regional or zone sales manager and upon definite reasons. The regional or zone sales manager is expected to have served a formal warning on the dealer, and to have given him a chance to mend his ways. In addition General Motors in a case of nonrenewal has the same obligation to repurchase the stock and to share in the lease of the dealer as if it had canceled the franchise.

These rules should take care of the routine. But there always remain a few cases where there is a genuine disagreement on the interpretation of the rules, and others in which they may be abused. Though numerically not important, such cases might produce a great deal of friction and of bad will; above all they might leave the dealer with the feeling that the rules are hypocritical and that the manufacturer tacitly tolerates or even encourages practices which he officially forbids.

Hence, in 1938, General Motors provided an administrative appeals board to which dealers can take recourse when they feel that they have been wronged by the divisional sales managers. This body—its official name is the Dealer Relations Board—consists of the four highest-ranking officers of the company none of whom has any direct concern with, or responsibility for, sales. Any dealer can appeal to it, though the board may refuse to hear trivial disputes. The appeal is decided without charge to the dealer, proceedings are informal, and the verdict is given within thirty days—provisions patterned after those of the quasi-judicial review bodies of the Federal government. In its seven years of existence the board has been appealed to only sixty-seven times, mostly over the cancellation or nonrenewal of franchises. Its real importance lies, however, not in the cases in which its decision has been invoked but in the cases—number unknown but believed considerable—in which the very fact of its existence has brought about agreement between dealer and sales manager. It has led sales managers to adhere to the rules; for no sales manager likes to be disavowed by the top officials of the company. It has convinced the dealers, who apparently were quite skeptical at first, that they are protected against arbitrary decisions and against an abuse of the sales manager's power to cancel the franchise or to refuse its renewal.

These policies of General Motors have largely removed the franchise as a source of friction from dealer-manufacturer relations. One point remains that cannot be covered by general rules—the safeguarding of the dealer's interests in the event of his death or retirement. A successful dealer undoubtedly feels rightly or wrongly that he has added greatly to the value of the franchise—not by building up equipment but by building up good-will. The value of his business will be considerably greater than the value of his tangible assets; of his profits only a small part will be attributable to his tangible investment, the larger part will be a return on effort expended and on reputation built up. Yet the dealer's legal title is confined to the tangible assets which alone he can sell or bequeath. And no automobile manufacturer—whether a private corporation or a state-owned automobile trust—could recognize a vested or hereditary title to dealership.

The General Motors solution for the problem is to make it part of the sales manager's duty to safeguard the dealer's extralegal and extracontractual equity as much as possible. If a dealer dies his son will be confirmed in the dealership if he has the necessary qualifications; to make this possible some of the divisions offer training courses for the sons of

dealers. If the son does not want to carry on or is not qualified—or if there is no son—the regional or zone sales manager will try to find a qualified buyer for the business who,
in taking over the dealership, will pay a fair price for the
going business of his predecessor. The same applies if a
dealer wants to retire. General Motors is under no legal—
probably not even under a moral—obligation to recognize
the equity of the heirs or of the retiring dealer. The franchise
has lapsed with the death of the dealer; and as the dealer
does not own it he cannot sell it upon retirement. But in
actual practice the unquestioned right of the manufacturer
is subordinated to the interest of the dealer wherever possible.
General Motors is even willing to provide acceptable candidates for a dealership with the capital to buy out a dealer
who wants to retire or the heirs of a dead dealer.

I have heard it said by some General Motors officials that
this method of recognizing the undefinable stake of an old
and successful dealer in the value of the franchise, is pater-
nalistic, dependent on the company's good-will and not, therefore, a permanent solution of a real problem. But the problem
of the invisible and intangible improvement made to the
property by a faithful lessee or tenant, though antedating
the automobile business by several thousand years, has never
been adequately solved. The only guarantee of an adequate
performance is the fact that of all the problems arising out of
the franchise, this is the one in which the dealer's interest is
least likely to clash with that of the sales manager. The sales
manager risks nothing by recognizing the moral title of the
dealer, and he stands to gain a great deal in good-will, confidence and loyalty.

The roots of the potential conflict between manufacturer
and dealer lie in the used-car losses. To build up the dealer's
efficiency and his economic position General Motors concerns

itself almost as much with the used-car market as with the new-car market in which its own direct interests lie. Every zone or regional sales manager has a used-car specialist on his staff to advise and help the dealers. The sales manager watches carefully the dealers' inventories of used cars and warns the dealers of any sign of congestion which might force used-car prices down. The Chevrolet Division for example has built up an entire used-car sales organization parallel to its sales organization for new cars. It makes constant surveys of the used-car market and research studies of consumer preferences and aversions when buying used cars. When at one time it became difficult to sell cars of its strongest competitor at second-hand, Chevrolet diagnosed the trouble and found a way to overcome it. To the people within his organization who complained that it was Chevrolet's job to sell its own cars, not those of the competitors, the sales manager simply answered that to sell used competitive makes was one of the ways to sell new Chevrolets.

Finally, General Motors has made concern for the used-car market one of the factors which decide its new-car production and sales policy. The company draws up each year a production program based on the best available analyses and forecasts of market conditions. On the basis of this program the sales managers of the car divisions allot new-car sales quotas to individual dealers. One of the determining factors in this program is the supply and price situation of the used-car market and the outlook for the dealers. This means that, instead of relying on pressure, the sales manager can base his demands for sales on a set of data which, while not infallible, are at least impersonal.

Harmony Out of Conflict

General Motors has realized that the dealer's interest, a healthy used-car market, is as much an interest of the corporation as the sales manager's interest in new-car sales. New-car sales determine the company's profit for the current year. But the used-car market determines long-term prospects and profits. To put it in a different way, General Motors has realized that it has not earned its profit on the car it just sold until the last in the chain of used-car buyers has paid his last installment. This approach turns the policies described here from concessions to equity and dealer pressure into necessities of prosperity for the manufacturer. As soon as the sales manager himself measures his performance by the twofold scale of current sales and used-car conditions, his interests parallel those of the dealer instead of clashing with them.

Resolution of the potential conflict between dealer and manufacturer finds expression in two organizations in General Motors through which the dealer and his interests are represented in the company's management: the Dealer Council and the Motors Holding Division.

The Dealer Council is an advisory body which meets regularly with the senior officers of the company (meetings were suspended during the war). Now in its tenth year the Council has a membership of thirty-six or forty-eight members organized in three or four panels. The members, usually holding office for two years, are selected to represent a geographic cross-section of the country as well as a fair sample of typical conditions. While not delegates in the sense of being elected or nominated by the dealership, they tend to regard themselves as representatives of the General Motors dealers in their territory, call meetings of these dealers to report on their work and to hear criticism, suggestions and ideas.

The Council brings before central management the views, problems and complaints of the dealers. Its discussions have ranged from technical questions of automobile design to merchandising and advertising techniques. In addition it was asked to review the whole problem of the franchise; the new franchise has largely grown out of its discussions.

Compared to the Council which meets with considerable fanfare in the Chairman's office, the Motors Holding Division seems rather inconspicuous at first sight. Whereas the Council speaks on behalf of all 12,000 General Motors dealers with a capital investment of about $300,000,000, Motors Holding never has represented more than 300 dealers; and the capital with which it operates has even in the busiest years remained below the ten-million mark. Nevertheless, it is more novel and more interesting an experiment than the Dealer Council. It may also have directly and indirectly contributed more to the solution of the dealer-manufacturer problem.

Motors Holding is an investment banker, advancing to qualified candidates for a General Motors dealership up to seventy-five per cent of total capital requirements. It is probably the only institution now operating in this country which successfully makes "character loans" of equity capital to small businesses. For this alone it deserves attention because the provisions of risk-bearing capital for small businesses is one of the greatest needs in our economy today.

The immediate aim of Motors Holding is to help dealers. It advances capital to qualified purchasers of the business of a dead or aging dealer. It grubstakes young men with drive and ability but with insufficient capital. It also enables the car divisions to give the franchise to the best qualified rather than to the wealthiest candidate. In purpose and function it is comparable to other service staffs of General Motors. Its value to the business does not lie in the profits it makes directly but in the greater profitability and efficiency of the units it serves. Motors Holding runs its business therefore on a basis which tends to limit its returns to a moderate interest and service charge. The lion's share of all profits goes to the dealer. In addition he alone benefits from any appreciation in the value of his business—usually the main source of profit in capital financing. He is not only entitled but compelled to buy Motors Holding's share holdings in his business at cost and as fast as profits permit. How well Motors Holding has done its job can be seen from the fact that altogether 500 dealers have been set up in business by its capital loans. At the time the war broke out about 300 dealers were carried on the books with an average investment of $25,000 to $30,000 per loan.

Motors Holding has the right to dissolve the partnership by buying out an unsuccessful dealer. This has proved necessary only in one case out of twenty—a rate of success which compares very favorably with the experience of other forms of investment, and which goes far to prove the contention of the advocates of "character banking" that a man's ability and integrity are better security than real estate or shares. Motors Holding thus proves two important points: that risk capital can be supplied to small business—as against the assertion that in the modern economy small business must choke for want of capital; and that the capital needs of big and small business do not conflict by necessity but may complement each other.

Perhaps even more important is the intangible result of Motors Holding's operations. The division is an organ of General Motors. Its capital funds come out of the company's treasury. Its losses have to be borne by General Motors. Its offices are in the corporation's central office. Yet its interests are the interests of the dealers—and not of that abstract thing "the average dealer" but of three hundred concrete, live dealers selling General Motors cars under all kinds of conditions all over the country. Motors Holding is thus not primarily interested in the formulation of general policies, but in concrete issues of dealer-manufacturer relations which are likely to affect its investment. If a sales manager's actions and policies are prejudicial to the dealers' interests and prosperity, Motors Holding will tackle the sales manager—not as an outsider appealing to equity but as an organ of the company protecting a General Motors investment. The sales manager will be much more willing to accept Motors Holding as unbiased and as likely to be right than he would be to accept a dealer. General Motors as a whole will also obtain a better and more sympathetic knowledge of the dealers' problems and point of view from Motors Holding than from surveys or conferences. It is hard to say how great the influence of Motors Holding has been in the development of the policies and practices through which the dealer-manufacturer conflict is being converted into a harmony of interests; for it has been mainly exercised through informal talks on specific issues. But that it has been a very considerable factor in the solution of the dealer problem is certain.

The relations between producer and dealer thus built up, represent an application of the principles of decentralization to a problem that is very different indeed from those in connection with which decentralization was first developed. The original task of decentralization had been to establish divisional autonomy within an institution. Applied to the dealers, decentralization was used to establish unity between independent businesses. This shows, or at least it indicates strongly, that decentralization is a general concept of indus-

trial order—a concept of federalism as we called it earlier
—rather than a mere administrative technique.

The experience of General Motors shows clearly the general rules that apply to the resolution of any economic or
social conflict in harmony. The mere will to get along is not
enough; but it is neither possible nor desirable that one or
either party give up its self-interest. Harmony can always be
achieved if there is at least one area where the self-interest
of the one is identical with the self-interest of the other. Then
co-operation can be anchored in the joint pursuit of this
common interest, to which the other and divergent interests
can be subordinated. Starting with the agreement on the one
area—for instance the long-term interest that General Motors
and the dealer have in common—the understanding of each
other's position on those issues where the interests are in conflict can be organized. General Motors' experience proves again
the old truth that a durable political structure is not one in
which self-interest is subordinated to altruism or vice versa,
but one in which the two become one or at least are made to
pull in parallel directions.

Finally the organization of General Motors' dealer relations is of general importance as an example of relations
between big and small business. Nobody will deny that there
is potential or actual conflict between Big Business and the
small businesses connected with it as suppliers, dealers, etc.
The question is only whether harmony can be created. Hence
the importance of General Motors' attempt to solve the problem.

No other industry will have precisely the same problem of
small business–big business relations as the automobile industry. To few other industries could these solutions be ap-

plied directly. But the general principles on which General Motors has solved the problem: federalism and the resolution of conflicts in harmony might well provide a model for a job that is still to be done in other branches of America's economy.

DECENTRALIZATION AS A MODEL?

OUR study seeks to examine General Motors primarily as a test of the achievements, problems and solutions of a free-enterprise system.

The leaders of General Motors themselves regard their concept of decentralization not as a technique of top management but as a basic principle of the industrial order. Hence the question arises whether their corporation below the level of top management can be organized on the basis of decentralization with its objective yardsticks. Secondly: even as a concept confined to top management there is the question of the general applicability of decentralization to American industry. This is particularly pertinent, as General Motors is basically different in structure from most other American corporations. It produces several hundred distinct finished products which are the result of independent though closely allied manufacturing processes. Also with a productive machine that is amazingly diversified in its products and processes, General Motors is integrated in actual operation, not only technically and financially but through producing for one market. Out of this juxtaposition of unity and diversity, the General Motors policies doubtless have been developed; but how much validity do they have beyond the specific problem with which they were originally designed to deal?

If decentralization is a valid concept of industrial order then the individual divisions within General Motors must be capable of being organized on and by it. If the concept can be applied with fair success to organization within the divisions, it can be safely assumed to have universal applicability to, and validity for, American business in general. For most American corporations are more diversified in their products and processes than the individual General Motors division— hence, a priori, more readily organized on a decentralized basis.

Obviously, conditions within a division are very different from conditions on the top-management level. Instead of an organization according to products, with each divisional manager the head of an integrated unit, divisional organization is on a functional basis with each executive the head of a functional department—engineering, for instance, or selling —which could not exist by itself at all. This difference is the greater the farther down we proceed. It is not possible to look upon the executives within a division as independent and to give them that freedom which the divisional manager enjoys. Above all, it is not possible to lay down a distinction between general policy and administrative decision. Finally —perhaps most important—the objective yardstick of competitive market position cannot be applied directly to the departments within a division. As far as they are manufacturing departments they can be measured by the yardstick of efficiency in terms of cost and of return on the investment; but they do not have a distinct marketable product the performance of which can be measured directly.

Still, in a considerable number of divisions, decentralization and the complementary policy of objective yardsticks have been made the basis for intradivisional organization. One wartime division, producing airplanes, applied the pattern of General Motors to the organization within the division. Its five plants were run very much as if they had been five divisions. This did not apply to the relations with the customer —the government—which was necessarily centralized so that all orders were obtained by the divisional manager. This also, of course, determined the production schedule of the five plants. But the work was distributed in such a way as to give each plant a complete and integrated job to do. Consequently, each plant manager could be left to his own decision how to perform his assignment. Methods and approach differed widely from plant to plant even though they were situated close to each other.

This particular division was built up in great haste in 1942 and 1943. It was necessary to train in the shortest possible time more than forty thousand workers and close to two thousand foremen. Many of the foremen had never before been in an industrial plant, not even as unskilled workers. Yet not only engineering and purchasing, but foremen and personnel recruiting and training were left in the hands of the five plant managers. As long as they did a good job and turned out their production quotas, the divisional manager did not interfere. At the same time, the divisional manager built up a small central staff of a dozen key men—comparable to the service staffs of General Motors—whose function it was to advise the plants, to help the plant managers whenever they felt in need of help, and to maintain unity in methods and approach between the plants.

Decentralization in this division was carried beyond the plant level and extended to superintendents and even to general foremen. Whenever possible, the subordinate departments were organized so that they did an integrated and complete job, which made it possible to give the man in charge full responsibility. Following the example of General Motors, all men of executive and supervisory rank were kept informed of divisional policy and divisional problems by frequent meetings with divisional management.

Other divisions achieve similar results by less novel

methods. In one accessory division with a conspicuously good record, both in war and in peace, decentralization is achieved through the organization of a small group of senior executives comprising chief engineer, production manager, works manager, sales manager and personnel manager, who work closely with the divisional manager. Each of these men has his own particular job. Each, however, is assumed to be capable of taking the divisional manager's place at any time, and has therefore to inform himself of all phases of the division's operations. The divisional manager thus gets a fairly good impression of the abilities of each of his associates for independent commands, and each of the men obtains a fairly broad education for leadership and a general understanding of business problems. This policy is supplemented by similar organizations farther down the line, by frequent meetings of supervisors and junior executives with divisional management and with colleagues in other departments, and finally by a policy of promotion which tries systematically to give to promising men an all-round training and to acquaint them at every stage of their career with all aspects of the business. This is particularly noticeable in the way foremen are handled in this division. They get comprehensive training when first promoted; they are also steadily shifted—first within the department, then within the business as a whole—so as to bring out their abilities and to force them to see the business, rather than their own specialized department.

In yet another division—one of the smaller car producers —the essence of decentralization is conserved through utilization of the tradition of craftsmanship which is particularly strong in this division. Superintendents and even foremen are frequently brought into the councils of management. They are informed of major problems that come up—whether they affect their own department or not. They are given opportunities to study the problems of other departments of the division, and their advice is sought on matters concerning their department. This division, too, emphasizes all-round training in its promotion and personnel policy; it is the only division of the company as far as I know where as much attention is paid in promoting a man to what he needs to learn as to what he is able to do.

Every one of these divisions is a big business in itself. The aircraft division with its 45,000 workers was very big business indeed and a good deal larger than most of the units of production found even in the biggest American corporations. Very few big businesses are as concentrated on one final product as was this division. Hence its experience proved both that decentralization can be applied to management within the productive unit of a large corporation, and that it can be applied to businesses producing one or two rather than a hundred final products. Not many American businesses could simply copy the General Motors model; but all—or practically all—could apply the General Motors principle.

What Good Is Decentralization?

One question, however, remains still unanswered: What is the advantage of decentralization? Would there be any point for any other large corporation in adopting the principle of decentralization? This question goes far beyond the problems of business management and touches upon vital issues of social organization.

Within General Motors itself, a minority of senior executives—small in number but of considerable experience and influence—inclines towards the view that decentralization is not necessarily the most efficient form of industrial organization except under special conditions.

The problem is best illustrated by the example of the Fisher Body Division—one of the largest within General Motors. Fisher Body decentralized its organization for war production. It divided itself into five major sub-divisions corresponding to its five major wartime products. The manager of each sub-division was in pretty much the same position as the manager of a General Motors division. He had his own staff and handled his own problems directly. Even within the sub-divisions there were decentralized units with their own management. And the Fisher Body central management was organized after the model of General Motors central management. It was a policy-making and supervisory body rather than in direct charge of production. It supplied the producing units with advice, help and direction through divisional service staffs. Before the war however Fisher Body was almost completely centralized. Its plants were dispersed all over the country; wherever there was a General Motors car assembly plant there was a Fisher Body plant contiguous to it. Yet even minor matters of local management usually had to be referred to Detroit for decision. And while—for reasons of its peculiar history—the division had the atmosphere of a large clan rather than that of a modern army, government was most decidedly exercised through orders from the top.

Within this division itself it is widely held that a centralized organization is the most efficient one for the Fisher Body peacetime type of production: one highly complex finished product of which only a few small parts—such as the hardware used on automobile bodies—could be separated out technically or economically. It was natural, efficient and altogether necessary to decentralize in wartime when Fisher undertook to turn out five distinct final products. It would, however, have been unnecessary and contrary to the logic of the productive process to decentralize Fisher's peacetime organization. According to this opinion, decentralization, while universally applicable, is not universally valid as the most efficient form of industrial organization. To present the argument in different words, Fisher Body is a conspicuously efficient producer. Its efficiency and performance account in large part for General Motors' rise to first place in the automobile business. While the internal figures of the corporation are not available, there is little doubt that the rate of return on which Fisher operates compares favorably with that of decentralized divisions. What advantage in efficiency could Fisher derive from being decentralized? What disadvantage is entailed in its centralization?

Very much the same question is posed by the experience of another one of the very large divisions, Chevrolet, again a conspicuously efficient producer—as responsible as Fisher Body for General Motors' growth. Yet Chevrolet also does not apply the principle of decentralization, or rather it applies it in a form which changes its whole meaning. Instead of using decentralization as a principle of industrial organization, it uses it—very successfully—as a mechanism to speed up administrative work. Where General Motors sees in decentralization an application of the concepts of constitutional government and of the rule of law Chevrolet regards it as a traffic rule. One might say that General Motors spells "Decentralization" with a capital "D," Chevrolet with a small "d." In spirit Chevrolet is probably even more centralized than Fisher Body was before the war. Yet no one can question its productive efficiency.

In Chevrolet we do not even have the factor which deprives the Fisher Body example of its representative character: that there is one very large, expensive and complex final product incapable of technical or economic subdivision. Chevrolet manufactures a considerable variety of goods. All of them go into the final car. But a good many of them are distinct as products as well as in the methods of their manufacture. Apparently this is a clear case for the application of genuine decentralization; yet the failure to decentralize beyond the initial stage has not, it would seem, resulted in impaired efficiency.

The importance of the question whether decentralization is absolutely more efficient than centralization does not lie, primarily, in its application to business management. It is actually the question whether a socialist economy can be as efficient economically as a free-enterprise economy. The issue between free enterprise and what for want of a better name may be called collectivism, should not be decided on grounds of economic efficiency. It is first of all a question of the organization of a free society and secondly one of full employment. Yet economic efficiency is an important aspect of the problem.

The Market Check

The difference between the free-enterprise system and state socialism or state capitalism is the dependence of the former on the market as the determinant of prices, profitability and production. The chief argument in favor of the greater economic efficiency of the free-enterprise system has always been the effect of the competitive market check. The main counter-argument has always been that the market check can be replaced by cost accounting and by "socialist competition," that is by cost efficiency alone.

All divisions of General Motors, even the biggest, are judged in the final analysis by their success in a highly competitive market. Yet the individual department or unit in one of the very big divisions is too far away from the market for its performance to be related to market success.

If it happens to manufacture a part or a sub-assembly which could not be sold or appraised independently, it is subject only to the yardstick of cost accounting. On the belief that this yardstick is insufficient unless supplemented by the yardstick of the market, General Motors bases its advocacy of decentralization which relates the individual producing unit again directly to the market. The very large divisions of General Motors, however, have attained tremendous internal efficiency without decentralization, that is, on the sole basis of cost accounting.

It would not be much of an exaggeration to say that the very large divisions of General Motors are run much like the units in a planned economy. They resemble remarkably, in their interior organization, the Russian "trusts" with their "socialist competition" regulated by base pricing as described in the most authoritative book on Russian industrial management.* Equally striking is the parallel between the approach of the management of the biggest General Motors divisions to problems of industrial organization and the reported approach of Soviet industrial managers. If a big business—and few Russian units are as big as Chevrolet or Fisher Body— can be as efficient a producer on a centralized as on a decentralized basis, free enterprise could hardly be maintained to be the necessarily most efficient producer—though, of course, efficiency of production is neither the only nor the supreme test of a social system.

One answer to this question might be that the biggest General Motors divisions are efficient not because but in spite of their centralized management. Their organization actually is less efficient. But this relative inefficiency is prevented from

---

* *Management in Russian Industry and Agriculture* by Gregory Bienstock, Solomon M. Schwarz and Aaron Yugow (Oxford University Press, New York. 1944).

making itself felt by the annual model change customary in the automobile industry which forces each car manufacturer to prove himself anew every year in a highly competitive market. In consequence, even the units of a centralized large division are under steady, though indirect, pressure from the market. Their results cannot actually be measured in terms of competitive market position since these units by themselves do not produce a finished product, but the competitive pressure is at work all the time throughout the division. Thus the effects of decentralization are achieved to a considerable extent even though decentralization itself is absent.

This corresponds to the well-known argument of theoretical economics that cost accounting is a sufficient yardstick of productive efficiency only if there is a real market. Without such a real market in the distance—a market that is "objective" in that it cannot be manipulated by those who are measured by it—cost accounting lacks a valid frame of reference. It ceases to be reliable and to be incorruptible. "Socialist competition," that is, cost accounting without the ultimate reference to the market, according to this argument, is like a game of poker in which one player could always change the rules to suit his hand. It cannot be as efficient as cost accounting subject to an indirect market check. And the latter in turn can only be as efficient as the direct market-check supplied by decentralization if the market is unusually competitive as in the automobile industry. Indeed, the market situation of this industry is so unusual—for the annual model is something few industries could have—that we would be justified in concluding from this argument that on the whole a *centralized organization, even if its cost accounting is anchored in a genuine market, is inferior in productive efficiency to a decentralized organization with its immediate double check of cost accounting and market.*

It is a good argument; and it shows both the function of the market as an *objective* yardstick and the validity of decentralization as a principle of industrial order. Yet it rests essentially on negative proof, and even the best negative proof always sounds a little specious. Another argument however roundly asserts that the centralized large divisions of General Motors are less efficient than they would be if decentralized. While they can produce goods as cheaply and as efficiently as any decentralized division, they fail to measure up to one of the most important yardsticks of institutional and administrative efficiency: they do not discover and develop industrial leaders.

Developing Leaders

This does not mean that people in Chevrolet and Fisher Body do not advance; perhaps there are greater opportunities for promotion—and undoubtedly greater opportunities for higher incomes—in the large divisions than there are in the small ones. The managerial employees of the large divisions may well enjoy a greater security than people in the smaller divisions. Yet a senior executive of one of the large divisions told me that he, himself, had advised one of his subordinates to accept a less well-paid job in an accessory division. "If he had stayed with us, he would undoubtedly have made more money and he would have had very good chances here. But he would not have received the training in an independent job and proper business experience. Above all, he would have remained a more or less anonymous member of a large organization. Now he will be forced to make himself familiar with all aspects of management instead of with engineering alone. He will be forced to learn to make decisions. He will be judged on his performance, rather than on that of a large organization. And if he has ability, as I think he has, he will have a good chance to become a divisional manager and to graduate to top management." In other words, in the big divisions, because of their centralized organization, men are likely to remain specialists with purely departmental knowledge right up to the very end of their careers. They do not receive a rounded experience which enables them to be leaders, nor do they get the opportunity to show their abilities in an independent command where they can be judged by their own individual performance. In a large centralized division there is thus a lack of that efficiency which alone holds out the promise of economic efficiency tomorrow, and without which there is no proper solution of the problem of survival, vital to any institution.

The assertion that the very big, centralized divisions are of inferior efficiency in leadership training and development could not be proved or disproved statistically. In fact while this book was being written, several Chevrolet executives were being promoted to top-management positions in General Motors. Yet, there is an impression throughout General Motors— intangible but real—that top management has been recruited to a proportionately greater extent from the smaller, decentralized divisions than from the centralized big ones. Whenever people talked to me about the bright young men who are likely to be on top ten or fifteen years hence there was an emphasis on men in the smaller divisions. While the very big divisions have undoubtedly done as good a war-production job as anybody in this country, the examples used by executives in their stories of managerial ingenuity and technical achievement were predominantly taken from the smaller divisions. When General Motors embarked upon its most difficult war job in which a division had to be founded to do an entirely new job that had never been done before—a job on whose successful performance the Pacific war depended to no small degree—the new manager as well as his chief assistants were taken from small divisions. By itself each of these impressions—and I give only a sample—would be meaningless. But while not adding up to proof, taken together they display too consistent a pattern to be mere coincidence.

Perhaps most telling is the fact that this conclusion seems to be fairly generally accepted as valid within General Motors, and even within the big divisions themselves. A senior executive of one of the big divisions after speaking at length about the advantages of his centralized organization, concluded by saying that they were attainable only because the smaller decentralized divisions supplied the top leadership. The efficiency of General Motors, he said, lies in its having a small number of big businesses to make the money, and a large number of small businesses to supply the leadership— "very much in the manner in which a big baseball club will get its talents from its small farms, but its revenue from the big-timers." Another very successful big-division man frankly charged his own outfit with a tendency towards bureaucratic rigidity that was stifling initiative and ability, and with creating discontent among the younger executives who had no chance of development in leadership and independent command. One of the favorite stories with General Motors executives is that of the large division which, some fifteen years ago, was split up into four or five new divisions. When the divisional manager who had built up the business, protested in the name of productive efficiency, he was told that the problem was not one of productive efficiency at all but of giving four or five times as many men a chance to develop, to become leaders and to test themselves against the responsibilities of an independent command.

Even more indicative is that Fisher Body has decided not

to return to its prewar organization in its conversion to peace-time production, but to attempt to maintain a decentralized management. The need for trained and independent leaders who cannot be obtained in sufficient quantity and quality in a centralized organization no matter how efficient it may be as a producer, was given as the main reason for this decision.

The importance of this conclusion for the controversy between free enterprise and controlled economy is very great. It enables us to assert that a collectivist economy, even if it should succeed in producing goods as cheaply as a free enterprise in a competitive market, would be of inferior efficiency in developing and training leaders capable of decisions and of assuming responsibility. The leadership of a socialized economy would have to be developed outside of industry; or recourse would have to be taken to emotional stimulants, such as revolutionary fervor or the appeal of a war, to bring out the full abilities of the individual. Furthermore, such an economy could not depend on the automatic succession of leaders on the basis of their performance, but would have to use periodic "purges" to bring in new blood. I believe that while by no means a complete explanation of the periodic purges of Russian industrial management during the last twenty years, the inability of a socialist economy to find, train and develop leaders in the normal course of business might have been an important component.

From the over-all point of view, the ability of an institution to produce leaders is more important than its ability to produce efficiently and cheaply. Efficient and cheap production can always be reached, given the human abilities and the human organization. But without an able, responsible and enterprising leadership, willing and capable of taking the initiative, the most efficient institution cannot maintain its efficiency, let alone increase it. The inability of a socialist enterprise to produce leaders and the failure of "socialist competition" to replace adequately the yardstick of the competitive market are very severe weaknesses. It may be maintained that to let the consumer decide what should be produced is dangerous for the survival of organized society, and that free enterprise pays too high a price for institutional efficiency. That, however, would be a political judgment, not one based on economic rationality; and if made, it should be based on the full awareness that in a socialist economy the major and automatic means for the steady supply, training and developing of economic leadership is absent.

Market and market price do not only have the economic role usually attributed to them but a social role as well. They supply objective performance tests for managerial ability, and thus furnish society with a principle of succession in the economic sphere. The test of the market supplies a principle of legitimacy to the economic sphere without which we may well be reduced either to purely bureaucratic criteria, to "purges" or to naked fights for power as a means of deciding who should run our economic institutions.

Finally in order to have a free enterprise economy it is not enough that its productive units be privately owned. They must also be so organized as to be subject in their entirety to the objective test of competitive market standing. To supply this is one of the major objectives of decentralization. General Motors has not worked out fully the organization of the large corporation, as long as its largest divisions tend towards centralization. Even so, decentralization has been proved to be a promising approach which seems capable of solving the institutional problems of the large corporation.

CHAPTER THREE

THE CORPORATION AS A SOCIAL INSTITUTION

1

THE AMERICAN BELIEFS

SO FAR we have dealt almost exclusively with questions of social and economic engineering, questions which, though not without their controversial features, by and large permit of objectively provable solutions. Now, in the realm of political beliefs, desires and values we enter a sphere in which the controversies are not merely on methods and techniques but on the goals of social life. Therefore we have to make clear, at the outset, that our concern here is with the particular beliefs, aims and purposes of American society with its roots in the Christian tradition.

It is characteristic of the American tradition that its political philosophy sees social institutions as a means to an end which is beyond society. It has never accepted society as an end in itself; nor has it ever seen social institutions as mere expediency, unconnected with the ultimate ethical ends of individual life. It has, at one and the same time, refused to accept that deification of society which endows the state, the nation or the race with absolute value, omnipotence and omniscience, and that degradation of society which makes the law a mere traffic rule without any ethical significance or reason.

Americans rarely realize how completely their view of society differs from that accepted in Europe where social philosophy for the last three hundred years has fluctuated between regarding society as God and regarding it merely as an expression of brute force. The difference between the American view of the nature and meaning of social organization and the views of modern Europe goes back to the sixteenth and seventeenth centuries. During that period which culminated in the Thirty Years' War (1618-1648) the Continent (and to a lesser degree England) broke with the traditional concept of society as a means to an ethical end—the concept that underlay the great medieval synthesis—and substituted for it either the deification or the degradation of politics. Ever since, the only choice in Europe has been between Hegel and Machiavelli. This country (and that part of English tradition which began with Hooker and led through Locke to Burke) refused to break with the basically Christian view of society as it was developed from the fifth to the fifteenth century and built its society on the re-application of the old principle to new social facts and new social needs.

To this social philosophy the United States owes that character of being at the same time both the most materialistic and the most idealistic society, which has baffled so many observers. This country can be materialistic because it gives an ethical meaning and an importance to the material institutions of social life. This seems outrageous to the European idealist who sees basic beliefs and ethical ends as existing in the realm of pure spirit and as completely detached from the sordid and humdrum human existence. It appears as dangerous nonsense to all those who maintain that society is its own goal and who therefore see in the demand that it justify itself in terms of individual fulfillment a demagogic appeal to the baser instincts of the rabble. At the same time America appears to be unbelievably, at times even childishly, idealistic because to an American material institutions and material gains are never an end in themselves but always a means for the realization of some ideal goal. Hence analysts have fluctuated between describing this country as completely obsessed by the drive for the "almighty dollar" and as quixotically engaged in reforming the world in the search for the millennium. Undoubtedly either characterization while grossly exaggerated, is essentially correct; but the true picture only emerges if we see the two as complementary. The American who regards social institutions and material goods as ethically valuable *because* they are the means to an ethical goal is neither an idealist nor a naturalist, he is a dualist.

To this philosophy of society this country owes its great political insight. The *Federalist* is a classic of politics precisely because it manages to be profoundly pragmatic and deeply moral at the same time. But to this philosophy America also owes its worst political blind spot: a refusal to see the existence of an irrational, emotional or naturalistic basis of allegiance. Thus the American people have repeatedly failed to see great emotional forces within their own country —the years before the Civil War are a good example—as they often fail to understand the behavior of foreign, especially of European, nations. It was almost impossible for an American to comprehend that, for instance, a German soldier would fight well even though bitterly opposed to Nazism. The proposition—elementary to every European whether German, French or Russian—that you owe allegiance to your country and nation as the permanent facts of human life rather than to the creed adopted by them for the time being, sounds like blasphemy to American ears. To an American too his country is the reality of his social life, but not because it exists but because it is the living embodiment of the American creed which thus receives the emphasis.

It does not concern us here whether this philosophy is a correct or a true statement of political reality.* What concerns us is that it is the only concept on which to base a meaningful analysis of American society. For Americans themselves see it that way and judge their society by the degree to which it realizes the basic purposes and beliefs of the individual. Hence Americans can afford to neglect many problems of social and political organization European nations have to face. At the same time this country has to take seriously any question relating to the relationship between American creed and American social performance. It must always ask whether its social institutions carry out the basic promises of American life or not.

It may be said that any complex society must contain many institutions which have nothing to do with the fulfillment of society's promises and the realization of society's beliefs. To have overlooked this and to have established the fiction of an absolute unity of culture and of the social "ideal type" is one of the weaknesses of cultural historians such as Spengler or of the cultural anthropologists of the modern American school. It can also be said that any society needs institutions which by their very nature cannot be related to social goals. This is, for instance, true of the family which finds its purpose in the biological survival of man, and which is thus a condition of society rather than conditioned by it; and the same is true of a church whose kingdom is not of this world, and which therefore transcends society. But if a social institution operates in such a manner as to make difficult or impossible

---

* I believe both that it correctly describes society and that it alone provides the basis for a free society as discussed in detail in my *The Future of Industrial Man.*

the attainment of the basic ethical purposes of society it will bring about a severe political crisis—and not only in America. A good example of this would be the conflict between the rising state and the universal church at the end of the Middle Ages; or—the reverse—the conflict between the religious purposes of the Christian churches and the ethos of nineteenth century society.

As far as the representative social institution of a society is concerned, even more is demanded than compatibility. For the representative institution must, in its very operations, promise to realize society's promises and society's beliefs. It is this promise which makes it the representative social institution. In other words, we not only have a political problem of functional harmony between corporation and society, we also have a political problem of ethical harmony. The very means which strengthen the corporation and which render it more efficient must also promise to bring about substantial realization of the basic beliefs and basic promises of our society. Otherwise we could not have a functioning industrial society in America.

We are not however looking for perfection or for the ideal, but for the possible. The strength and cohesion and ultimately the survival of every society depend on its ability to realize its basic promises and beliefs sufficiently to be acceptable to its members as meaningful and rational. But no society can ever realize its promises in full and for every one of its citizens; perfection does not pertain to the kingdom of man. On the other hand no society could survive if it failed completely to carry out what it promises. Such a society would be worse than a failure; it would be a threat. It would appear as irrational and as a mockery of its own, proclaimed beliefs. But how much ethical efficiency a society has to have in order to be acceptable and to appear as rational and successful is not known and can probably not be ascertained except in a purely pragmatic test. It is probable that the minimum ethical efficiency needed to keep society going is fairly low. The individual citizen is willing to accept not only a fair degree of chance but a fair degree of failure, provided that they appear to him to be the exception rather than the general rule.

Refusal to accept the inevitable shortcomings of any society is responsible for a good deal of what is best in political life. The demand that society be made to live up fully to its promises and beliefs underlies the activity of the reformer and accounts for many social and political advances and improvements. And nothing is more contemptible than the smug resignation to the inevitable imperfections of society which in all ages has characterized the Philistine.

At the same time refusal to understand that society and social institutions cannot be perfect, and that by the very nature of human activity their efficiency is low (though no lower than that of any other man-made thing such as, for instance, a steam engine) accounts for some of the worst mistakes in political analysis and political action. Time and again and in every society there have been men who considered their own society and its institutions doomed and ineffectual because they did not run at a hundred-per-cent efficiency. As long as this leads to nothing worse than premature predictions that this or that institution (capitalism, democracy, the British Empire or Russian communism) are doomed, no real harm is done. But it very often leads to a cynical willingness to give up what we have because it is not perfect. It is, for instance, certainly true that the United States will not be a perfect democracy as long as the American Negro is treated as an outcast. But to conclude therefrom as did a section of the Left that American democracy is nothing but a sham and might as well be scrapped entirely is not only illogical but dangerous. It is political smugness surely as con-temptible as that of the Philistine and perhaps more destruc-tive.

Analysis of the degree to which our society and its institu-tions fulfill our basic beliefs and promises has to start with the realization that without some considerable ethical effi-ciency no society and no institution can survive. Yet it must also be accepted that not more than partial success can be expected or should be demanded. To paraphrase words of Edmund Burke, it is not enough to prove a society to be less than perfect to justify its overthrow; one must also prove that a new society or new institution is likely to do better.

Fundamental Promises

It will never be possible to obtain anything resembling unanimity on the concrete ways to realize the basic beliefs and promises of American society. But on these beliefs and promises themselves the American people agree apparently with hardly a dissenting voice. Fundamentally, American political philosophy stands on the Christian basis of the uniqueness of the individual. From this follows (a) the prom-ise of justice or, as we usually phrase it, of equal opportuni-ties. From it also follows (b) the promise of individual fulfillment, of the "good life," or, in a perhaps more precise formulation, the promise of status and function as an indi-vidual.

While not confined to America, the dogma of the unique-ness of the individual is nowhere else emphasized so strongly or made so exclusively the focus of social promises and be-liefs as in this country. This exclusive emphasis certainly sets the United States apart from the rest of the Western Hemi-sphere. It shares, however, with the modern West—at least with that part of it that is in the Protestant tradition—the projection of its basic beliefs into the secular sphere. It is to the social and economic sphere that this country looks for the realization of its beliefs and the fulfillment of its promises. Whether this is still true of Europe—as it was undoubtedly true up to 1914 and probably up to 1929—is very doubtful indeed; and here may well lie a major cause of future conflicts and collisions between this country and the Old World.*

Projected into the secular sphere, the concept of the uniqueness of the individual becomes what in this country is usually called "middle-class society." This concept was undoubtedly in the minds of the people who, in a public-opinion survey conducted by Fortune Magazine a few years ago, defined themselves in an overwhelming majority of more than ninety per cent as belonging to the "middle class"—a declaration of faith in the principles of American society as well as in the reality of its fulfillment.

Like every other slogan, that of the "middle-class society" makes no sense if taken literally. A middle class clearly requires a class above and a class below; yet a "middle-class society" clearly implies that all—or almost all—members belong to and number themselves among the middle class. This discrepancy between literal and actual meaning of the term has not escaped attention. Indeed for a hundred and fifty years it has served the extremists on both Right and Left as an easy target at which to shoot their accusation that the concept is a hollow sham, a delusion and ridiculous propaganda.

Probably very few of the people queried in Fortune's public-opinion poll knew the exact figures on income distribution or had worked out the mathematical odds on their own

---

* This whole question has been discussed extensively in my book *The End of Economic Man* (New York and London, 1939) ; but it does not concern us in this study which focuses on the United States, and which, for reasons given in Chapter I, assumes the basis of our social beliefs as given.

social and economic advancement; but even fewer, if any, will have labored under the delusion that in this country there are no rich and no poor, no weak and no mighty. What they meant by calling themselves almost unanimously "middle class" was first that in this country there is only one mode of life. The millionaire who wants to live in an "upper class" home has to import a château from France, and the worker rides to the plant in a car of the same make as that of the boss. This is what Americans usually mean when they talk of "equality," a specifically American phenomenon for which no parallel could be found in Europe. It explains those features of American society which have always struck visitors from abroad: the friendliness and neighborliness, the absence of envy, the genuine pleasure people take in somebody else's success, the absence of any special reverence or awe for the man on the top—but also the preference so often shown for "safe" mediocrity or the premium on conformity. There has been a great deal of discussion whether this concept of equality is the product of the frontier or whether the frontier life was based on it. Whatever its origin, it pervades all American life. It shows in such small details as the general accessibility of even the highest official and the absence of special elevators for the bosses in office buildings, and in such major traits as the deep resentment against anyone—man or nation—who "throws his weight around."

"Middle-class society" also means in our minds a chance for each member to have a meaningful, a useful, a full life. Indeed, the traditional argument in favor of a middle station is that it alone allows a man to lead a dignified and meaningful life—a life in which he has status and function as an individual.

Finally—and above all—implied in this concept of a "middle-class society" is the demand that in this country position in society is, or should be, determined by nothing but the individual's contribution to society. In this sense there is indeed no upper and no lower class because, strictly speaking, there is no class. The "middle-class society" of the American dream is thus really a classless society but one based not on equality of rewards as is the utopia of the Marxists, but on equality of justice.

All this is familiar. But what is often overlooked is that equality of opportunity and the human dignity of status and function stand in a very peculiar relationship to each other. On the one hand they are Siamese twins neither of which can exist without the other. They must be realized at the same time and through the same social instrumentalities to give us a "middle-class society." Yet they stand in a dialectical contradiction to each other that makes them appear incompatible. One principle demands that each individual have status and function because of his uniqueness as an individual; the other that his status and function depend exclusively on his contribution to society. The first leads to the demand that each member find individual meaning in society—that society be seen as existing exclusively for him. The second leads to the demand that social position be based on individual achievement and ability, that the individual be judged on his social performance alone. The one seems to lead to a hierarchical concept of society, the other to anarchy.

It is deceptively easy to resolve the conflict by throwing out one of the concepts. This was the way of the decayed feudal society of eighteenth century France or of the seventeenth century Levellers in England—to name only two attempts. Yet every such attempt at a one-sided solution has proven that the beliefs can only be realized together. It is not possible within the Christian tradition to give status, function and meaning without giving a rational chance of equal opportunities. It is not possible within the Christian tradition to give equal opportunities without giving individual dignity. Those two concepts stand in the same relation to each other as the North Pole and the South Pole: neither can be where the other is, yet neither can be without the other. In the American concept of a middle-class society this is clearly recognized; and from this recognition the concept derives much of its strength and all of its appeal. But this recognition also poses for American statesmanship a constant problem of synthesizing and balancing.

If the big-business corporation is America's representative social institution it must realize these basic beliefs of American society—at least enough to satisfy minimum requirements. It must give status and function to the individual, and it must give him the justice of equal opportunities. This does not mean that the economic purpose of the corporation, efficient production, is to be subordinated to its social function, or that the fulfillment of society's basic belief is to be subordinated to the profit and survival-interest of the individual business. The corporation can only function as the representative social institution of our society if it can fulfill its social functions in a manner which strengthens it as an efficient producer, and vice versa. But as the representative social institution of our society the corporation in addition to being an economic tool is a political and social body; its social function as a community is as important as its economic function as an efficient producer.

The demand for status and function as an individual means that in the modern industrial society the citizen must obtain both standing in his society and individual satisfaction through his membership in the plant, that is, through being an employee. Individual dignity and fulfillment in an industrial society can only be given in and through work. Hence the painful futility of all the brave attempts to give the modern citizen individual fulfillment in "cultural," "recreational" or "leisure-hours" activities. The first demand thus is that our citizens are citizens because they are engaged in industry. This is the problem with which Social Security has tried to grapple. For you are not a citizen if your status in society depends on forces over which you have absolutely no control such as the business cycle. Equally important is that the individual must be able to realize through his work in industry that satisfaction which comes from one's own meaningfulness for society and which expresses the basic conviction of the uniqueness of the person. The industrial society must give its members that sense of importance which cannot be produced by propaganda or by other psychological means, but can only come from the reality of having importance. This is not a demand for "industrial democracy" if by that is meant a structure of industry in which everybody is equal in rank, income or function. On the contrary it is basically a hierarchical concept in which positions of widely divergent rank, power and income are each seen as equally important to the success of the whole because of the subordination of one man under the other. To attack industrial society, as would the sentimental equalitarian, because it is based on subordination instead of on formal equality, is a misunderstanding of the nature both of industry and of society. Like every other institution which co-ordinates human efforts to a social end, the corporation must be organized on hierarchical lines. But also everybody from the boss to the sweeper must be seen as equally necessary to the success of the common enterprise.

At the same time the large corporation must offer equal opportunities for advancement. This is simply the traditional demand for justice, a consequence of the Christian concept of human dignity. What is new is only that we today look for the realization of justice in this life and in and through the industrial sphere. The demand for equal opportunities is not, as is often mistakenly assumed, a demand for absolute equality of rewards. On the contrary equal opportunities automatically assume an inequality of rewards. For the very concept of justice implies rewards graduated according to unequal performance and unequal responsibilities.

Equal opportunity means obviously that advancement not be based on external hereditary or other fortuitous factors. But it also means that advancement be given according to rational and reasonable criteria. This question of the criteria for advancement constitutes the real problem the modern corporation has to solve in this area.

There is nothing new in these beliefs and demands. But never before have we looked to the industrial sphere for their realization. In spite of a century of industrialization the American, in common with all Westerners, has been pre-industrial in his mentality and consciousness until the most recent years. He has looked for the realization of his promises and beliefs to farm and small town regardless of the reality of big industrial plant and big city. Only now have we realized that the large mass-production plant is our social reality, our representative institution, which has to carry the burden of our dreams. The survival of our basic beliefs and promises —the survival of the very meaning of our society—depends on the ability of the large corporation to give substantial realization of the American creed in an industrial society. The task which the corporation is asked to carry out is both a very heavy and a very new one. No one in the world knows yet the answers to the problems of this brand-new thing, the industrial society. We shall be very satisfied and happily surprised if we find as much as promising beginnings.

Are Opportunities Shrinking?

A characteristic of an industrial society is that it should be able to realize most easily what has traditionally been regarded as the most difficult achievement of society. Justice has always been something that could not be attained in this world, at least not to any substantial extent. But in an industrial society substantial equality of opportunity should be obtainable, as it is inherent in the structure of the society. The demand for managerial and technical ability in the modern industrial society with its mass-production technology is so large as to be almost insatiable. One should therefore expect to find that equality of opportunity in our industrial society is taken for granted. Indeed whatever meager statistics are available show uniformly that the ratio of foremen to workers and of superintendents to foremen is much higher today than it was thirty or fifty years ago and that it is still rising.

Yet there is no doubt that popular opinion on the whole, in this as in all other western countries, is convinced that opportunities are shrinking under the modern industrial system and that equality of opportunities is shrinking even faster than opportunities themselves. One does not have to take a formal poll to know that a great many—perhaps the majority—of the people in our society would answer "Yes" to the question: Do you think that the modern corporation offers fewer opportunities than the small business of a generation ago?

In such a clash between statistical fact and popular impression, the engineer or statistician is prone to dismiss the popular belief as "pure prejudice" and worthless. But political actions and reactions are based not on statistics but on political belief. Facts and figures determine the effectiveness of an action, but not the action itself. Moreover it is the first rule of political analysis that a strong popular belief must be held to have a rational basis, however irrational it might appear at first glance. It is always the vague and inarticulate but plausible answer to a very concrete and real question. Hence it is all-important in politics to find the underlying cause of a widely held belief.

The popular conviction that modern industrial society fails to realize equality of opportunities and justice of economic rewards to a substantial degree is therefore in politics conclusive evidence that the modern industrial corporation does not perform adequately its social job. It may well give more men more opportunities than the small business society which it succeeded. But it certainly does not do it in a way and through methods which appear rational and meaningful to the individual in our society. This is true both for advancement from worker to foremanship—advancement into the industrial middle class—and for advancement from foreman to superintendent, that is, the advancement of the middle class itself.

Three reasons for the failure to provide a satisfactory system of equal opportunities are readily apparent.

(1) However many opportunities there may be, they are rarely anywhere in the modern industrial plant organized in a rational and comprehensible system and according to objective criteria. From the point of view of the worker—and increasingly from that of the foreman as well—selection for promotion is irrational and bewilderingly haphazard. It seems to be based on nothing but the arbitrary whims of a management quite remote and personally almost unknown to the men

in the ranks. Every manager will reply hotly that this belief is nonsense, and that he and his staff give a very large part of their time and very serious attention to the selection of the right man for promotion. Needless to say, this is absolutely true almost everywhere; but it is also irrelevant. What matters is that the deliberations and decisions of personnel management are not based on any clear policy and on any impersonal criterion. In the absence of such a basis for decision the worker and the foreman—who are not "in" on managerial deliberations—cannot see any pattern; and in the last analysis there isn't any. Very few managers even realize how irrational their procedure on promotion must appear to the men in their plants. There is often a glaring contrast between the sincere attempts of a plant management to do a conscientious job of promotion and the almost unanimous conviction of the workers in the plant that promotion is based on rank favoritism, whims and accidents. This is inevitable because there is no observable rational pattern of managerial behavior visible to the worker—just as the most fantastic rumors are inevitable and will be believed by sane people if no facts are available.

The first task in the field of equal opportunities for workers and foremen is thus to have a clear, comprehensible and reasonably impersonal policy. Not as a strait jacket forbidding any movement beyond its narrow limits but, like all good policies, as a compass bearing by which decisions can be organized in a pattern while still decided according to their individual requirements. It will be anything but easy to work out such a basis. The industrial plant by its very nature does not permit the application of such routines as graduated examinations. It demands a criterion of promotion based on those most elusive factors, performance, ability and character. Yet without a rational policy all plants may be forced to accept the most constricting and desiccating principle conceivable—advancement by seniority alone. General and rigid application of the seniority rule would deprive the industrial plant of its leadership supply from below, and would thus endanger our industrial society the efficiency of which depends on the maximum supply of leaders. It would certainly limit severely the opportunities for promotion out of the ranks. But the worker and the foreman will not only be willing to take this loss of opportunity to better themselves socially and economically; they will demand it if the alternative is a system of opportunities which seems to be devoid of rationality and incapable of comprehension.

(2) Another reason why the actual performance of the corporation is not accepted as a substantial fulfillment of the promise of equal opportunities seems to lie in the increasing emphasis on formal training and education as prerequisite to supervisory or managerial jobs. It is not our business here to discuss whether this emphasis is actually justified or whether it represents an attempt on the part of management to unload the job of judging a man's abilities and attainments on the professional educator. However great the advantage which the character of modern industrial enterprise and of modern technology gives to the formally trained man over the man who has picked up his education in the shop or the office, we certainly suffer from a tremendous overvaluation of the formal education offered today and of the diploma as a proof of attainment or ability. I hope that the trend towards an ever-increasing formalization of educational requirements will be reversed soon. But at present we have to accept as a social reality that, while formal education is no guarantee of advancement, the absence of a diploma constitutes a handicap.

Even today it is the exception rather than the rule for an

American plant to recruit its entire supervisory and managerial force among the graduates of colleges and engineering schools, and to exclude the men in the shop from any possibility of advancement. On the whole such a policy is followed only by plants employing exclusively or mainly women. But there is increasing justification for the widespread charge that personnel managers pay more attention to a man's school record than to his ability and character.

To a certain extent this tendency is counteracted by the steady increase in the number of people who finish high school and college—especially notable in the Middle West and Far West. Still the emphasis on formal education puts a substantial premium on superior financial standing. For while it is true by and large that an able, industrious child, however poor, can always work his way through high school and college if he wants to, it is also true that the child of well-to-do parents doesn't have to be particularly able to get the same formal education. The quantitative importance of this factor probably is not very great. But qualitatively it is a real problem. For it puts into question the promise to youth to be judged on its performance rather than on its origin which is one of the most treasured traditions of this country. Unwillingness to tolerate any breach of this promise accounts for the almost ridiculous fierceness with which the Middle West and Far West condemn the mild and innocuous nepotism of Boston and Philadelphia. It accounts for the ruthlessness with which the children of very rich parents are excluded from political or business careers—to a point where it is almost impossible for the son of a very rich man to lead a useful life. The emphasis however slight on financial ability which is implicit in the preference for people with a long formal training is thus seen as a substantial weakness of the industrial system and as a substantial failure to fulfill the promises of our society.

It is therefore imperative for the corporation to make it possible for men of ability to gain preferment regardless of the formal education they were able to acquire before going to work in industry. Opportunities to acquire a formal education must be provided for those willing and able to carry the extra work involved but not able to carry the financial burden of an education through the normal channels. Furthermore it would seem advisable for every corporation to think over the whole problem of educational prerequisites and to eliminate them where they are nothing more than devices to enable personnel managers to evade their duty of testing the ability of the men under them.

(3) Finally, the popular impression that the corporation fails to give substantial equality of opportunities can be traced to a failure of the corporation to provide opportunities in which a man can show his latent abilities. This is partly the result of the tendency towards excessive specialization which would be counteracted by the training of generally educated men. But failure to provide an adequate proving ground for ability is also inherent in the nature of modern Big Business. In the mass-production plant there is a natural tendency to keep a man on one job without attempting to find out whether he is capable of doing more than unskilled work. Also, in a big organization it is almost impossible to provide that contact between the man at the bottom and the executive which was natural in the small business; and thus the executive cannot pick out likely-looking youngsters. This is what people mean when they say they would rather go to work in a small business than in a large organization. Although the opportunities are infinitely great in a big organization, the chances of being overlooked and the danger of being mis-

placed and forgotten in a corner are even greater. It is symptomatic that it is believed to be easier for young people to advance from subordinate clerical jobs in the financial, accounting, legal and sales departments than it is to advance in the plant; for those nonproduction departments still retain much of the flavor of small business organization.

Thus the corporation has to find ways of giving its workers, especially its young workers, a chance to show what they can do and a personal contact with somebody interested in what they can do. Perhaps none of the lessons which the war has taught industrial management is more important than that of the extent to which talent and ability in the plants had been allowed to go to waste in the years before the war. The success of the various "suggestion plans" and the success of the mass-upgrading should have taught us that the prewar corporation had not learned how to give scope to the abilities of its employees.

Dignity and Status in Industrial Society

All these complaints are familiar to anyone who has ever studied the social problems of American industry. But even more familiar is the complaint that it is more difficult today for the individual to become independent than it was fifty years ago. Again it would probably be useless to try to prove or disprove this assertion statistically. What is really meant is that advancement in the modern corporation does not give the same satisfaction as was given by advancement in the small business society. The corporation of today undoubtedly advances a great many more people than ever became independent in the small business society of yesterday. It offers much higher economic reward—and perhaps less economic risk—to those it advances. But it seems to believe that economic rewards are in themselves enough, whereas the essence of "independence" is a social and psychological satisfaction which cannot be replaced by economic satisfaction alone. Even a responsible executive in a big corporation is often not "independent" but dependent. He has no sphere of authority in which to fulfill himself as a responsible personality. And he does not have the social standing which the independent small businessman of yesterday had in his community; in fact he has no standing in his community at all if he, as often happens, works for a branch plant or a subsidiary of a big corporation not domiciled in the community.

That this is one of the basic problems of the modern corporation in America is proved by the recent attempts to unionize foremen. It can be proved statistically that as many foremen have a chance to advance into executive ranks as ever before—they may even have a better chance than they used to have. Certainly their economic remuneration is fully as good as that of the independent small businessman, if not better both absolutely and in relation to national income levels. During the last depression foremen were discharged wholesale by panic-stricken managements, in deplorable contrast to the sound traditional policy of keeping intact the supervisory force. But they certainly fared no worse than the average small businessman. Yet a substantial number of foremen seem to have come to the conclusion that theirs is not a middle-class position, and that foremanship is not, as it traditionally has been in this country, the first rung on the management ladder, but a dead end. Foremanship in short does not give adequate individual satisfactions. To a considerable extent this was the result of special wartime conditions and dislocations. But a feeling as general and as widespread as the unrest among foremen—which incidentally could be found in a good many plants long before the war—can only be explained with an inherent failure of the rewards of foremanship to measure up to the promises of a middle-class position. And what is true of the foreman is to a much greater degree true of the worker.

This shows that the problem of dignity and fulfillment—of status and function—is real. It also shows that the problem cannot be solved alone by more or better opportunities for advancement or greater economic rewards. It is futile to argue that there can be no question of a "proletarization" of the middle class because its economic position or its economic opportunities are improving. To maintain a middle class with a middle-class mentality and a middle-class acceptance of society as meaningful, industrial society must also offer psychological and social satisfactions. It is even likely that the lack of dignity and fulfillment which is so obviously the major problem of industrial society, may only be aggravated by emphasizing economic opportunities and rewards. It is an oversimplification—but not altogether a falsification—that dignity and individual fulfillment are so difficult to achieve in industrial society because of its exclusive concern with economic advancement.

"Getting ahead" is seen as the exclusive criterion of success. But inevitably only a minority can advance, only a minority of workers can become foremen, only a minority of foremen can become superintendents. If, as is the case in our society, advancement is seen as the only social goal, if every other satisfaction is regarded as subsidiary, the majority must necessarily feel dissatisfied. It is very likely that most of our present-day concern with "shrinking opportunities" has little or nothing to do with those opportunities for advancement with which it professes to deal. It rather refers to the shrinking of the opportunities for self-fulfillment except in advancement. If this diagnosis is correct, it would explain the prevalence of the conviction that opportunities are shrinking. For total opportunities, opportunities for advancement plus opportunities for self-fulfillment, would indeed be shrinking as the industrial system expands, even though this expansion brings about an increase in the opportunities for advancement. The realization of human dignity, the achievement of status and function would thus emerge as the major unanswered question of industrial society.

The modern corporation as a child of laissez-faire economics and of the market society is based on a creed whose greatest weakness is the inability to see the need for status and function of the individual in society. In the philosophy of the market society there is no other social criterion than economic reward. Henry Maine's famous epigram that the course of modern history has been from status to contract neatly summarizes the belief of the nineteenth century, that social status and function should be exclusively the result of economic advancement. This emphasis was the result of a rebellion against a concept of society which defined human position exclusively in terms of politically determined status, and which thus denied equality of opportunity. But the rebellion went too far. In order to establish justice it denied meaning and fulfillment to those who cannot advance—that is, to the majority—instead of realizing that the good society must give both justice and status.

In its refusal to concern itself with the unsuccessful majority, the market society was a true child of Calvinism with its refusal to concern itself with the great majority that is not elected to be saved. Following Herbert Spencer, this belief is now expressed usually in the language of Darwinian "survival of the fittest" rather than in theological terms. But this does not alter the fact that the philosophy of the market society only makes sense if the unsuccessful are seen as "rejected by the Lord" with whom to have pity would be sinful as questioning the decision of the Lord. We can only deny

social status and function to the economically unsuccessful
if we are convinced that lack of economic success is (a)
always a man's own fault, and (b) a reliable indication of
his worthlessness as a human personality and as a citizen.
But we have not been willing for a long time to accept Calvinism, at least not in this respect. It appears to us an absurd
non sequitur that a man who does not make good in economic
life will therefore also be a drunkard and beat his wife and
children regularly—a proposition which, judging by their
popular novels, seemed perfectly logical to the early Victor-
ians. We either are not prepared to regard economic success
as conclusive evidence of a man's worth, or we are not prepared to cast the worthless, that is, the unsuccessful, into outer
darkness. We therefore have today the problem of giving
social status and function to the masses without at the same
time giving up the equality of opportunity for the sake of
which the eighteenth and nineteenth centuries destroyed the
politically-determined status of the *ancien regime*. It is perhaps the biggest job of the modern corporation as the representative institution of industrial society to find a synthesis
between justice and dignity, between equality of opportunities
and social status and function.

Assembly Line "Monotony"

What causes this lack of status and function, of individual
satisfaction and fulfillment in the industrial system? One
standard answer has been that work in the factory—particularly in the modern mass-production factory—is so monotonous as to deprive the worker of all satisfaction. Instead
of being a challenge to the worker's creative faculties, work
becomes a job to be done for the pay check. Monotony instead of creation, subordination to the machine instead of

craftsmanship and workmanship—these are the traditional terms in which the problem has been discussed from William Blake's bitter denunciation of the "Satanic Mill" to Charlie Chaplin's satire of "Modern Times." And it is the one critical statement about modern industry that even those industrialists are willing to accept who otherwise believe their system to be perfect. The labor-relations expert of a large corporation who said that "nobody with an IQ above moron should be allowed to work on the assembly line" was fairly representative.

There is a good deal to the traditional view. Charlie Chaplin's movie was a gross parody, but a parody of something that exists. Specifically the assembly-line system of industrial production deprives the worker of satisfaction in his work in two ways: by the rigid subordination of every worker to the speed of the slowest man in the line, and by the confinement of the worker to one manipulation repeated endlessly which denies the satisfaction of finishing a job. An ex-automobile foreman turned garage mechanic said: "When I finish a repair job here and the car rolls out, I have done a job; back in Detroit the stack of sheet steel always remained the same however many fenders we turned out." Unfortunately, these features of assembly-line work are encouraged by an "assembly-line mentality" among modern management which believes that a worker is the more efficient the more machine-like and the less human he is.

But it is also true that even in the highly mechanized mass-production plants assembly-line operations employ only a small part of the labor force. Above all it is true that the assembly line as employed in the final stage of automobile production and as caricatured by Charlie Chaplin, is neither the only nor always the most efficient application of mass production. The war has shown that the imposition of one working rhythm and speed and the confinement of the worker to one elementary manipulation are incidental rather than essential features of efficient mass production.

Altogether it is probable that to blame "monotony" is both superficial and sentimental. Clearly, assembly-line work even of the most unskilled kind, is less monotonous than the great majority of agricultural pursuits such as weeding the corn patch, picking potato bugs off plants or setting out tobacco seedlings. Yet, the agrarian life is usually set up as the ideal against the "monotony" of modern industry—only too often by people who have spent all their life in the city. The slogans of "monotony" and of the "lack of creative fulfillment in industry" are based on the same totally false analysis of human life and human work as the "artistic temperament," the "poet who writes with his heart's blood" instead of with ink, or the actor who "lives his part"; that is, they are adolescent and dilettante romanticism. Only the dilettante can afford to forego monotony and to look for "creative fulfillment." The professional is always the man who does a routine job. If there is anybody who, in the traditional explanation, stands for all the modern industrial worker lacks, it is the artist. Yet very few assembly-line jobs are as monotonous, as empty of creative fulfillment, and as tedious as to practice scales.

The charge of "monotony" not only overlooks that monotony is inevitable, it overlooks that a considerable amount of it is necessary and certainly good for the great majority of men. The opposite of monotony is insecurity. Monotony means simply that we know what is going to happen next. Complete monotony is certainly unbearable except for a moron. But complete insecurity is just as unbearable except for a madman. Any normal human being requires a fair amount of routine to remain sane; "battle fatigue" or "shell shock" are but the mental strain that results from too little monotony and too much insecurity. The more creative ability a man has or the more responsibility he is willing to shoulder, the less monotony he needs.

But real creative ability—ability to live largely in a world based on one's own inner resources—is the rarest quality in the world. And the willingness to shoulder responsibility, while much more general, is still confined to a small minority. The well-known reluctance of most workers to accept a foremanship is not entirely due to a fear of responsibility; reluctance to break established social relations with one's fellow-workers is often a potent and a very understandable reason. But the fear of responsibility certainly plays a large part and leads to a desire for monotony, that is, for security.

There are much deeper causes for the lack of industrial citizenship than monotony. To find them we must turn from the emotional argument of "monotony" to the few facts we have.

According to all reports, women in mass-production industry do not suffer from "monotony" nearly as badly as men. This has shown up strikingly during this war when millions of women, mostly without any previous industrial experience, came to work on assembly lines and conveyor belts. Is it likely that there are such profound differences between the sexes as to make a woman like the routine work which a man detests? If that were true what about the tradition that it is Eve and the daughters of Eve who always yearn for novelty? Is it not more likely that the difference between the psychological and physiological effects of routine work on men and women is a consequence of the obvious fact that women do not look on their work in a plant as permanent, as their life's work, as that which gives meaning and standing to their life? They see in it usually an interlude between school and marriage from which they expect no satisfaction but the pay—and perhaps the chance to find a husband. Expecting no satisfaction in the work itself, they are not hurt by "monotony" and the absence of "creative fulfillment."

Such a line of thought is corroborated by the famous experiments conducted in the late twenties by the Western Electric Company at Hawthorne, Illinois. In some of these experiments the conditions under which the worker operated were intentionally worsened and his work was intentionally made more monotonous. Yet his productivity increased, his fatigue went down and his satisfaction rose steadily *as long as the attention and recognition he received were increased.* These experiments thus showed clearly that it is not the character of the work which determines satisfaction but the importance attached to the worker. It is not routine and monotony which produce dissatisfaction but the absence of recognition, of meaning, of relation of one's own work to society.

Wartime experience has gone even further in teaching us the same lesson. In Great Britain, according to all observers, the war brought the industrial worker a satisfaction, a feeling of importance and achievement, a certainty of citizenship, self-respect and pride which he had never known before. Yet this went hand in hand with a tremendous increase in mechanization. In this country there is the example of the aircraft manufacturer on the West Coast who, in the early stages of the war, was faced with what appeared to be an unsurmountable problem of bad morale among the workers: absenteeism, "quickie" strikes, slowdowns and slipshod work. Increases in wages brought no improvement; nor did better hours, better transportation, good nurseries for the children of employees, improved shopping facilities. Finally it was found that the workers had never seen any of the planes they were producing, had never found out where the part they worked on fitted and had never been told how important this part was to the total functioning of the plane. A big bomber was brought in and displayed on the factory grounds; the workers were invited to inspect it, to sit in it and to bring their wives and children along. When finally they were shown the part they were making in the bomber, and its importance was explained to them by a crew member, the bad morale and unrest disappeared at once. What had happened was that the worker was shown his status and function in the war effort as a responsible and valuable member of society and of the nation at war.

These facts show very clearly what the problem is. There is a minor problem of "monotony." In many unskilled jobs in modern mass-production industry those workers who have ability and who are willing to take initiative and responsibility, have little or no opportunity to assert themselves. In the assembly-line jobs proper there is a good deal of frustration—resulting from the imposition of a uniform working rhythm and speed which are unnatural because they are not developed according to the worker's own co-ordination, but are geared to the rhythm and speed of the slowest man on the line and then speeded up. There is also the muscular and nervous fatigue of unbalanced body motions and one-sided concentration which results from the confinement of the worker to one endlessly repeated manipulation.

The major problem, however, is not mechanical but social: in mass-production industry the worker has not enough relation to his work to find satisfaction in it. He does not produce a product. Often he has no idea what he is doing or why. There is no meaning in his work, only a pay check. The worker in his work does not obtain the satisfaction of citizenship because he does not have citizenship. For as very old wisdom has it, a man who works only for a living and not for the sake of the work and of its meaning, is not and cannot be a citizen.

In the war we made tremendous efforts to establish this relationship between the worker and his product, and in the emotional tension of total war this was comparatively easy. But how to attain it in peace when production again is for the individual consumer rather than for national survival? Hitler faced this problem; and his only answer was to make war the only goal of society. American industry will have to find a solution under which we can produce meaningfully for peace.

Can Unionism Do It?

Two attempts have been made so far to solve the problem of industrial citizenship: industrial paternalism and industrial unionism. Both have failed to solve the problem.

The failure of paternalism is obvious. Except for a few survivals which are just barely kept alive by respect for the "Old Man" who built the business, paternalism has become as good as extinct. The reasons for its failure are obvious too. It has been proved not only a false answer but a false answer to the wrong problem. It rests on the basic fallacy that people will take propaganda for reality. Paternalism attempts to give the individual in industrial society status and function by telling him that he has status and function. The problem of status and function in industrial society arises because in the modern plant the worker does not have the dignity and responsibility of an adult but is kept in the dependence of a child. Paternalism tries to make him feel like an adult by treating him like a good child. The result has been—at least in this country—that paternalist management has often led to greater dissatisfaction than the rule of a "tough boss."

Management has large responsibilties for the worker

which it cannot shirk. But the solution of the problem of function and status in the industrial system cannot be found in doing more for the worker, in giving him more social security, more welfare and recreational agencies, in looking after him better. It can only lie in giving him the responsibility and dignity of an adult.

To say that unionism has failed in any of its objects may seem a joke—and one in questionable taste—now that collective bargaining is the law of the land and the union shop all but compulsory. At the outset it has therefore to be made clear that the statement is not meant to deny obvious facts or to question the permanency of unions as the general and virtually compulsory organizations of industrial labor. It is most improbable that, even with the sharpest imaginable anti-union reaction in this country, the fact of unionization or its extent will be seriously questioned. The only major question will be whether the unions are to be, as today, independent, self-governing associations or bureaucratically run organs of the national government. Nationalization of the organizations of labor would certainly not lead to a relaxation of labor laws and restrictions on management. On the contrary it would lead to extreme government control over business exercised in the name of the rights of labor—and it is thus surely in the interest of corporation management to make it possible for the present unions to remain autonomous.

But nevertheless the unions we have today in the mass-production industries do not succeed in giving the worker citizenship in industrial society and are not capable of giving such citizenship. The effectiveness of these unions lies largely in their concentration on economic issues. They can add security measures—an annual wage, or seniority—to their demands for higher wage rates and shorter hours. They can attempt to seize a share of managerial power, power over prices, policies or profits. But they are quite unable ever to subordinate demands for economic advantages or political power to the demands of society even though the members themselves seek in the union above all social integration in a community.

A second point is that unions are in inception and basic nature negative; they are anti-bodies. They were designed to protect the worker *against* management, *against* society. What is needed however is an integration of the worker as a partner *in* the industrial system and as a citizen *in* society. The most powerful union leaders are unable to get their own unions to drop practices which are clearly anti-social, and which, unless discontinued, will make government control of unions a certainty: jurisdictional strikes—clear blackmail against society; the initiation fee racket—a clear denial of equal opportunities; the penalizing of efficiency and progress through "feather bedding" which in levying a private toll on the nation comes close to highway robbery. I do not think that a single one of the major union leaders of this country—with the possible exception of John L. Lewis—considers these practices justifiable or as in the interest of labor. Yet their combined efforts have been completely unavailing, simply because these practices are an essential manifestation of the basically negative tradition of unionism.

Altogether the union, like the corporation, is a basic institution of an industrial society. It has therefore to be in such harmony with society that the achievement of its own ends furthers the realization of society's basic beliefs and promises. But there is a deep conflict between the negative—anti-industry, anti-society—leitmotif of American unionism and the demand of society that the unions, as institutions, contribute positively to the welfare and fulfillment of society.

This should not be an irresolvable conflict. It may not be grounded in necessities of unionism—though unions everywhere have been afflicted with it;* it may be only the result of historical circumstances which no longer apply. And it is to be hoped that the unions can eventually become institutions of society rather than institutions against society, and can participate in the great and difficult job of integrating the worker as a citizen into industrial society. So far, however, they have hardly even tackled the job.

---

*An extremely interesting study of this problem from the pro-labor side is Adolph Sturmthal's "The Tragedy of European Labor" (1943) which convincingly argues that the impotence and collapse of the apparently so powerful labor unions on the continent of Europe was the result of their inability to be anything else but the representative of a special interest *against* society.

THE FOREMAN: THE INDUSTRIAL MIDDLE CLASS *

IN a theoretical analysis of industrial society such as is given in the preceding section, the problems tend to crystallize around the two conceptual foci, equal opportunities and status and function. As we project this analysis into the concrete reality we see that the problems to be solved are quite different in the case of the industrial middle class, the foreman, and in that of the hourly worker. The foreman's unsolved problem is almost exclusively that of middle-class status and function. The worker lacks equal opportunities as well as status and function.

Only two generations ago, there were a few plants in this country where the foreman was a semi-independent contractor who had undertaken to supply a certain product or to do a certain process at a stipulated rate. If he could do the job more cheaply, the difference was his profit—in some cases his only compensation; if he lost out on the transaction the loss was his. In other words, the foreman was close to being an independent businessman, except that he did not own his capital equipment.

It is clearly impossible to run foremanship in modern mass production industry along similar lines. But traditionally, foremanship is still regarded very much as being the highest position within the ranks of the working class and the first rung on the management ladder. This concept of foremanship

---

* This chapter was written several months before the American Management Association published its report on the foreman situation in May of 1945; there is considerable agreement between that report and my conclusions.

distinguishes the American industrial system sharply from the European. In this country, the foreman group is traditionally a middle class into which any able member of the lower class can graduate and from which any able man can graduate into the upper classes. Even in those countries in Europe which, like the Scandinavian countries, developed furthest towards a middle-class society, the industrial sphere has never been included in the middle-class concept. Foremanship has indeed been the highest position within the European working class. But in no country in Europe has it ever been the first position within management. Management was not recruited from among the foremen, but from the outside—the college-trained engineers, the clerical, accounting, and selling departments. Foremanship in Europe has been a dead end—not a middle-class position, but in the working class. It may be said that in Europe the foreman has been very much like the long-serving, non-commissioned officer who will never get a commission. The American foreman too can be compared to a platoon sergeant; but traditionally he is at the same time a second lieutenant, and a member of the same social group as the commanding general.

On this unique position of the foreman depends to a very large extent American middle-class mentality and social structure in an industrial age. If we want to maintain this middle-class society, we must maintain the traditional position of the foreman. That means, as far as the foreman is concerned, that we must maintain the opportunities to rise into management and the middle-class function and status of foremanship.

The Foreman's Opportunities

The foreman of the 1870's who ran his own department at his own risk was in most cases unable to advance any further. Sixty years ago the only means of advance for a foreman was to obtain enough capital to start his own business with his own capital equipment. It is still only a minority of foremen who can expect to be promoted. But today there are scores of jobs as superintendent, or plant manager, which have to be filled, and which are filled largely by promoting foremen. Capital accumulation was undoubtedly much easier two generations ago when there were no income taxes. Personal loans of capital credit could be obtained under the banking methods of those days. Yet the opportunities were still so limited as to be almost beyond comparison with the opportunities for advancement in Big Business today where the capital is already supplied and where a foreman can advance exclusively on his merits as an executive.

The question is, therefore, not whether there are enough opportunities, but whether the opportunities are "equal"; that is, whether selection for promotion is according to a rational and comprehensible scheme which the foreman can understand, and which makes sense to him.

This is one of the problems to which the concept of decentralization is supposed to supply the solution. We can therefore legitimately ask how a corporation which, like General Motors, is organized on the basis of decentralization, tackles the foreman problem.

There are three lines of attack. (1) In the first place there is considerable emphasis throughout General Motors on applying to the foreman the objective yardstick of base pricing and cost analysis. Each year the foremen make an efficiency budget of costs and output for their departments which focuses on three main criteria of productive efficiency: output per man-hour or (where labor with different skills is used together) output per dollar of wages; output per dollar invested in machines; rate of wastage of material and of tools through breakage, faulty work, etc. The budget, and the extent to which a foreman lives up to it, express the foreman's abilities both as a leader of men and as a mechanic; for shortcomings in either capacity will at once become manifest in lower efficiency. In drawing up these budgets the foreman works with the division's efficiency experts but theirs is primarily a service function—to render help and advice to the foreman. There is a close parallel to the service staffs maintained by central management for the use of the divisional manager. The necessary check on the foreman's efficiency is supplied, as in the case of a divisional manager, more by the competition with other foremen and their performance than by dictation from above. This way it is not only possible for each foreman to know precisely how he is doing, but management is given an objective, though incomplete, yardstick for the determination of a foreman's abilities as an executive.

(2) Equally important, though far less general, are attempts to train the foreman for executive positions, and to test promising foremen in more responsible jobs. The first is done in a number of divisions in special foreman courses. The aim of these courses is not only to teach the foreman the rudiments of personnel management but also to give him an understanding of the whole business and of the function of his department in it. At least as much time is spent on discussing the problems of other departments and of the business in general as on the specific training of the foreman for his immediate job. In some few divisions an attempt is made to

rotate a foreman within the plant—usually by calling on him to substitute for a colleague on vacation or sickness leave. Occasionally, foremen are in similar ways tried out in bigger jobs, such as assistant to a general foreman.

In a good many divisions, especially those in which the tradition of craftsmanship is still strong, the top executives themselves take active part in the foreman training programs and thus come to know the men and their individual abilities. In a few others which are particularly personnel-minded, it is made very clear through words and deeds that the divisional management is on the lookout for promising men and that it is in the interest of superintendents and plant managers to give their foremen all the opportunities possible.

(3) Finally, in half a dozen divisions definite attempts are being made to bring the foreman into the councils of management, if only in an advisory capacity. Management problems which concern either all foremen or the business as a whole are brought before informal meetings. The foremen are encouraged to speak their minds, and to ask for information; and an attempt is being made to make the foremen see the problems of business and the reasons for policy decisions and rulings. These meetings, seldom formal, seem to afford a particularly good opportunity for management to find out who is a good man, and seem also to be regarded by the foremen as the best means, next to the yardstick of cost analysis, to arrive at a fair basis for selection and promotion.

But all this, even if developed to the fullest extent, would not achieve very much. Hence the question what could be done is very actively discussed in General Motors both from the point of obtaining an adequate supply of executives and from that of creating adequately equal opportunities for the foreman. Of the many suggestions for improvement mentioned to me by General Motors executives, the following sound both promising and practical:

A foreman, before being selected for promotion to a bigger job, should get some experience outside of his own field, if not outside of production altogether. This would avoid over-specialization and would also give a broader basis for a rational judgment on promotion. The assembly-line foreman, for instance, should be asked to work as a foreman in a machine shop, if not in a clerical department or a service department. It was frankly admitted that in the short run this might be an expensive procedure as a good assembly-line foreman could hardly be expected to make a very valuable contribution to the accounting department. But the belief was also expressed that, whatever the short-term cost, it would be repaid many times in increased efficiency and understanding on the part of the foreman when returned to his old field, and in increased understanding and knowledge on the part of management of the quality of each foreman.

Along the same line was a suggestion to work out a definite policy of trying out foremen in bigger jobs, such as that of assistant to a superintendent. It was felt that thereby management would not only learn a great deal about the real abilities of its junior executives; above all, the foreman would learn himself whether he is really able and willing to assume the added responsibility. To give the foreman a chance to find out for himself what a bigger job is like should result not only in a better and more satisfying selection, but also in much more contentment on the part of those not selected for promotion.

It was suggested several times that promising foremen who had given proof of their fitness for bigger jobs should be given an opportunity for some intensive training—either in courses for senior foremen or through some other form of "post graduate" training for promotion. This would eliminate what was considered a particularly unsatisfactory feature of the present system: that a number of men who are promoted from foremanship to a higher position, fail to do a good job because of lack of training, and have to return to their old job as foreman which makes them feel disgraced and discontented.

None of these ideas is put forward as a panacea. They illustrate however the fact that the problem of equal opportunities for the industrial middle class is mainly one of technical imagination and organization; for the opportunities themselves exist. They also show that, while still far from a completely satisfying solution, the problem is a soluble one.

The Foreman's Job

Far less favorable than the foreman's equal opportunities are his status and function as the industrial middle class. It is actually doubtful whether there is a place for such a middle class in the industrial system. Certainly, during the last fifty years—and especially during the last fifteen—the foreman has lost rapidly in status, in function, and in the chance for individual fulfillment in his job. He has become, or at least tends to become, the "forgotten man" of American industry.

It is ironical that perhaps the gravest threat to the function and status of the foreman group has come from the increase in his opportunities. The foreman of seventy years ago was directly under the owner or the chief executive of the business. This severely limited his chances to become more than a foreman without accumulating capital; it is the development of the hierarchy of executives between the foreman in the plant and the president of the corporation which has given the foreman group the chances for advancement which it has today. But the absence of this hierarchy also gave the foreman an autonomous status and a vital function, comparable to that of the divisional manager of today.

Seventy years ago, the foreman, even if not a semi-independent contractor, was a partner in managerial decisions and in policy making, and the undisputed boss of the workers under him. Today, with a large group of executives above him, most of this function and authority of the foreman has been taken away. Managerial decisions are made on a level so far above his that it takes a determined effort on the part of management to keep the foreman in contact with these decisions. To make him a partner in them is practically impossible. Production methods have become largely a matter of specialized technical training instead of being based on the foreman's lifelong experience; the work is thus necessarily almost completely in the hands of process engineers, time-motion-study experts and trained production men. At the same time the growth of the industrial unit has made it necessary for the business to have a labor policy binding on the foreman. This means that he no longer can hire and fire as he sees fit, that the decisions how to use the men under him is largely in the hands of a trained personnel manager with aptitude tests and time-motion studies, and that there is very little scope for the foreman's traditional job of training skilled workers. The growth of Big Business has tended to deprive the foreman of all managerial function and to make of him a gang boss, whose job it is to see that executive orders are carried out.

Even this function has largely disappeared, as a result of the unionization of the workers, which has substituted the impersonal authority of a contract for the personal authority of the foreman. Also unionization means that questions of labor policy—whether raised by employer or employee—have to be handled on a level of management far above that of foreman since they are likely to involve the entire plant. The insistence of most unions on carrying grievances and other questions of labor policy and treatment directly to plant management instead of to the foreman, on a centralized agency for hiring and firing, and on pushing aside the foreman in practically all such matters, is usually regarded by management as a sinister attempt to undermine discipline and managerial authority in the plant. But even if union leadership were most desirous to collaborate with management, it would still tend to go over the head of the foreman simply because, from the point of view of the union, it is a waste of time to negotiate with someone who lacks the power to make a decision, and who cannot commit the company to a definite policy. The foreman, caught between a strong union and a strong management, will normally try to shirk an issue in which he might have to decide between two so powerful groups.

That the foreman himself regards his position as threatened shows clearly in the success of the recent drive to unionize foremen. True, this drive was caused as much by special and transitory wartime dislocations as by long-term disturbances. True also that a group can unionize without losing its middle-class character. The Newspaper Guild has not made "proletarians" out of reporters; nor has the American Teachers' Union made school teachers any less middle-class minded. Altogether a good case can be made out in favor of a professional association of a large middle-class group working under similar conditions and beset by the same problems. All this, however, misses the point. Foreman unionization is only a symptom. It is not the cause but only one expression of a pretty general change in the foreman's outlook. This change in outlook is itself only the result of a change in basic conditions under which the foreman has become less of a second lieutenant and increasingly a long-serving sergeant.

This shows very clearly in the twofold way in which the terms "executive" and "management" are used. So far in this book, I have used both terms so as to include the foreman. This is, indeed, the usage of General Motors top officials and of some of the divisional managers. This usage is however opposed by some of their associates who feel that the foreman is not a part of management, cannot be organized on the basis of decentralization, and does not have any share in managerial decisions.

This split terminology reflects a split in the actual position of the foreman in the company. As a deliberate policy the foreman is put on a basis essentially different from that of the hourly worker under him. He is on a straight salary which has to be at least one-third higher than the average of the five highest paid men working under him. He enjoys seniority rights in layoffs over the hourly workers. In regard to vacation with pay, retirement pension, and severance pay, he is treated as a salaried junior executive. In addition, several divisions have tried to set the foreman apart by providing special cafeterias for him, exempting him from time-clock punching, etc.

Beyond these formal provisions, there is however no unity in the position of foreman. Some divisions try to make the foreman actually a member of management. In some of the smaller car manufacturers or accessory divisions the foremen not only feel themselves a part of management but *are* a part of management actively and responsibly participating in managerial decisions, production planning and labor policy.

But there are also divisions, among them some very large ones, where the foreman is at best a gang boss. In one he is hardly even that. A special department of divisional management handles all hiring and firing, and also determines where each worker is to work and how. For each worker and each job, this department works out the best procedure through time-motion-studies, aptitude tests and discussions with the worker. The foreman is hardly even consulted. His only job is to see that the production method arrived at in collaboration with the individual worker is observed. He has no right to change it, though he may ask for a revision; the only thing he can do is to ask for the transfer of a worker with whom he cannot get along.

In spite of these disparities of thought and practice, General Motors experience is clear enough on two points. The first is that the foreman himself does not want to give up his middle-class position, and that he will support managerial attempts to preserve it. This shows for instance in the fact that so far there has been comparatively little pressure for foreman unionization within General Motors. Yet the Detroit area is otherwise one of the strongholds of the foremen's union; and the wartime dislocations usually held responsible for the unionization drive were particularly noticeable in General Motors with its tremendous wartime expansion. Even men within the foremen's union itself told me "off the record" of the conviction of General Motors foremen that there is a genuine desire on the part of their top management to give them real authority, status and function.

The second conclusion is that the extent to which the foreman can retain his middle-class status in modern mass-production industry depends on the extent to which decentralization functions. Wherever decentralization—at least in part —has been made to reach the foreman, he is a junior executive; wherever it has failed to integrate him into management he is no better than a gang boss.

We can now answer the question whether foremanship in

modern mass-production industry is a middle-class position or not. It is not correct that the foreman *is* a member of management and that he has status and function as such as the employers' organizations maintain in their fight against the unionization of foremen. It is equally incorrect that the foreman in modern mass-production industry *is not* a member of management as is asserted by the foremen's union. What is correct is that the position of the foreman in modern mass-production industry is marginal. He can be made a member of management at the cost of serious effort and hard work. Yet he can never be quite secure in his middle-class position; decentralization cannot be pushed all the way to the foreman's level because of modern technology as well as because of modern labor relations.

American industry in general not only has to work out systematic policies on foreman training; it will also have to make it a general practice to bring the foreman everywhere into the councils of management. These attempts will be well worth the cost—not only from the point of view of society but from that of the corporation as well. Without the active support of a consciously middle-class foreman group, management would be unable to maintain itself within the plant; and without the active support of the industrial middle-class free enterprise would soon cease to enjoy popular support. Yet even if much more is being done to strengthen the status, function and authority of the foreman than appears possible at present, the social position of the industrial middle class is likely to be ambiguous. It is an in-between position between worker and management pertaining of the nature of both. If the working class is proletarized, the foreman will be proletarized too.

If our industrial society splits into the civil war of the class-war concept, the foreman who lives between the two camps cannot but be deprived of the autonomy and dignity of his traditional middle-class position. The foreman problem can never be solved by attempts on the managerial level alone. His position depends as much on the position of the worker under him as on his relation to the manager above him. If the worker too is integrated into the middle-class concept of American life—if in other words the worker too has status and function in industrial society—the foreman's position in our society will be secure as a middle-class position. Otherwise it will at best be very precarious. In the last analysis the key to the solution of the foreman problem lies in the solution of the problem of the worker.

THE WORKER

THE analysis of the foreman's opportunities and middle-class position has made it clear that decentralization as a principle of industrial order can be applied only where there is at least a rudiment of genuine executive functions. It cannot possibly be the basis for an integration of the worker into industrial society; for it is almost the definition of the industrial worker that he does not direct but is directed.

Nowhere can the problem of the worker's industrial citizenship be seen in purer form, and nowhere is the absence of a solution as grave a matter as in the American automobile industry. The automobile industry stands for modern industry all over the globe. It is to the twentieth century what the Lancashire cotton mills were to the early nineteenth century: the industry of industries. The performance of all industry is likely to be judged by it. Any solution it might find to give the worker citizenship in industrial society would become the general solution. No solution found elsewhere would have much meaning unless it could successfully be applied in the automobile industry. Detroit is *the* industrial city *per se;* and, for better or worse, as Detroit goes, so goes industry.

The automobile industry is also the industry with about the worst relations between labor and management—surpassed by none in mutual bitterness, and matched only by such traditional sources of industrial infection as coal mining and rubber. The main cause of this industrial antagonism which belies the very foundation of American beliefs and promises is the absence of a workable solution of the twin problems of equal opportunities and of status and function of the worker.

There are a good many other contributory causes of the bitterness, distrust and hostility with which the labor situation in the automobile industry is charged. There is, first, the legacy of the 1937 sit-down strikes, which more than anything else prevents either side from approaching a common problem in a spirit of understanding and sympathy. Because of 1937, far too many people in management prefer even today to escape into the belief that workers are a race apart and almost subhuman, and that all labor leaders are crooks and gangsters, rather than face a difficult and dangerous problem. Because of 1937, there are also far too many workers who avoid thinking by convincing themselves that all bosses are fiends. The years of sniping and backbiting of which the sit-down strikes were the climax have warped the perspective even of the sanest men on both sides.

An additional cause of conflict in the automobile industry is its concentration in a few counties of southeast Michigan, which isolates it from the rest of the country. There is furthermore a latent antagonism between the managerial group with its roots largely in the "old stock" of the mid-western small town, and the workers who are very largely first or second generation immigrants from eastern or southern Europe, recent arrivals from the West Virginia and Tennessee hill-country or Negroes. Thus, there is a tendency, especially among the lower ranks of management, to feel superior to the worker, or at least to see him as an alien.

All these disturbing factors are effective only because of the absence of an integration of the automobile worker into industrial society through equal opportunities and through status and function. The memory of the labor troubles of the thirties, the lack of homogeneity between management and labor, supply only the sparks; the dynamite lies in the fact that the automobile industry, as our youngest and most representative mass-production industry, exhibits the unsolved basic problem in its clearest form. In other fields this problem is still obscured by the traditions of the small shop, or by the rich lore of an old craft as in printing and steel making. In the automobile industry the problem is in the open. Detroit and its smaller satellites in the automobile country are the industrial centers which most clearly pose the vital problems of industrial society. From one point of view this means that conditions in the automobile industry, in spite of all appearances to the contrary, are comparatively healthy; at least the wound is a clean one. Seen from another angle, however, this makes conditions in the industry most difficult and their solution most urgent.

The extent to which the worker lacks equal opportunities to advance shows clearly in the way in which both management and labor look upon the worker's chances. There is an ever-growing tendency among plant managers to depend on outside sources rather than on the men in the plant for their supply of foremen and other junior executives. The degree of an engineering school or a college, or work in the clerical, accounting or sales departments, today constitute the preferred qualifications for foreman and junior executive in many mass-production plants. This is particularly pronounced in all assembly-line processes; even where an assembly-line foreman comes out of the ranks of the workers, he has rarely been an assembly-line worker.

The worker shows his estimate of his opportunities in the demand for seniority as the basis for promotion instead of achievement. Even more revealing is the common belief of mass-production workers that the only chance for a smart man to advance today lies in work in the union and not in work in the plant. Finally, there is the fact that the mass-production worker, on the whole, does not want his children to follow in his footsteps; he is convinced that their best chance for social and economic advancement lies in avoiding work in a plant by going to college—a glaring contrast to the pride of the old craftsman in his traditional and often inherited profession.

Even so, the opportunities for the hourly worker in the mass-production plant are much better than his status and function. The modern mass-production plant needs so many executives that, even with a growing reliance on sources outside the plant, a comparatively large number of workers achieve promotion eventually. But there is little chance for anybody below the executive level to find satisfaction in a job whose relation to reality is very obscure. For the great majority of automobile workers, the only meaning of the job is in the pay check, not in anything connected with the work or the product. Work appears as something unnatural, a disagreeable, meaningless and stultifying condition of getting the pay check, devoid of dignity as well as of importance. No wonder that this puts a premium on slovenly work, on slow-downs, and on other tricks to get the same pay check with less work. No wonder that this results in an unhappy and discontented worker—because a pay check is not enough to base one's self-respect on. Perhaps the best way to sum up is by quoting a craftsman of the old school whom I met years ago. He had just decided to leave a well-paid job in the automobile industry. When I asked him why he was unhappy in Detroit, he said, "The whole place is on relief; even if they have jobs, they still behave and act as if they were unemployed."

There are two standard reactions to these facts. The one is to pretend that things are as they should be. This is the attitude both of the confirmed stand-patter and of the confirmed

Marxist; for both conditions are precisely as they have to be under the capitalist system. That the one uncritically endorses, while the other uncritically condemns, everything connected with this system, makes little difference in their basic negativism. Even less constructive is the second reaction: that of the agrarian romanticist who considers industry the great betrayal, and who knows no answer except to make undone all that has happened during the last two hundred years.

I am well aware that we have no workable solution to the problem; and nothing would appear to me to be more dangerous than the attempt to conceal this by rhetoric or—the most dangerous deception of all—by advertising some "infallible" nostrum. But it also seems to me that the failure to find solutions so far does not prove that they cannot be found through hard work and hard thinking. We could not possibly have found lasting solutions in the very short time—not much more than fifty years—since we first became aware that such a problem exists; and it was much later, probably not before the Great Depression, that this country first realized the central importance of the problem of the worker's citizenship in industrial society.

Equalizing Opportunities

The first and most obvious step to give the worker equal opportunities is to offer him a training that will put him on an equal competitive level with people who have had a chance to go to engineering school or to college. In General Motors this is being attempted by the General Motors Institute which offers many courses on basic as well as on special subjects, ranging from mechanical engineering to such lesser skills as operating a comptometer.

One division on its own goes considerably further and has

an elaborate system of apprenticeship schools supplemented by special work offered at a near-by engineering college for employees of the division. These courses are devised in such a manner as to make anyone who successfully finishes them eligible for promotion to a supervisory position. They are partly given on company time though, in addition, six to eight hours of the worker's own time are required each week. It is the policy of this division to try to have every new worker in the plant enroll in the program. The program has the full support of the foremen, who in many cases are themselves graduates of this apprentice training scheme and who also furnish most of the teachers for it. Yet just enough men have the energy and drive to go through the program to fill the division's need for junior executives—a good indication that there is little to the fear voiced sometimes that offering training facilities to employees will lead to an unusable surplus of overtrained people.

A second line of approach is to give men the opportunity to show latent talent and to acquire knowledge and training within the plant. This is done in some divisions by rotating workers periodically from job to job which shows what kind of a job the man is most fitted for. In some of these divisions an effort is made to give workers with ability a chance of proving themselves in responsible positions by trying them out in such jobs as that of jobsetter or instructor for new employees.

Less promising in my opinion are several attempts to "screen out" capable workers for jobs requiring greater skill or greater independence through formal psychological or aptitude tests, as is advocated by some of General Motors' personnel experts. Such tests never measure the important thing, the integration of specific traits and skills into a personality. While they can say with a fair degree of reliability that a man

is unfit for a particular line of work requiring definite qualities of the mind or of the hand, they can never tell what a man
is fit for, let alone whether he is fit for a position of leadership. But even if an infallible test could be devised, its use as
a basis for promotions would be ill-advised, for it would lack
precisely that element of rational comprehensibility which a
scheme of promotions must have to fulfill the promise of
equal opportunities. However, in deciding where a new man
should start, there is probably a field for tests, particularly
if used as a complement to experienced judgement rather than
as a substitute for it; perhaps as suggested by one executive,
we could thus direct the least able and least ambitious workers into the most mechanical jobs.

Finally, some divisions use methods of stimulating the
worker's interest in his work. These include not only information about his job but also definite rewards for inventiveness
and for an analytical attitude on the part of the worker. These
methods, while definitely designed to provide tests of individual abilities as a yardstick for advancement, find their
widest application in respect to the problem of status and
function.

The Plant Community

As for the worker's status and function the war showed us
how much there is to be done and a few things that can be
done. The war brought into the plants hordes of people who
had never before been inside a factory, and who did not
just accept industrial conditions as a matter of course but
wanted to know why they were doing what they were expected
to do. The difficulties in using these new employees in the
traditional fashion forced a good many plant managers to
develop new methods. In addition, the war supplied an
emotional factor which made production meaningful—in

marked contrast to peacetimes. This, too, showed what should be done as well as a few things that could be done. While the emotional stimulus of war production was ephemeral, some of the lessons of war should—and perhaps will—be remembered now that the war is over.

The first great lesson which might be applied to peacetime industrial society is the flexibility of the concept of modern mass production. Prior to the war, mass-production techniques were on the whole applied with a rigidity which saw in the automobile assembly line the only valid use of the concept of mass production. The war showed that this type of assembly line is neither the only application of the concept, nor in all circumstances the best. It showed further that the concept of the human contribution to production as a minor appurtenance to the machine that was inherent in the orthodox assembly line, is neither the only possible concept, nor always the best. We learned that mass production is much more than a technique. It is a broad concept based on the combination of three factors: standardization and interchangeability of parts; a principle of production which sees each process as a composite of elementary and unskilled manipulations; and a principle of materials control which aims at bringing all pieces needed for any given step of the operation to the operator at the same time.

The new understanding has tremendously expanded the field to which mass-production methods can be applied. We have learned that any operation can be handled by modern mass-production methods if the volume is only large enough. Neither the difficulty of the operation nor the precision required make much difference. This is perhaps the greatest single technological advance made in this generation. At the same time we have learned that it is neither necessary nor always efficient to organize all mass production in such a manner as to have the majority of workers confine themselves to doing one and only one of the elementary manipulations. We have learned that we can, though not always, organize mass production in such a manner that the individual worker is not tied to the speed and rhythm of an assembly line, that is to the speed and rhythm of the slowest and most uneven member of the chain. And it is the subordination of the individual speed and rhythm to that of a line that is responsible for most of the fatigue and nervous disturbance caused by assembly-line work. We have also learned that it is not necessary, in all operations, to confine the worker to one endless operation which is never finished, and which never finishes anything—the factor most responsible for the lack of satisfaction in assembly-line work.

There are countless examples of our new freedom in using mass-production methods. Again and again during the war, unskilled workers had to be used for a new and highly skilled job, simply because skilled men were not available. It was impossible to "lay out" the job in the usual assembly-line fashion in which one unskilled operation done by one unskilled man is followed by the next unskilled operation done by the next unskilled man. The way out of this dilemma was to reconstruct—as in a jigsaw puzzle—a skilled job out of its unskilled components. The operation was broken down into its unskilled components like any assembly-line job. But then the unskilled components were put together again with the result that an unskilled worker, doing a series of unskilled operations, actually performed the job of a highly skilled mechanic—and did it as reliably and as efficiently as had been done by skilled men. Yet each man turned out a complete part at the speed and with the rhythm best suited for him. Each new employee worked through the analysis of his job. "We take him into our confidence" was the way one personnel manager put it. He was then given a chart which showed the operation, step by step; for every step it gave a list of the things the worker had to look out for—temperature, speed, etc. Finally the chart gave for every step the reason why it was being done and what it achieved.

An even more radical departure from the layman's picture of the assembly line as something based on gadgets could be found in a General Motors accessory division in Michigan which was making bomb sights for the Royal Air Force. Here the main problem was not one of speed and precision but one of balancing several dozens of extremely delicate instruments against each other in the final assembly, something like the well-known children's game in which several little beads in a closed case have to be coaxed into holes. This required not only infinite patience but a complete absence of tension which was finally achieved by standing the assembly-line technique on its head. The most advanced methods of materials-flow were used and every worker on the final assembly line received at the same time all the parts needed for his job. But the object of this was not, as on the traditional conveyor belt, to impose speed on the worker but to slow him down to a leisurely and relaxed pace. Each assembly-line worker did the entire assembly job. The parts for the next job did not arrive until he signaled for them. On the final job of balancing there was no time limit at all—in some cases the parts "clicked" in a few minutes, in others it took days. If the balance was not achieved on the first few tries, the worker had to take out some time, either resting or working on another purely mechanical job.

This was admittedly a freak. Yet it contained important lessons. The job had been tackled by several first-rate engineering firms in this country and in Britain. They all had tried to use the orthodox assembly line and had failed to get any production. They concluded that the bomb sights could not be made by modern production methods at all; and that was undoubtedly a correct conclusion as far as traditional assembly-line techniques were concerned. The final solution, however, not only showed that modern methods could be used. It also showed that properly, that is imaginatively, applied, these methods would produce bomb sights many times faster than the skilled craftsman could, and at a fraction of the cost. And though they have no data to prove it, the executives responsible are convinced that these methods, developed to cope with an emergency, would prove faster and cheaper if applied to several products normally turned out on the orthodox assembly line.

Equally illuminating is the experience of another division producing electrical accessories. This division was suddenly called upon to increase the production of an item badly needed by the Navy. It had been producing this item all along; moreover it was a product closely resembling one of its main peacetime products. There should have been no problem of design or production methods. But the manpower shortage in its own area forced the division to move the job to another city with a surplus of labor, though of completely unskilled and inexperienced labor. Hence the job—originally semiskilled—had to be redesigned for unskilled men. The solution, apparently developed independently, was the same as in our first example. The skilled job was reconstructed as a series of unskilled operations to be performed in sequence by the same worker. Each worker was taken individually through the process of designing the whole series of operations. He was shown the finished product and its functions and led back, step by step, to the first manipulation. Several thousand new workers, practically all without previous industrial experience, produced a precision product within a few months, though there had been fewer than fifty men from the old plant to instruct and to lead them. This new and improvised plant apparently produced as fast and as cheaply as the old methods used in peacetime. Exact comparison is not possible, but as far as the available data go, they seem to show that the new technique which replaced the assembly-line-in-space by an assembly-line-in-concept, and which thus enabled one man to turn out a finished product all by himself, was as efficient technically as the old methods. And of course it was many times more efficient in terms of human satisfaction, identification of the worker with his work and understanding of product and process by the worker.

The second great lesson of the war was that it is really not true that the worker is happy and contented if he gets nothing out of his work except the pay check, or that he is not interested in his work and in his product. On the contrary, he yearns for a chance to know and to understand as much as possible about his work, his product, his plant, and his job. Plant management was forced to use its imagination to establish a relation between the war-worker and his product, not out of humanitarian reasons but for the sake of greater efficiency. The result of such attempts was everywhere an increase in efficiency and productivity, as well as in worker morale and satisfaction.

One of the smaller divisions of General Motors in northern Michigan converted from the production of steering gears to army carbines. This made necessary a considerable expansion of production and employment with most of the new workers entirely alien to industrial processes; at the same time, the job required great care and precision. The management worked out a plan under which a special department of skilled men was entrusted with the training of new employees. The new worker was first put on a machine and left there working for a few days to become familiar with the "feel" of industrial work, the atmosphere, noise and smell of a big plant. Then a man from the special department took him—or her; most new workers were women—out to the target range, showed him a carbine, took it to pieces, explained how it works, and showed the part on which he himself worked. Then the new-comer was asked to fire a few shots with the carbine. How important precision is, was being shown by direct demonstration. After the new worker had fired a carbine in which the part which he himself produced was accurate according to specifi-cations, he was given a carbine in which his part was too small or too big; the effect on the functioning of the rifle was imme-diately apparent. After this, the representative of the special department and the worker sat down together to work out the most efficient production methods based on time-motion-studies of the job and on the individual's rhythm. In each case, the precise procedure was worked out individually and with due consideration for the worker's individual physical and psychological characteristics. Most important, it was the worker himself who worked out the procedure and set the schedule, with the trained expert confining himself to guid-ance, advice and assistance. The final result was then drawn up in a chart. The worker knew not only what he did at every step but also why. This established a direct relationship be-tween the worker and his contribution to the war effort through his work, and an acceptance of the most advanced methods of production on his part as something he had worked out himself. In a district known for its high labor turnover and absenteeism, this plant succeeded in keeping both below the peacetime ratio. Perhaps even more important was the fact that the production schedule established by the worker himself topped in almost all cases the norm set by time-mo-tion-studies; and the actual performance exceeded in a good many cases that of the production schedule. So successful has the plan been that this division is firmly determined to maintain it after reconversion to peacetime production.

A good many managers have realized under war-pressure that the worker who takes pride and interest in his work is a better worker and a better citizen. They have also come to understand that, in the past, they have been deficient in imagination and have failed to see both the worker's need for a relation to his work, and the ways in which this need can be answered. Early in the war one divisional manager of General Motors—a model employer with very good welfare and training facilities for his workers—almost turned down an offer from the Army to bring to the plant one of its big bombers for, which the division was producing several hundred vital but small parts. It seemed to him not only a waste of time that would be better spent on production, but also without interest to the workers. To his amazement, this visit created the most intense excitement among the workers and resulted in an almost unbelievable increase in morale and productive efficiency. It was not, however, the story of the exploits of the bomber in combat which made this impression but the interest of the bomber's maintenance crew in the production of the plant. It was from the maintenance crew that the workers first learned what the parts were which they had been producing for two years, where they were used in the bomber, and how important they were. It had never occurred to management to inform the workers of such elementary facts; nor had it ever occurred to management that knowledge of these facts might have any effect on worker morale and productivity. The manager has himself concluded from this experience that it is his most important reconversion job to establish a relationship between the workers and their peacetime product as close and as satisfying as that established by the bomber visit.

The third lesson for postwar policy that is to be found in the war experience is the extent to which in our prewar economy we let go to waste that most precious of all creative assets, human inventiveness and imagination. The wartime suggestion plans aimed at improving technological efficiency by providing a mechanism for workers to make suggestions, and by rewarding them for successful suggestions. They were a real help to war production wherever new products or new processes had to be developed. And even in plants which continued pretty much on their prewar basis, they were a tremendous success as far as the interest of the workers was concerned—proving again the fallacy of the argument that the worker is interested only in his pay check and not in his work.

In the one year 1944 the 400,000 employees of General Motors made more than 115,000 written suggestions for improvements. Even taking into account the emotional stimulus of the war and the fact that—in contrast to the carefully planned peacetime production—there was much room for improvement in the hastily improvised and continually changing production of war goods, the total of suggestions is staggering. And it should not be forgotten that for every suggestion made in writing there was probably another made orally and without a record, and another which a worker meant to make but never did.

At the same time only one quarter of the 115,000 suggestions made—some 28,000—were usable, the rest were useless. Divisional managers on the whole leaned over backward to accept suggestions; all suggestions were carefully investigated by a committee of plant executives who had instructions to use as many suggestions as possible. A worker did not have to have the answer for his suggestion to be accepted; it was sufficient for him to have had the germ of a usable idea. Yet, three quarters of all suggestions could not be used. That the great majority of workers had not learned enough about the plant to understand their own work, shows that the plant does not offer them adequate facilities for learning, just as the number of suggestions made proves that they want to learn and are eager to take an active part.

Where to Begin?

There are three conclusions to be drawn from this analysis of the war-experience. The main job lies in the field of imagination and attitudes—on the part of management as well as on that of labor. The best place to start are such non-controversial, purely technical fields as working methods, products and community life in the plant. Finally it must be realized that, at present, we do not know enough to treat the problem itself; we can only doctor the symptoms. But while such "social gadgeteering" will not solve any of the problems it may give both management and labor the imagination to work on the problems themselves—imagination they lack at present.

There are several areas in which work—even though only "gadgeteering"—seems possible: The one in which important results might be achieved fastest is clearly that of the imaginative use of mass-production methods. For work in this area requires precisely the technical imagination in which modern management excels. Not that results will come fast. In the reconversion period most plants are going back to the orthodox methods used before the war; and we would not want them to do otherwise as, during this period, our first consideration must be maximum speed and maximum employment rather than experimentation. Also, there are a good many processes

—the final car assembly is one—where the orthodox assembly line will remain the only efficient method of production. But because industrial managers are trained to think in terms of cost per unit, the imaginative application of mass-production methods with its promise of greater efficiency may come more easily to them than work or thought not directly related to costs. For this reason we need a systematic evaluation of the haphazard, almost accidental developments of the war period, and a sound and consistent theory of the mass-production concept. Listening to engineers and production men talking about their experiences with mass-production methods—many of them quite oblivious of the fact that they were actually doing new things—I was struck again and again by the need for a new theory of mass-production technology, more or less a complement to Frederick Taylor's famous studies but with the focus on the individual worker rather than on the individual manipulation.

In the relationship between worker, product and plant—the second area in which constructive work is possible—we should try to attain in peacetime the same identification with the product and the interest in it that were the result of patriotic fervor and of the glamour of war production. Admittedly, to turn out hinges for automobile doors is less dramatic than to turn out the same hinges for airplane cockpits. Yet even work on ordinary door hinges is more satisfying and more meaningful to the worker if he knows what the product is, what it is being used for and how it is being made. Not that we should make the worker into an expert engineer or a production man; but it is unnecessary and demoralizing that so many workers in the modern plant know neither how their machine works nor what mass production is.

This is not the place nor am I competent to discuss the techniques of this new job of labor relations. But it is fairly obvious that they would have to be based on a complete reversal of what normally—and wrongly—is considered the basis of such relations: to tell the worker what he is supposed to be wanting to know. The basis must clearly be a willingness to listen to the worker in order to find out what he really wants to know, and what he does or does not know. For this purpose the unusable majority of workers' suggestions for technical improvements might be used. For "worthless" suggestions should tell a great deal about the worker's wants, needs and desires. The very fact that a suggestion has been made, attests not only to the worker's interest in his job but also to his feeling that the job is not done as well as it could be. And because every suggestion is concrete and arises out of the worker's own experience, conversation, demonstration or instruction based on it is directly relevant to the worker, in marked contrast to leaflets, speeches or "educational literature." For this reason alone, every effort should be made to retain the suggestion plan in peacetimes.

This is generally accepted. Yet few suggestion plans have ever been really successful in peacetimes. There are two major obstacles:

First there is the foreman's attitude toward a plan under which his subordinates are expected to make suggestions for better working methods. During the war when most of the products and processes were new and untried, it was easy for the foreman to admit that the workers under him knew more or better than he himself; for nobody knew much about the product or the process at the start. In peacetime, however, the average foreman is apt to resent it as criticism of his efficiency and ability if one of his workers is able to suggest an improvement which had escaped the foreman himself. In the past this has been a serious problem. Perhaps the answer would be to have the foreman himself benefit financially from successful suggestions for improvement made by members of his department.

Much more difficult is the reluctance of workers to suggest an improvement which will make production more efficient and thus deprive fellow workers of their employment. During the war, when every plant could use more people than it could get, this was a comparatively minor problem. Even so, employers found it advisable to compensate workers affected by an improvement suggested by one of their fellow workers; otherwise, even under wartime conditions, there would have been terrific pressure against such improvements as contrary to the interests of labor. In peacetime, as all past experience has shown, this pressure tends to become so heavy as to make it virtually prohibitive for any worker to suggest an improvement. Obviously this is intimately connected with the problem of full employment. But even in very good times there is an apparently irreconcilable conflict between the worker's desire to show his ability, and his loyalty to his fellow workers. However much this loyalty may be deplored by the theoretical economist who holds that labor in the long run will benefit most from technological advance, it is not only an ineradicable, it is a commendable attitude.

To resolve this conflict several industrial plants have tried to eliminate the features which make a successful suggestion appear a threat to the plant community. One accessory division of General Motors which for twenty years has operated a suggestion scheme with good success promises that for a considerable period no suggestion will lead to decrease in employment or to an increase in the number of pieces each worker on the job is supposed to turn out per dollar of pay. A successful suggestion thus means higher production but also higher pay for all and unchanged employment—at least for a considerable period. But while this minimizes the conflict, a resolution can only be reached if we succeed in enlisting the worker's loyalty to his fellow workers on the side of the suggestion plan, that is, if we make the individual worker's suggestion profitable and advantageous for the plant community.

This is the principle on which Soviet Russia has been running its industrial suggestion plan which is the perhaps most successful feature of the Russian industrialization drive. We might well study seriously the Russian policy which sets aside half of the savings resulting from a suggestion during the first twelve months for such services to the plant community as housing, a plant hospital or a plant school. However, the forms in which the workers of a Russian plant benefit from a suggestion made by one of their number could hardly be adopted in this country; they are straight paternalism. But it might be effective to use part of the savings resulting from a suggestion to insure the plant community against the three things the modern worker fears most, chronic sickness, old age and unemployment. Such insurance funds would not put the worker and his private life under the paternalist control of his employer; and they might well be supervised by joint labor-management boards. The chronic-sickness provisions would probably be restricted to cases not covered by the ordinary sickness and accident insurance in force in plants today, but to those rare but particularly dreaded cases of uninsurable chronic illness which stop a man's earning power completely. These suggestions may be entirely impractical or ineffectual. But they indicate how the problem could be tackled.

Suggestions, while the obvious, are not the only means to enlist the worker's active participation in his work, and to promote his understanding of the plant and of his place in it. Our experience indicates that we might make him a party to the laying out and planning of the job he himself is doing. We have mentioned several instances where this was done during the war, for instance, in the production of carbines at a plant normally making steering gears. Of course, the worker would not and could not actually plan more than the details of his job. The main responsibility for production and processes must always remain in the hands of trained men. But the man on the machine could find out for himself what it is that has been worked out for him and why. And he could, by working through the process under an instructor, fit the job to his own best speed and rhythm. Thus he might not only derive much greater satisfaction from his work but might become capable of seeing his own job from the management's angle of vision.

At the same time, an attempt should be made to satisfy the worker's interest in the business that employs him. The need for this has been recognized increasingly during the last decade or so, which has led to such things as the publication of annual "reports to the employees" which try to give all the facts management believes to be of interest to the worker. As far as I can see most of these reports fail because they are transparent and rather inept propaganda and because they are condescending and written with a "papa-knows-best" attitude. What is needed is a serious and adult effort to supply the answers the worker wants to know, instead of giving him the answers management expects him to want to know. In any event the questions should come from the worker.

But measures and policies to give the worker a relation to his work or an understanding of it, in short psychological satisfaction, while essential, are not enough. Feeling, knowledge, understanding, satisfy only if they can express themselves in initiative and responsibility, that is, in doing. Without the reality of active participation, psychological satisfaction will not only be ineffective, it will boomerang and become the basis of even greater frustration. Not to have seen this was the fundamental weakness of industrial paternalism and the chief cause of its fall. In order to give the worker industrial citizenship, status and function in an industrial society, a determined attempt will have to be made to give him initiative and responsible participation.

There is another reason why such an attempt seems particularly important: it is the most direct way to better labor relations. No one who has ever participated as an outsider in the settlement of a labor dispute can have failed to notice that one important cause of the trouble is mutual misunderstanding. The so-called issue is usually nothing but a surface phenomenon; the real issue arises very often out of a failure of management to imagine what goes on in the minds of the worker, and a failure of labor to imagine what management is after and why. A shrewd and experienced labor arbitrator once put it: "I never attempt to settle the apparent issue; I always try to make each side see why the other one has raised the issue at this point. Once they understand that, they can almost always settle the issue themselves." This of course overlooks the fight for power between labor and management that so often hides behind grievances and wage demands. But it is true that it is not the issue that counts but the bitterness behind it, which in turn is frequently caused by narrowness of imagination and understanding. The measures we have been discussing so far would, if successful, give management that understanding of the worker's angle of vision which it lacks today. But it is also necessary that the worker understand the management's job and its angle of vision. Today that may perhaps be even more important than that management understand the worker. Otherwise labor will neither respect nor support the managerial function; and modern industry, which is based on organization, cannot work unless management is left respected and undisturbed in the exercise of its job. The best way in which the worker can acquire the understanding of what management is, what its functions, its problems, its rationale and rationality are, is through the personal experience of initiative and responsibility. To promote it would be a major contribution to industrial peace.

Hence, though difficult, the attempt should be made to bring the worker into the administration of the community services of the plant that are run for his benefit. It is doubtful whether management is not today doing far too much for the worker, instead of letting him do it for himself. An example of the damage that can be done by such well-intentioned paternalism was given in one General Motors division, where Red Cross and War Loan drives were started within the plant by individual workers. Unthinkingly, management took these drives away from the workers and entrusted them to professionals in the personnel department. The professionals undoubtedly did a much better job and raised much more money than the workers themselves would have done. Yet, they deprived the worker of the satisfaction of himself doing something for himself, and thus created real resentment in the plant. It shows how hard it is for management to understand the human problem, that this resentment not only surprised the divisional executives but also was interpreted by them as yet another proof of the perversity of labor.

It must be possible to run such services as accident prevention, the cafeterias, the health service, or, in places where women work, the day nurseries with the active participation of the worker, if not to entrust them entirely to committees of workers and foremen. This would provide an outlet for the desire of recognition among the workers which today finds satisfaction only in union activities, if at all. It would give a good many workers managerial experience. It would also be a step towards making the plant a community in which people live a meaningful life, with a status and function in their community.

The Wage Issue

All these are admittedly palliatives rather than real remedies. Even though it will be hard enough to work out any one of these "social gadgets" all of them together, working successfully, would at best prepare the ground for attempts at real solutions. And even this effect will not be achieved unless the wage issue is eliminated from industrial relations as a source of poisoning and bitterness.

In the traditional discussion, "labor relations" are often assumed to center on the wage issue. To show that this view is mistaken has been one purpose of this study. Actually, the wage issue is, properly speaking, an extraneous issue. Wages are determined not by the policies of labor and management but by objective economic facts of productive efficiency of labor, price for the product and size of its market at a given price. This means that wages are capable, by and large, of being determined objectively; they should not and need not be a contentious issue.

In the reality of today, however, the wage issue is a contentious issue, and one which constantly generates bitterness and stirs up strife. It is also a fact that no constructive social action is possible within the plant as long as the wage issue sets management and labor against each other at every step. The strike against General Motors, for instance, which was called just as this book went to press—November 1945—seems likely to undo all the constructive social lessons of war production on both sides. True enough, the real issue of this strike is not wages; both sides would have been perfectly willing to settle for a wage increase somewhere between the thirty per cent demanded by the union and the ten per cent offered by the company. The real issue is the demand of the union to be ceded a share in determining the company's profit margin and its pricing, that is, a share in management. Yet the strike would never have occurred had the wage issue been solvable on a noncontentious, that is, an objective basis.

There is only one objective basis for wage rates: the productive efficiency of the worker. The worker can be paid only out of what he produces; his wage is a part of the unit costs —the largest part, normally—and must come out of the unit price. Any increase in wages that does not come out of an increase in productivity is not only deceptive; it is harmful to the worker himself. It either penalizes him directly by narrowing the market for his product, or it penalizes the consumers, that is, the workers in other employments who are forced to pay higher prices. Hence only productive efficiency can give us a basis for the determination of wages that is both just and workable.

It will be by no means easy to work out a system under which wage rates are objectively determined by productive efficiency. Apart from the difficulty of obtaining reliable data, there is the big problem of how improvements in efficiency are to be divided between the worker and the consumer, that is, between higher wages and lower prices. But since this, in the last analysis, is a decision between the worker's interest in a higher rate of pay and his interest in greater and more stable employment, the problem should be solvable on the basis of such objective data as the elasticity of demand for a product and its competitive price position. It is encouraging that some of the most responsible union leaders, such as

Harold Ruttenberg of the Steelworkers, have lately shown willingness to accept wage-determination on this basis.

Much more difficult will be the decision how to divide the gains from increased efficiency between wages and profits. Since it is, after all, management whose efforts are usually alone responsible for any increase in productive efficiency, profits certainly deserve a major share. Also, we want to make it worth while for management and owners to exert themselves and to risk their capital as well as their efforts. Hence the least the employer is entitled to is the difference between the rate of efficiency at which his plant operates and the average efficiency of the industry. But the premium on managerial efforts might well have to be a good deal higher. However, net profits are so small in relation to the total wage bill of modern industry that they really are of very little interest to labor, except as a propaganda issue.

An objective basis for wages in productive efficiency would be incompatible with "collective bargaining." But surely collective bargaining has not achieved what its advocates promised—industrial peace. Collective bargaining, that is, bargaining between equally strong partners, is certainly juster than one-sided dictation; and the present law is thus an improvement over former conditions even though it largely replaces the former excess power of management by an excess power of labor. But unless two contending parties of equal weight have a principle of decision in common, their bargaining is not likely to end in peace and harmony but in deadlock, frustration, mutual recrimination and bitterness—precisely what we are having now. Compare with this the amazing results of our wartime policy. The War Labor Board was a makeshift agency, and the "Little Steel Formula" was absurd and arbitrary as a basis for decisions. Yet, wartime labor policy was highly successful simply because the "Little Steel Formula" gave an objective basis for decisions.

The Annual Wage

As important as basing wage rates upon productive efficiency—and much easier of attainment—would be the elimination of the conflict between labor and management on what "wages" are.

To management wages mean the amount of money paid out to workers for each unit produced; it is inevitably a part of unit cost. For the individual unit is what the plant produces and what the consumer buys; the plant does not sell its "output" but individual boxes of matches, mattresses or automobiles. Hence for management wages—the only wages that matter—are the wage per hour or per piece worked.

But to the worker wages are necessarily the total amount he receives at the end of the week or in the course of a year. They are the source of his family income out of which he pays for food, rent, clothing and education, all of which are permanent expenses. He is primarily concerned not with wage rates—what he receives per hour or per piece—but with wage income. Hence management and labor talk of two different things when they talk of wages. And a great many wage disputes which are nominally fought over hourly or piece rates are really fought over the wage income.

If the worker today, with few exceptions, lacks the imagination to see the connection between wage and productive efficiency, management as a whole lacks the imagination to see wage as the source of family income. It also does not see that to the worker wage income is much more important than wage rate, and that he can only be willing to settle questions of *wage rates* on an efficiency basis, if his *wage income* is assured.

It should be possible without too much difficulty to settle this conflict without abandoning the principle of wage rate as a part of unit cost which no management—capitalist or communist—could ever abandon. And it would be to the supreme interest of American industrial management today to work out such a solution right away; for otherwise it is fairly certain that the government will, during the next few years, impose annual-wage plans on industry without, necessarily, paying much attention to the necessities of industrial production.

To be satisfactory a guaranteed-wage plan neither should nor could include all workers. But if such a plan were confined to men with a few years' seniority in the plant—usually the older men with families who most need a predictable income—it would satisfy the workers. And in very few companies does the number of men with more than four or five years of continuous service exceed the number the company would employ anyhow even in a depression. Also it is neither necessary nor possible to guarantee fifty-two weeks of paid work in the year. If the worker knows for sure that, saving catastrophes or offenses on his part, he will receive two-thirds of a full year's pay, he can budget. If we assume that two-thirds of all men have the necessary security—a generous assumption—such a guarantee of two-thirds of the full wages would amount to a commitment for less than half of normal labor costs. Even in 1932, the worst depression year, most industries worked more.

The guaranteed wage raises very difficult problems for companies owning more than one plant which normally, in case of depression, shut down one or several plants altogether and concentrate production in the remainder—for very good reasons of efficiency and cost. It also raises serious difficulties of computing pay for work done in excess of the guarantee, of adjustment for seasonal fluctuations, etc. And in a really severe depression the scheme might break down in some industries; an escape clause releasing the company from its guarantee should orders fall below a certain point—such as fifty per cent of normal—will have to be included in every guaranteed-wage plan. But a bridge over the gulf between "wage" as part of unit costs, and "wage" as the source of family income will have to be built. Otherwise wages will always remain an issue dividing management and labor. And only if wages are eliminated as a perpetual source of disturbance can we ever hope to come to grips with the fundamental problems of social life in an industrial society.

Conclusions

We can definitely state that collectivism—whether state socialism or state capitalism—is not the answer to the basic political problems of industrial society. Indeed it has no relevance whatsoever. State-ownership or state-management of industry would in no way result in a realization of equal opportunities or of self-fulfillment for worker or foreman. The problems to be solved are not problems of ownership or of political control. They are problems of the social organization of modern technology. And there is absolutely nothing to indicate that a state-owned or state-controlled economy would possess any characteristics, would have any scheme of social order that would promise a speedier or a better solution of these essential problems of modern industrial society.*

---

* It is very interesting in this connection that in the Soviet Union today, the industrial managers and planning officials, who together account for a

Indeed this shows very clearly in the actual developments in all countries that have adopted a collectivist order. Everywhere—whether in Soviet Russia or in Nazi Germany—collectivism promised to give citizenship to the members of industrial society. Everywhere it failed to make good this promise. The worker in a Soviet Trust or in a Nazi armaments plant is much less related to his work, much more of a mere cog than the worker in the most mechanized, most de-humanized American plant; and he has far fewer chances of advancement in the plant. This failure has forced all collectivist experiments to seek the fulfillment of their promises of citizenship outside of the industrial sphere. The Nazis tried to organize all society on the noneconomic pattern of the armed camp. The Russians attempted first to give social meaning to the individual through the concept of "permanent revolution," and to create opportunities for advancement in the party bureaucracy; later they have been substituting for the citizenship in an industrial society they cannot give, the emotional satisfaction of nationalism, of building up the "Socialist Fatherland," or of fighting a "Holy War." These experiences show clearly that the attempt to solve the basic political problems of modern industrial society through collectivism must lead to a pseudo-solution which is by its very nature unstable such as the armed camp or the emotion of a patriotic war, and which is likely to block the way to any real solution.

The final conclusion from our diagnosis is that a solution of the problems of equal opportunities and of citizenship in

---

large part of Communist Party membership, have come to the conclusions that "socialism" means simply state ownership, and that any discussion of the traditional question of a "classless society" or of the status and citizenship of the worker is pointless, if not outright seditious. *Bienstock* et al., op. cit.

industrial society is in the interest of the large corporation itself.

There is little need to expand on this as far as the foreman is concerned. The foreman is the first line of management and anything that makes him stronger, more satisfied in his job and prouder of his responsibility strengthens management altogether. Also the foreman group constitutes the largest reservoir of potential executives at the disposal of the large corporation. To utilize this reservoir to the utmost, that is to give the foreman the maximum of opportunities, is clearly in the best interest of the corporation.

The same holds true for the worker. Altogether any policy that aims at making available to the corporation the ability and drive of the workers must result in greater efficiency and productivity. To find the able and ambitious men in the ranks for promotion to supervisory positions or, as in the suggestion plan, to enlist the active participation of the worker in improving the efficiency of production and organization would strengthen the corporation noticeably. As a matter of fact, any other policy would be harmful to the large corporation. Faced with an ever-growing need for executives and engaged in a technological and efficiency competition which is becoming fiercer all the time, the corporation simply cannot afford to deprive itself of the intelligence, imagination and initiative of ninety per cent of the people who work for it, that is, the workers. It can neither afford to reserve its executive positions for that small minority that managed to get a college degree; there simply are not enough *good* people with degrees around to satisfy the demand. Nor is it compatible with the interests of the corporation to give a small group of professionals— such as process engineers—a monopoly on technological advance. These experts have to supply the leadership; but the more the individual worker considers technological improve-

ment as his concern, the stronger will the corporation be. And
few, if any, would question that the satisfied worker, secure
emotionally in his relationship to his product and his plant,
is a better, a more efficient, a more productive worker, let
alone a more co-operative one.

A question might be raised however over the suggestion
to give the worker actual management experience by entrusting to him a share in the running of the community services
within the plant. Frightened by the attempts of some unions—
notably the United Automobile Workers—to take over plant
management, a good many industrial executives feel today
that any participation of the worker in management within
the plant, will lead to encroachment and to an usurpation
of legitimate management functions by organized labor.

There can be no doubt that such union attempts constitute
a severe threat to the functioning of industry. Without a
unified management, organized under one authority and
accepting one and the same criteria of success and the same
focus of allegiance, industry simply could not function—in
Soviet Russia as little as in Cleveland, Ohio. Hence there
can be no participation of the worker in the management of
the business which, in the worker's own interest, must be in
the hands of trained executives working for the business, and
not for the union or for the government. But no such argument holds against the participation of workers—preferably
not union officials with their divided allegiance—in the management of the services which are only incidental to production proper. Any plant has a considerable number of those.
And to make workers responsible for their proper running
should give the men on the machines some of the understanding of the functions, motives and problems of management
on which a free enterprise depends and which is almost entirely absent today.

The benefits the corporation would derive from the successful solution of the problem of the worker's industrial citizenship could not always be expressed in dollars and cents or measured by a cost accountant. Nevertheless they are real and tangible. It may well be the most important domestic result of this war to have made industrial management aware of this and conscious of the fact that the corporation is not only an economic tool but a social institution.

To understand that the modern large corporation is the representative institution of our society; that it is above all an institution, that is, a human organization and not just a complex of inanimate machines; that it is based upon a concept of order rather than upon gadgets; and that all of us as consumers, as workers, as savers and as citizens have an equal stake in its prosperity, these are the important lessons we have to learn. To make it possible for this new social institution to function efficiently and productively, to realize its economic and social potential and to resolve its economic and social problems, is our most urgent task and our most challenging opportunity.

CHAPTER FOUR

ECONOMIC POLICY IN AN
INDUSTRIAL SOCIETY

1

THE "CURSE OF BIGNESS"

WE can define the relationship between the corporation and society in several ways. We may say that legally the corporation is a creature of the state, endowed in the interest of society with legal existence, legal rights and privileges. Or we may use the terminology of the political analyst and talk of the corporation as an institution of organized society which has to fulfill basic social tasks. Or, economically, we may talk of the corporation as the unit in which our industrial resources are organized for efficient production. Whatever the terminology, the large corporation is a tool and organ of society. Hence society must demand of the corporation that it be able to discharge the specific economic functions which are its *raison d'être*. This is an absolute, a supreme demand—as absolute and supreme as the demand that the corporation meet the necessities of its own functioning and survival.

How do these two absolute commands relate to each other? Is there conflict or harmony between the demand for efficiency in terms of corporate functioning, and the demand for efficiency in terms of functioning, stability and prosperity of society? Clearly, a functioning free-enterprise society can only exist if the two sets of requirements can be satisfied by one economic policy. If the economic policy needed in the interest of society were in constant conflict with an economic policy needed in the interest of corporate functioning and efficiency, we would have perpetual, paralyzing friction.

There are, broadly speaking, three aspects under which this interdependence can be discussed:

What is the relation between the requirements of social stability and the structural requirements of the large corporation? Is the survival of the corporation which dominates its internal policy, in the social interest or contrary to it? And what about the specific policies that follow from the survival interest of the corporation? Here we shall analyze corporate policies for their effect on social stability; in this area also belong the questions of monopoly and of the social effects of "bigness."

The second aspect is that of the relationship between the corporation's criterion and yardstick of institutional efficiency, profit, and society's criterion of economic efficiency, maximum production at the lowest cost. Is there a conflict between "production for profit" and "production for use"? What about profitability as a criterion of economic action, and the "profit motive" as an incentive?

Finally, there is the question whether the free-enterprise system, an economy based on politically uncontrolled corporations, motivated by the desire to make profits, and regulated by a competitive market, can satisfy society's demand for stable, expanding employment—politically the most important question today.

The Stakes of Society

Whatever its social beliefs, modern industrial society must organize its economy in the large units of Big Business. Whatever contributes to the stability, survival and efficiency of these units, contributes directly to social stability and efficiency.

On the whole, this is so obvious as to require little amplification. Society has as much of a stake in the solution of the leadership problem of the modern corporation as the corporation itself. Any advance the corporation may make in discovering and developing talents and abilities within its organization directly benefits society as it finds immediate expression in more efficient production. Just as vital is the stake of society in the development of a responsible, well-trained and well-tested top management and in the provision of an orderly method of succession in industry. Society stands to lose as much as the corporation from the failure of an improperly prepared and insufficiently tested big-business manager; for the decline or collapse of one of our large corporations would threaten the stability of the entire economy. Even greater is the danger inherent in a haphazard or arbitrary scheme of succession. In fact, we may expect society to demand of all our big businesses that they institute a rational recruiting and testing system for top leadership such as is provided for example by the policy of decentralization. Social and economic stability in this country today is gravely threatened by the existence of a few very big corporations that depend entirely upon one rapidly aging man, without independent associates or tested lieutenants able to prevent a precipitate decline or disintegration of the business in the event of his death.

Harmony also exists between the interest of society in a clear and carefully planned corporation policy and the interest of the corporation itself. If the corporation does not have a clear policy and a definite organ of policy decision, its actions and behavior become unpredictable. This must introduce elements of insecurity into economic life which directly threaten social stability. Society has an overriding interest in predictable pricing policies, predictable employment and personnel policies and predictable business practices, which can be obtained only through managerial policy decisions.

Also, society, even more than the corporation itself, has a direct interest in the objective yardsticks which measure success and failure of corporate decisions and actions. Without such objective yardsticks mistakes might go without correction till they endanger economic prosperity and employment. Without them we would also lack the means to judge efficiency and to distribute rewards and recognition on an impersonal basis; and nothing would tend to disrupt social and political life more than to make rewards and recognition in the economic sphere depend upon political favor or personal decision. Management would become subordinated to personal ambition and factionalism instead of to the interest of efficient production. It is no accident that in Soviet Russia, which has deprived itself completely of the most impersonal yardstick of economic achievement, the competitive market, cost accounting has been elevated to top rank among the social sciences.

We have, however, to say a few words about the interest of society in the survival of the corporation and of its organization. Today we are conscious of this interest, but our consciousness is of very recent origin. Traditionally it had been held that society has no stake in the survival of the corporate organization, and that indeed any policy aimed at perpetuating corporate identity and unity is contrary to full economic efficiency.

This traditional view was a result of the pre-industrial mentality of classical economics which saw in the individual trader doing business alone and for his own account on a day-to-day basis the model of economic activity. Of course, this individual trader—the jobber in the stock market was clearly the example Ricardo had in mind—cannot function except in a most elaborate economic institution, the modern market. But assuming the market to be "natural," the classical economists could indeed not only overlook the importance of organization in the economic process, they could come to the conclusion that any attempt to maintain an economic organization is contrary to best economic efficiency.

In an economy based upon industrial production, the organization of the productive resources is not only a prerequisite; it is itself an essential resource. Traditional economics knew three factors which must be combined to obtain production: labor, raw materials and capital equipment. But the simplest industrial operation requires a fourth one, managerial organization. This fourth factor has become the most important one in modern mass production and the only one for which there are no substitutes. We can replace one raw material by another, substitute manual labor for machines and vice versa. But organization is irreplaceable. Under modern industrial conditions it is the one resource that must be carefully conserved in the interest of society. We may express this economically in the concept of the "going concern" which has an infinitely greater economic value than the sum of its parts. Or we may use social terms and stress the fact that the organization of human resources cannot be improvised. The fact remains that society has an overriding interest in keeping alive the integrated producing unit.

This does not mean that any and every big business is a unit whose survival is in the interest of society. There can be, and undoubtedly there are, many corporations which are not efficient and integrating producing units. Some of them are conglomerations of several efficient units in the survival of which society has an interest, though there is no social necessity to preserve the present corporate structure. This, of course, was the contention of the drafters of the Public Utilities Holding Company Act who asserted that it was in the interest of the survival and efficient functioning of the actual unit, i. e., the producing company, to be freed from dependence on the socially and economically unproductive unit, the holding company.

Or, an individual corporation may be an efficient producing unit only as part of another corporation. It is an independent corporation in name and law but only a subsidiary in social reality. Society would then be interested solely in maintaining the integrity of the complex of corporations which together make up a productive unit rather than in maintaining the corporate integrity of one corporation. A good example of this is the legally and financially independent railroad company whose track is leased to another railroad and forms part of a unified system. It is symptomatic that in railroad reorganizations the legal rights of this formally independent organization are regularly subordinated to the maintenance of the entire system as a functioning unit. These qualifications do not, however, create any conflict between the survival interest of the corporation and the interest of society in the survival of the corporation; for it is as much to the interest of the corporation to be an integrated producing unit as it is to the interest of society to maintain an integrated producing unit.

It can be said that in actual economic policy we have been striving to maintain intact the producing unit of the corporation ever since the beginnings of modern industry; that at least is the interpretation of traditional monetary policy given in one of the most brilliant analyses of economic policy.*

---

* Karl Polanyi, *The Great Transformation*, New York, 1944.

Up to the great depression, however, this parallelism between the survival interest of the corporation and the social interest of society in the survival of the producing unit was more felt than understood; the policies adopted to the end of corporate survival were usually regarded as concessions to political pressure rather than as rightly in the interest of society. Since 1929 we have learned that no society can afford to jettison its basic producing unit—in this country, the large corporation, which has to be defended against international as well as internal economic forces. This is very largely the meaning of the new monetary policies which, by divorcing the domestic structure from the fluctuations of the international system, guarantee the producing units against disintegration through international deflation. This is also the meaning of the policy of government subsidies which was independently inaugurated in all industrial countries at the onset of the depression—in the United States through the Reconstruction Finance Corporation—as well as the purpose of the radical revision of the bankruptcy laws in all industrial countries.

This new realization of the social interest of organized society in the survival of corporate identity and productive integrity poses difficult problems of economic and political organization. It is not compatible with the traditional tenets of international monetary organization and the traditional concepts of international trade. It may even be said that we today tend to overemphasize society's interest in the survival of the corporation at the expense of other equally important social interests. This does not, however, concern us here. For our purpose in this book, the agreement between the corporate necessity of survival and the social interest in this survival is the important thing.

Is Monopoly in the Corporate Interest?

The assertion of the social importance of corporate stability and survival raises at once the issue of monopoly. Traditionally a monopoly position has been regarded as the best safeguard of the corporate survival; indeed, the nineteenth century theory of monopoly rested squarely on the assertion that the self-interest of any business will force it to seek a monopoly position. Yet, a monopoly, by definition, is antisocial; its purpose is to satisfy the interests of the monopolyholder at the expense of society, and to reward him for producing less at higher price.

Many attempts have been made, especially during the last two decades, to claim that monopoly is socially beneficial. The most sweeping of these attempts was the National Recovery Act (NRA) in the first years of the New Deal which demanded the conversion of all American industry into compulsory monopolies in the interest of social stability. Today several British industrial associations—notably the British Iron and Steel Federation—and a good many labor unions on both sides of the Atlantic are arguing along similar lines.

It should therefore be asserted uncompromisingly that a monopolistic enterprise or a monopolistic industry always impairs social stability and economic efficiency. This effect of monopoly is inherent in its nature—simply because absolute power always means abuse of power. The "enlightened monopoly" is a myth, whether it is to be entrusted to Big Business as in the NRA, or to labor unions as proposed by Sir William Beveridge for England. Finally, wherever there are "natural" monopolies, that is monopolies which are unavoidable because of the nature of the productive or distributive process—electric power supply in a given area or central banking in a given country for instance—they have to be under the regulatory control of consumers' representatives.

The textbook type of monopoly, domination of the market by one product or one producer, is indeed neither very frequent nor particularly frightening. When the theory of monopoly was developed by Adam Smith and his disciples almost every commodity was irreplaceable; control of the market of one commodity or of one product thus gave an absolute monopoly. In our developed economy there is tremendous interchangeability between raw materials and increasingly between finished goods. A good example of the competition between finished goods is offered by the automobile market. Even if there were only one car producer there would still be a highly competitive market. For every used car actively competes with the new cars; and over the used-car market no producer of new cars can exercise any control.

Hence monopolistic control of the market of one commodity will usually be broken within reasonably short time by the shift to existing substitutes or the development of new ones. The only exceptions are very cheap articles consumed in tremendous numbers, such as matches or patent medicines, because the individual consumer spends so little on them that he is not conscious of the burden imposed by a monopoly. The late Swedish "Match King," Ivar Kreuger, imposed a monopoly profit of ten per cent on consumers simply by reducing the number of matches per box from 50 to 45, without reducing the price. Nobody noticed it; and certainly no individual consumer cut down his consumption of matches or looked for a competing brand the boxes of which contained full measure.

But in the place of the former monopolies based on direct control of the market we have today a steadily growing number of monopolies based on control of the access to the factors of production. There is the cartel—European style—which rests on a monopoly of the access to capital, the patent pool which is built on the control of managerial skill and knowledge, the "feather-bedding" and jurisdictional rules of the unions which impose a monopoly of a craft or of an obsolete technique on society through the union's control over labor, the monopolistic practices in the commodity field—for instance the "corners" in cotton and silver—imposed by interest groups through their control of governmental power. And these newly fashioned monopolies are not self-defeating as the old ones had been. They rest on control over the producer so that they cannot be touched by consumer action in the market like the old monopoly; they also are usually backed by political power or by law as in the case of union rules or patent pools.

Finally, we have to realize that monopolistic practices in one sector of the economy inevitably bring about monopolistic practices in all the other sectors. Monopolistic union practices force managements to behave monopolistically and vice versa. The monopoly of administrative government agencies forces the economy to organize itself in monopolistic units, and so forth.

Monopolies, whether of business, government or labor, are anti-social; and there is undoubtedly a tendency towards monopoly in the organizations of modern economic life. Monopolies are a serious problem of economic policy, not a mere theoretical contingency. Nevertheless, the conclusion drawn from these facts by the traditional theory of monopoly is false: that monopoly best satisfies the interest of business and that, therefore, there is an inherent conflict between the social interests of society and the survival interest of business enterprise. It is not correct that monopoly is necessarily in the best interest of business enterprise. Actually, it is incompatible with the demands of modern mass-production industry.

It was the essence of the nineteenth century theory of monopoly that maximum profit for the longest period could not be realized by maximum production for the lowest price— the social criterion of efficient production—but only by following the opposite, "monopolistic" policy. If this theory were a correct expression of social reality, industrial society could not exist, at least not in the form in which we know it, as a society of independent, self-governing corporate units. If it were true that the independent business must try to be monopolistic for its own best self-interest, we could not hope to be able to enforce anti-monopoly laws; for no institution can accept rules which go counter to its basic survival interest and purpose. On the other hand, we could not permit business to be monopolistic; for this would deny the basic demands and needs of society. From the classical theory of monopoly no other conclusion is possible than that a free-enterprise economy is impossible once society has become an industrial society. On the basis of the classical theory of monopoly there is no other conclusion but state socialism or a society of compulsory cartels; and in actual practice there is little difference between the two.

This theory of monopoly which is still widely accepted as gospel truth, rests on the assumption—correct in the eighteenth century—that supply will always be limited, whereas demand will always be unlimited. On this assumption, monopolistic behavior will indeed yield the maximum profit. But under modern industrial conditions, it is not supply that is limited, but demand; supply in modern mass-production industry has, by definition, no practical limitations. It is simply not true that contraction of production and artificial maintenance of high prices will always yield the highest profit to the producer. On the contrary, under conditions of modern technology, the maximum profit is obtained by maximum production at the minimum cost. To have first realized this was the great achievement and the original contribution of Henry Ford. The essence of the mass-production process is the reversal of the conditions from which the theory of monopoly was deduced. The new assumptions constitute a veritable economic revolution. Like all revolutions, it has created as many problems as it solved; the threat of mass unemployment is very largely a reflection of this change in which supply has become more elastic than demand. But as far as the problem of monopoly is concerned, the new technology can resolve the conflict between social purpose and corporate purpose. For in modern mass-production industry monopolistic behavior (artificial contraction of production in order to maintain an artificially high price) is uneconomical and unprofitable. Instead, that behavior has become most profitable for the producer which is also most beneficial to society, namely, maximum production at minimum cost.

Under modern mass-production conditions maximum profitability depends on maximum efficiency. In a monopolistic business, competitive market standing is eliminated as a measure of efficiency; and we have seen in the preceding chapter that without the yardstick of the market, the objective checks of efficiency function very poorly, if they function at all. In other words, under modern mass-production conditions, a business will realize the highest rate of profit on its invested capital only if it is subject to that check of the competitive market which a monopolistic business eliminates.

When General Motors in the twenties began to expand rapidly, it was laid down by the top executives that it should not aim at complete control of the automobile market but should in its own best interest keep its market quota low enough to make possible the existence of strong and healthy competitors—not for philanthropic or political reasons, but simply from the point of view of the corporation's efficiency and profitability. It is clear that there is a certain tension between corporate interest in the existence of strong and vigorous competition and the way in which success is measured in terms of a steady tightening of the corporation's hold on the market. In other words, there may be a point where a business may succeed too well for its own good. But this in itself is a complete contradiction of the nineteenth century theory which denied the existence of such a point. According to that theory, the point where a business enterprise begins to lose its social usefulness is the point where it begins to be most profitable. Actually, the point at which a business reaches its maximum social usefulness is also the point of its maximum profitability. Under conditions of modern mass production, there is no conflict between corporate interest in profitability and social interest in maximum production.

In political or academic discussions, it is still not understood on the whole how completely the coming of mass-production technology has changed the nature of monopoly. This can be seen in such a book as Mr. Thurman Arnold's "The Bottlenecks of Business" in which the attempt to apply the traditional concepts of monopoly to radically altered conditions enmeshes the very brilliant author in one contradiction after another. Yet the public as a whole apparently senses that monopoly is no longer the major issue of economic policy it was forty or fifty years ago. One has only to compare the feverish excitement created by "trust-busting" under Theodore Roosevelt with the polite boredom with which the public has been watching the anti-trust drives of the last few years in spite of "sensational disclosures" and excellent staging.

A comparison of the assumptions on which the theory of

monopoly rests with the actual conditions of modern industrial production brings out yet another important fact. The
classical theory of monopoly—like all classical economic
theory—knows no time element; its model of economic behavior is the jobber in the stock market who "covers" a deal
as fast as he makes it. Hence to the traditional theory all
attempts to control fluctuations and economic change are
equally restrictive, equally monopolistic. But in industrial
reality economic activity extends over a very long period of
time. Actually, the business cycle of seven to fifteen years is
the unit of industrial activity; the average profit or loss over
this period corresponds economically to the immediate profit
or loss the jobber in the stock market realizes when he
"covers." This is partly owing to the length of time it takes
to develop a new product or process today, but mainly because
industrial production today requires a tremendous fixed capital investment. The capital of the stock-jobber is freed the
instant he "closes his book" that is, with every transaction;
industrial capital has to stay invested, and can only be liqui-
dated, if at all, by production over the long period of the
business cycle.

In the modern industrial economy we have therefore to
distinguish sharply between restrictive activities that attempt
to smooth out cyclical fluctuations, and restrictive activities
that try to restrict output or to perpetuate inefficient methods
and obsolete equipment. The latter are truly monopolistic,
hence anti-social. But the former are actually in the interest
of efficient production and therefore in that of society; they
result in a greater utilization of labor and of productive
capacity over the business cycle, hence in larger production
both absolutely and per unit of cost.

It is by no means easy to draw the line between these two
different kinds of regulatory action; nor is there likely to be

agreement on any one formula. Whoever suffers as the result
of economic change will always be convinced that he is the
victim of transitory and accidental forces against which he
ought to be protected for the good of society. Whoever benefits from a change feels conversely that the change is in the
best interest of society. The attempts made so far—for instance the distinction made by the U. S. Supreme Court between a "reasonable" and an "unreasonable" trust or Mr.
Thurman Arnold's juxtaposition of "good" and "bad" monopolies—have not given us a clear or a reliable principle of
analysis. Yet, it is important that we recognize the basic difference between these two superficially so very similar types
of economic action; for otherwise monopolistic abuse will
always be defended as in the interest of social stability and
of productive efficiency. It is for lack of this distinction that
we exempt labor unions altogether from the provisions of the
anti-trust laws, and thus condone some of the worst monopolistic abuses in our economy, instead of drawing a line between legitimate and illegitimate union attempts to protect
labor against economic change. It is also for lack of a dividing line between regulatory and restrictive practices that we
lack a consistent and enforceable anti-monopoly policy which
would be in the interest of both business and the society.

Bigness—Asset or Liability?

When the late Mr. Justice Brandeis coined the catch phrase
of the "curse of bigness" some thirty years ago, he was convinced that bigness was not only socially destructive but economically and technologically unjustified. He saw its cause
mainly in the greed or the drive for power of the "tycoon."

Uncurbed individual ambition is, of course, one cause of
bigness, and the bigness resulting from it is as anti-social and

as unjustified as Mr. Brandeis said it was. Also, it is not confined to business; as Mr. Brandeis towards the end of his life realized very clearly, "Little Napoleons" are just as likely to arise in labor unions or in the government as in business. We may even say that in a free-enterprise system they are least likely to entrench themselves in business; for there we possess a brake in competition in the market which is lacking in other spheres. Incidentally, the "tycoon" flourishes best in times of crisis and emergency, such as a war, when there is undue emphasis on the kind of organizing ability and drive which is his typical asset. Hence today we have in our society quite a few ramshackle and jerry-built personal empires which truly are under the "curse of bigness"—some the domain of war production "wizards," some that of union bosses, some that of overextended government agencies. And it will be a painful process to bring these structures down to normal size.

But the real problem of bigness lies elsewhere: it lies in the *economic and technological necessity of bigness in modern industry*. Mr. Brandeis maintained that bigness was economically inefficient. We know today that in modern industrial production, particularly in modern mass production, the small unit is not only inefficient, it cannot produce at all. It is, of course, still true that there is an upper limit to the efficiency of bigness to overstep which results in decreasing efficiency. But there is also a lower limit; and in most modern industries it is very high. It is an interesting commentary that Henry Ford who, in his sponsorship of small "village industries" is the most faithful follower of Mr. Justice Brandeis, owns, in his River Rouge plant, the largest, most concentrated and most highly centralized industrial unit in this country— and one which a good many observers have judged definitely to exceed the most efficient size.

We thus have a situation in which bigness—not that of the

"tycoon" or "boss" but that of the large integrated corporation—is economically necessary and economically efficient. Hence from the economic point of view, bigness is socially productive. But is it also conducive to social stability and to the functioning of society? Or is there a conflict between the requirements of efficient production and those of social stability and well-being?

There can be no doubt that size creates problems. We have devoted most of the second chapter to a discussion of these problems. We have maintained that these problems exist because Big Business does not automatically provide safeguards and controls which are given in a small-business economy. We have, however, also shown that it is fully as much in the interest of the large corporation as in that of society that these handicaps be overcome. It is not correct that the maximum profitability is reached under conditions of centralization and bureaucracy. On the contrary, it is in the most urgent survival interest of the corporation to prevent bureaucratic ossification, top-heavy centralized management, and a drying up of the sources of leadership supply. In the policy of decentralization, the large corporation has a means to overcome the functional disadvantages of bigness—provided always that the outside check of the competitive market is given. In fine there is no inevitable clash between the economic and the social effects of bigness, provided Big Business has a definite policy and organization by means of which it can derive all the advantages of a small-business economy without losing any of the advantages of bigness.

For—and that is a point that is often overlooked—bigness is not only advantageous from the point of view of efficient production. It carries with it considerable social advantages—advantages which permit the large corporation not only to produce more cheaply and more efficiently, but also to contribute to social stability. These advantages are exclusive to Big Business; small business could not attain them under any system of organization whatever.

In its service staffs, General Motors has an organization which enables all units of the company to produce more efficiently and at lower cost than any of them could as independent units. This is obvious in regard to the research laboratories. Even if everyone of the General Motors divisions would support a research laboratory two or three times as large as its proportionate share in the General Motors research institutions, the result in terms of new products, new and cheaper ways of producing, etc., would be many times smaller than the result of the one big research laboratory. Very few divisions would be able to hire research men of the caliber represented in the central research laboratory; and the effectiveness of the laboratory is very largely the result of its ability to put to work as a team a considerable number of men with different training, backgrounds and approach. The same applies to less publicized services, such as that rendered by the engineering, the manufacturing, the sales and public relations staffs—not to mention the savings in time and money made possible through the existence of a centralized accounting system, centralized financial management, and the centralized handling of legal affairs. These service staffs supply even units of small size—such as the very small divisions— with the most up-to-date, cheapest and most productive methods of engineering and manufacturing, with the most advanced research, and with a comprehensive knowledge of the whole field of mass production.

Another important advantage of bigness is that it enables the business enterprise to have a policy and to have a special policy-making body which is sufficiently far removed from the actual day-to-day problems to take the long view, and to take into account the relationship between the organization and society. Society as a whole certainly has a direct interest in good relations between the big corporation and the retailers of its products. As we have seen, the social interest in small business is not in conflict with the *long-term interests* of the automobile producer which require a strong and healthy dealer organization and a strong and healthy second-hand car market. However, the social interest in small business is in potential conflict with the *short-term interest* of the corporation in maximum sales of new cars. In the ordinary small or medium-sized business, top management cannot detach itself sufficiently from immediate concerns to pay much attention to the long-term problems and to build a policy which, in satisfying the long-term interests of the corporation, also satisfies the interest of society in the small business man. The president of a smaller automobile company may be forced to devote all his time and energy to the current problems, thus slighting not only the best long-term interest of his own business but the interest of society as well. In General Motors, top management is detached enough to act as an arbiter between these two interests. With divisional management taking care of current problems, central management can take the long view. It is both able and expected to formulate policies which satisfy long-term requirements, and to create organs through which this long-term interest—which is also an interest of society—is directly represented within the company.

This leads us to the next point: bigness can contribute to social stability because a big business can subordinate temporary gains to long-term policies. This applies to such questions as pricing, merchandising and purchasing. It also applies to employment policies; General Motors, for instance, has been able to put into effect a foreman employment program under which the supervisory force is to be maintained even in bad times. A small business could rarely afford to sacrifice the immediate saving in cost to be obtained by laying off superfluous foremen, to the long-term interest of keeping intact its skilled personnel.

Finally, bigness—if organized on a decentralized basis— makes it possible to go further in discovering, developing and promoting able men than small business ever could. If small business tries systematically to find the able men within its organization and to train them for leadership, it will soon have more potential leaders on its hands than it can employ. When this happens the trained people either leave the organization or they grow weary and bitter waiting for the death or retirement of their superiors. In either case, the leadership development program will be given up very soon. General Motors, because of its very bigness, has been able to build up a reservoir of trained men without running up against over-training or overstaffing. In so big an organization there is always a place for a trained man. If there are no vacancies in the division in which he has grown up, there will sooner or later be a vacancy in another; he may be shifted to the central office staffs in New York or Detroit; he may be used in overseas operations, etc. In any event he will neither be lost for the organization nor grow stale in the anteroom. In such a big organization, it is possible to make leadership development a natural function of management and to overcome the fear so common to the small-business executive that, by training a capable subordinate, he will train himself out of his own job.

All this is obtainable only in a *decentralized* big business. Hence decentralization is the condition for the conversion of bigness from a social liability into a social asset. Bigness, if centralized—whether for lack of a policy or because the units of production have been allowed to grow too large for effective decentralization—carries with it dangers to the stability and functioning of society, just as it carries dangers to the stability and functioning of the corporation. But in itself that bigness which is required in the interest of economic efficiency under modern technological conditions, is not in conflict with the requirements of social stability and social functioning.

PRODUCTION FOR "USE" OR FOR "PROFIT"?

TAKEN literally, there is hardly any slogan that makes less sense than that of "production for use versus production for profit." It seems to imply that the products of our economic machine, say for instance the bread produced by the National Biscuit Company, are not being used or that they are being abused. But even if we overlook the literal meaning of the slogan and concentrate on what the slogan intends to say, we will find that it has several not necessarily compatible meanings.

To contrast production for profit with production for use very often implies a rejection of profit as a condition, and of profitability as the yardstick, of economic actions and results; we are being asked to substitute "service" for profitability as the rationale of economic behavior.

The slogan also often implies a rejection of the "profit motive" as the guiding principle of economic behavior in society.

Another meaning implied in the demand that we produce for "use" instead of for "profit" is the rejection of an economic system in which the individual consumer decides what he wants to have, in favor of a system under which government would decide what he should have in his interest as well as in that of society. This is, of course, an attack upon the institution of the competitive market and of market price as the governors of production and distribution.

Common to all three meanings of the slogan is the assertion that "production for profit" is not only unnecessary and "unnatural" but that it leads to an economic structure which is contrary to the best interests of both society and the individual. "Production for profit" is the principle of rationality and efficiency on which the corporation must base itself. The demand for "production for use" thus asserts a conflict between the needs of society and those of the corporation.

The demand that some criterion other than profitability be used as the yardstick and determinant of economic actions and results, rests on a misunderstanding of the nature of the economic process. Every economic transaction is by definition a gamble on the future. In every economic transaction there is thus a considerable element of risk. In primitive economics the risks are those of crop failure, pests and plant diseases, natural catastrophes, etc.; and even the most stationary and most elementary economic system can neither avoid nor control these risks. The more complex the economy becomes, the more complex become the risks incurred in any economic activity.

What applies to a stationary economy applies with doubled force to an economy in expansion. To the ordinary risks of economic life are added the risks of expansion. Some idea of the magnitude of these risks is given by the research engineer's rule of thumb according to which only one out of ten new products developed will prove an economic success; yet the modern research engineer has come closer to converting expansion into an orderly, organized and predictable process than anybody else. To these risks is added the uncertainty which arises from the fact that no one can tell how much time it will take till even the most successful new venture is established. It may take fifteen years—and it rarely takes much less—before a new product or a new process can be regarded as proved. Profit is thus an inevitable risk premium and the basis of all economic activity, whether capitalist, socialist or cave man. An economy which does not make due provision for risks must eat up its substance and must become poorer and less productive.

Profit, in addition to being the insurance premium against the risk involved in the gamble on the future, is also the only source of the new capital equipment without which expansion would be impossible. New capital can only be created by keeping resources or their products for future use, that is out of a margin between total production and production currently consumed. This margin is the profit margin. The higher it is, the faster can an economy advance, the more jolts can it take, the faster can it recover from setbacks. Both, the growth of an economy and its stability are directly proportionate to the profit margin.* It is no accident that of all industrial countries today, the Soviet Union has the highest profit rate on industrial production. This does not mean that the Soviet Union is a "capitalist" country; it only shows that the Soviet economy expands at an extremely fast rate and, because it is a "planned economy" without automatic control of mistakes, under unusually risky conditions. The key to industrial expansion has always been to increase the capital investment per worker; the curve which illustrates the increase in this figure runs parallel to that showing the rise in productivity and output. And the only source of capital equipment is profit.

Actually, the profit margin on which the American economy operates, is definitely too low. We will have to increase it not only to obtain the economic expansion needed for stable

---

* I have refrained here intentionally from going into the important Keynesian distinction between "investment" and "saving," that is between profit used as the basis for expansion, and profit kept out of economic usefulness. In the first place it does not affect the over-all argument; profit is still the only source of new capital equipment. Secondly, the problem of obtaining "investment" rather than "saving" is discussed extensively in the section on stable employment following this.

employment, but in the interest of national strength and survival.

In the past this country has depended to an altogether unprecedented extent on a substitute for genuine capital formation: the exploitation of nature's bounty, the appropriation and the "mining" of virgin soil, the depletion of lumber, oil and ore resources. Henry George's belief that the appropriation of new land is the sole source of capital, was a mistake; the sole source of capital is profit. But his mistake was a natural one as the United States during the nineteenth century certainly based its expanding economy as much on the bounty of nature as on man-made capital. And to a lesser extent the same was true of the rest of the Western World, especially of England, except that there the natural resources of colonial territories were appropriated and used up rather than resources at home. We can no longer base our economy on the appropriation and depletion of nature's bounty. In the future we are going to be increasingly dependent on profit.

In the first place, the capital requirements for industrial expansion under modern technological conditions are too great to be satisfied out of "natural" resources. They can only come out of profits on production.* Secondly, industrialization has become a world-wide process which means that the formerly colonial, raw-material producing areas will now need for themselves the "natural capital" on the appropriation and exploitation of which European, especially English, industrial expansion during the last one hundred fifty years

---

* This does not mean that capital investment has reached the point of "diminishing returns" where more and more new investment is needed to produce less and less increase in productivity. On the contrary, all evidence shows that productivity per unit of capital investment has been increasing quite rapidly these last twenty-five years and is still increasing. Our economic machine is simply too large to rest on the narrow foundation of appropriating accumulated "natural capital" such as land, just as our monetary system is too large to get its monetary material from bonanzas.

was so largely based. Finally—and most important—we can no longer afford to use up the productive resources of nature at the rate at which they have been used up. Soil erosion and depletion of soil fertility, destruction of timber resources, overconsumption of irreplaceable fuels and ores has been a world-wide phenomenon. But nowhere has it gone further than in this country; especially during the two World Wars we indulged in a veritable orgy of natural-capital consumption. In the interest of national defense, national prosperity and national survival we must surely preserve and build up our natural resources. They cannot be allowed to be used in lieu of capital. Capital formation will have to be based on the one resource which, instead of being destroyed by being used, reproduces itself, namely profit.

Just as it is nonsense to say that economic life is possible without profit, it is nonsense to believe that there could be any other yardstick for the success or failure of an economic action but profitability. Of course, it is always necessary for society to go in for a good many unprofitable activities in the social interest. But all such activities which are undertaken in spite of their economic unprofitability must be paid for out of the profits of some other branch of economic activity; otherwise, the total economy shrinks. Profitability is simply another word for economic rationality. And what other rationality could there be to measure economic activity but economic rationality?

The reason for the frequent failure to understand this elementary proportion lies in the customary confusion of *profitability* which is an objective principle of social action, with the *profit motive* which is a subjective principle of individual motivation. The confusion between these two entirely different things began with the utilitarian philosophers and economists of the classical period of economic thought who mistakenly derived profitability not from the objective conditions of economic life but from a thoroughly fallacious psychology of individual behavior. This mistake in turn was possible because they, though living in a period of violent economic expansion, based their economic thinking on the concept of a stationary economy—the concept of the equilibrium. Of course, even a stationary economy needs profits to make good the inevitable losses; but the losses of a stationary economy are not inherent in the economic process itself, but are caused by some outside agent, such as the weather, insects, pests, etc. While the disregard of the inevitability of such outside disturbances imparts to classical economics the abstract character of a chess problem, the classical economist intentionally aimed at a purely theoretical, quasi-mathematical formulation.

Today, we know that the assumption of an equilibrium is not only unrealistic but that the equilibrium itself is undesirable. Under modern industrial conditions there is no greater threat than a stationary economy which must lead to wholesale unemployment. We can no longer follow the classical economists or Marx in regarding profit as, at best, a provision against outside interferences with the equilibrium. In an expanding economy, profit and profitability are of the very essence of the economic process. In our theoretical economics this has been fully recognized.* Even in Russia the Marxist dogma of profit as typical of "capitalism" has been officially

---

* The two books which pioneered in the development of the modern concept of a dynamic economy are Frank Knight's *Risk, Uncertainty, and Profit* and Schumpeter's *Theorie der Wirtschaftlichen Entwickelung*. It is interesting that, though absolutely independent of each other, they wrote their books at about the same time in the years immediately preceding the first World War. The contribution of these two books to economic thought is fully as great as that of Mr. Keynes, if not greater; while Keynes represents the last and most advanced formulation of equilibrium economics, Knight and Schumpeter have opened up a new field of economic dynamics.

revoked; the recent revision of Soviet official theory which caused so much comment in this country, consisted mainly in accepting profitability as the yardstick and determinant of production under any social or economic system. It takes time, however, for new ideas to seep into popular consciousness so that popular discussion is still under the spell of the confusion between profitability and profit motive.

This is much more than a theoretical question. The confusion is responsible for the failure of our economic policy to understand that profits are necessary for economic expansion. It is a legitimate and serious problem of economic policy to decide where the profits shall go, how they shall be invested, and what activities should be furthered. But to question whether we want profits or not makes simply no sense —provided we want economic expansion. The confusion also underlies our failure to see that the present rate of profitability on which American economy operates is too low for the economic expansion which we expect.

The Profit Motive

Profit and profitability are objective criteria of economic action. They have nothing to do with the beliefs of a given society or with particular institutions but apply to any society however organized. Essentially profit and profitability are nothing but reformulations of the law of the conservation of energy in economic terms.

The "profit motive" on the other hand pertains to man's actions and reactions. In capitalist society, moreover, it is institutionalized in special institutions, and behavior according to the "profit motive" receives social sanctions and rewards. It is this "profit motive," the socially sanctioned behavior of the individual to obtain the maximum material gain, which is under attack as "unnatural" and "antisocial." And since the corporation in a free-enterprise economy is directed by, and dedicated to, the satisfaction of this "profit motive," the question arises whether the "profit motive" is indeed incompatible with a stable, functioning and good society.

The attack on the profit motive as "unnatural" and conflicting with socially and individually more beneficial and more fundamental human motives is, like the attack on profitability, partly the result of an excessive reaction against the wrong psychology of the utilitarian economists. They had proclaimed that man has a natural instinct to "truck and bargain," and they deduced from this instinct the laws of classical economics. We know today that there is no such thing as a natural instinct to "truck and bargain." If we ever needed proof of the fallacy of the utilitarian concept, it has been abundantly supplied by modern cultural anthropology and modern psychology.* We also know that in most human activities, motives are thoroughly mixed, and that we will never find anybody acting on the basis of that "simple and clear calculation" of possible gain against possible effort on which the classical economists based their theories of economic behavior. Finally, we know that the orthodox economists were completely mistaken when they used the utilitarian "pleasure-pain calculus" to equate "work" with "pain." The psychological and social ravages of unemployment have certainly shown that idleness, far from being pleasing, is destructive, and that work, far from being disagreeable, is a necessity of human existence and self-respect and in itself a source of pride and satisfaction. There is little left today of that psychology from which the profit motive emerged as the con-

* The reader will find a brilliant summary of this evidence in Karl Polanyi's *The Great Transformation* (New York 1944).

troller of human destinies and as the natural law of human behavior.

To say that the profit motive is not inborn in man and the expression of his true nature is, however, something very different from asserting that it is vicious, unnatural and socially undesirable. This assertion rests on two beliefs which are both as untenable and as fallacious psychologically as the dogma of the preordained profit motive which they tried to replace. The first of these is the belief that man's "creative instinct" is not only good in itself but alone sufficient to make man socially constructive—the belief which is expressed in Veblen's famous juxtaposition of "industry" and "business." The second of these beliefs asserts that, but for the profit motive, human society would be one of equality and peace, and that all drive for power and privilege, all conflict and all inequality are the result of the lust for gain. In other words, both beliefs see in the profit motive the one, or at least the main, obstacle to the millennium.

It cannot be said too emphatically that no society can be based on man's "creative instincts." In order to make social life possible there must always be a principle of organization which reduces individual fulfillment and individual drive to a social purpose. Otherwise that co-ordinated human effort on which social life rests becomes impossible. If we do not use profit and profitability as the reduction gear, we would have to work out some other social mechanism to convert the subjective drive of the individual into the objective performance of society.

If we take, for instance, the people employed in the production of an automobile, we shall find that the "instinct of workmanship" leads in totally different directions, depending upon whether we look at the engineer, the production man or the sales manager. For the engineer the highest standard of

achievement and craftsmanship lies in the most functional
and most up-to-date car embodying the best and newest in engineering research, in materials and in design. He may be
inclined to regard as alien and as in conflict with his ideas of
workmanship such considerations as cheapness and ease of
production, habits of automobile users, their comfort, etc.;
and he would want to change his design all the time in order
to incorporate the latest engineering improvements. The
standards by which the production man will measure his
workmanship and achievement would be above all cheapness,
speed and ease of production. His ideal is an engineering design that will never change. His attitude towards the consumer's preference and desires was summed up perfectly in the
epigram attributed to that prince of production men, Henry
Ford, when he said that "the customer can have any color as
long as it's black." The sales manager finally—or anybody
whose business it is to distribute cars—sees maximum
achievement in the most salable car, a cheap car that "looks
like a million dollars" and satisfies the consumer's desire to
keep up with the Joneses—however unreasonable this may
appear to the engineer or to the production man. Each has
"instincts of workmanship" which are creative. But the instinct of the one can find free rein only at the expense of the
instinct of another. If society wants automobiles, it must be
able to subordinate the instincts of each man to an objective
principle of social satisfaction. However much such an objective principle "violates" individual integrity—a point
mooted since the dawn of history—society must have it.

The profit motive may not be the best reduction gear. It
certainly is not the only possible one. But to denounce it because it is a reduction gear—Veblen's procedure—begs the
question. What we have to answer is not whether the profit
motive is good or bad, but whether it is efficient or inefficient

as a principle of social integration of individual motives and desires.

In a society which accepts economic advancement and economic goals as socially efficient and as socially desirable the profit motive is socially the most efficient device. In any other society, it is not an efficient mechanism. In the Middle Ages, for instance, the profit motive was clearly socially inefficient from the point of view of an order which regarded economic goals—beyond mere physical survival—as socially irrelevant and as morally suspect. In a society which believes in the desirability of economic progress, as has ours for the last two hundred years, the profit motive is an efficient mechanism of integration, because it relates individual motives and drives directly to accepted social purposes. Obviously, this creates problems in those spheres of social life to which economic rationality is not applicable, such as the arts. But these problems are no greater than those faced by the Middle Ages in applying their noneconomic objective principle of social integration to the economic sphere with its necessarily economic rationality. In other words, while no society and no principle of social integration can be perfect or automatic, the profit motive is the most efficient and the simplest mechanism for the conversion of individual drives into social purpose and action under the given conditions and beliefs of *our* society. It is, perhaps, the best commentary on this conclusion that the Soviet Union has gone as far as any capitalist country—and further—in using economic rewards and incentives in industry. For, however different its social tenets and institutions, Russia shares with the West the belief in economic goals.

The Lust for Power

What about the second count in the popular indictment of the profit motive: that it is the cause of the lust for power and dominance and the sole or main obstacle to peace and equality? Certainly the "profit motive" is not necessarily inherent in human nature. But inherent in human nature there is a drive for power and distinction of which the profit motive is only one possible form. If we eliminate the profit motive, the result will not be the equal and peaceful society of the millennium but the emergence of some other outlet for man's basic lust for power.

The weakness of the traditional argument is beautifully illustrated by the first great sermon on the profit motive as the original sin, and on its abolition as the key to the earthly paradise—Thomas More's *Utopia*. More's ideal society is perfect, peaceful, free of strife and ambition simply because property and gain have been eliminated. At the same time—almost on the same page—More proposes an elaborate system of honors and preferments as the basis for social power and political rulership. And he never sees the obvious: that the competition for these honors and preferments would at once bring back the ambition, the strife, the factionalism and the lust for power and prestige which he had just driven out by banishing the profit motive. Plato—and More was a Platonist—knew better. But his proposal in the *Republic* not to admit anyone to rulership until he be old enough to be past ambition is hardly more realistic; is there an age limit on ambition and pride? Wherever in history a man was kept out of power until very late, his lust for power, his ambition, his dominance and factiousness increased, often to the point of pathological exaggeration.

If I may again point to the findings of modern anthropology: the sentimental concept of "primitive equality" popularized by Rousseau and Marx has been exploded completely. There are many primitive tribes which do not know individual property in the sense in which we use the term. There are however no examples of real communism among primitive tribes; communism is far too complicated a social arrangement to be attainable for a primitive society. And in every single culture we know of, there is a socially accepted motive of advancement to power and prestige around which the social organization is built.

Actually, we should not have needed anthropology to teach us that society is based on man's innate drive for power and social recognition. We have known for thousands of years that Pride is an essentially human quality. We may, with the ancient Greeks and the Renaissance, accept Pride as a virtue. Or we may with the Christian doctrine regard Pride as both cause and result of man's fall from grace and as the center of his corruption. But we can never hope to have a society without it. The statesman may, as a Christian, deplore the weakness of man and strive to overcome it in himself. As a statesman, however, he has to accept the fact that Pride and its manifestations are both, the reason for the existence of society, and a constant in any social organization. The problem of the statesman is not to suppress or to overcome the drive for power; that is the concern of philosopher and saint. The political problem is how to direct the drive for power into the socially most constructive or least destructive channels.

To say, as is customary, that the profit motive is bad because all drive for power is bad, evades the issue; it may be good theology but it certainly is not relevant to politics. To say that the profit motive is bad because without it there would be no drive for power, is not even bad theology; it is nonsense. The only relevant and meaningful question is whether the profit motive is the socially most efficient one of the available directions in which the drive for power can be channeled.

I do not think that anyone can give a dogmatic answer; the absolutely best lies in the field of religion or philosophy, not in that of politics or social organization. But we can say that of the channels available and known to us, the profit motive has a very high, if not the highest, social efficiency. All the other known forms in which the lust for power can be expressed, offer satisfaction by giving the ambitious man direct power and domination over his fellow men. The profit motive alone gives fulfillment through power over things. It is an old truth that the richest and most overbearing millionaire in a capitalist society has less power over the individual worker than the worst paid official in a collectivist state, who can grant or withhold a license to do business or a work card. Certainly there is the danger that the power over things may develop into a power over men. But it is not an inevitable danger, and it can be checked by social action.

It has been long contended that we can also control the exercise of power over men—for instance, by a Bill of Rights, by popular vote, or by substituting rules of law and procedure for arbitrary decision; this is the case for "democratic socialism." The argument fails to take into account that paternalism may be benevolent but will always tend to be arbitrary and uncontrolled—simply because it substitutes the best judgment of the ruler for the composite judgment of the ruled. And who is to control the ruler if his power over men has once been accepted as "legitimate power"? The profit motive is the one way known to us to divert ambition from the socially destructive goal of power over men, into a socially constructive channel, that of economic production. This, though not by itself sufficient, is a protection against the danger that the lives and the livelihood of the individual citizen will become pawns in the game of human ambition and fair prey for the drive for power. It is no accident that the great villains of history are not found among the "economic royalists" but among the "incorruptibles," whose aim was power and power alone. Neither Robespierre nor Hitler could have been bought off by money; they lacked economic acquisitiveness entirely. But this hardly made them any more beneficial for mankind; their indifference to anything but naked power over men only heightened their inhumanity.

One of the most brilliant writers of our time, Arthur Koestler, recently put forward the thesis (in his book *The Yogi and the Commissar*) that fundamentally there are only two types of social behavior, renunciation of social effectiveness and pursuit of naked power. This, though not new, is a stimulating thesis, but also a most destructive one. It denies all meaning to social life and with it the possibility of a good or of a free society. To have a free society we must make it possible for man to act and to live in society without destroying himself or enslaving his fellow men. We must harness the lust for power to a social purpose. This, in a society accepting economic goals, the profit motive can do.

We do not have to regard the drive for gain as noble or as the best man is capable of. But noble or base, it directs the drive for power into the least dangerous channel. Of course the profit motive does not bring about a free society; the identification of capitalism with democracy, so current today, is utterly superficial and is the result of a truly shocking confusion. But while the profit motive by itself leads to a free society as little as any other human drive, it is more compatible with it than the other forms in which the lust for power may manifest itself socially. A free society is not based on man's drives but on his reason; it always has to guard against the danger of its perversion by the drive for power or by any other drive. The profit motive contains potential threats like all other manifestations of human pride. But unlike the other forms in which the drive for power may become socially effective, the profit motive of a free-enterprise society also contains powerful safeguards against the politically most dangerous consequence of human pride, the tyranny of the power-drunk.

The Market

The most consistent and the most serious criticism of profit is directed against its use as the organizing principle of the economic life of society, that is against the institution of the market.

Every society must perform somehow the functions which a free-enterprise society discharges through the market. It must allocate scarce goods. It must integrate individual motives and individual actions into social effectiveness. It must have a determinant of the direction of economic activity and a control over mistakes.

If we had real abundance of goods we would indeed not need any mechanism to distribute scarce goods. Real abundance means that goods would produce themselves without any human effort. This is not only impossible except on the lowest stage of economic development and in a tropical climate; it is also extremely undesirable. If by some miracle we could obtain the goods we want without effort, we would have to invent something that requires effort in order to have a civilization at all. Not only is work in our society the main claim to social standing and self-respect. We also know that wherever there is any cultural achievement in a primitive tribe living under conditions of natural abundance of subsistence goods, it rests on an artificial and socially created need for effort. A human community can only be organized on the basis of joint effort. And while the purpose to which the effort is organized may be varied—a religious cult, war or economic progress—its basis must always be the organization of productive work.

The need for a principle of social integration has been discussed a few pages back where we talked about the function of the "profit motive." We only have to add that this integration depends on society's having one standard of values, one common denominator in which the different contributions of different people can be expressed, and by means of which they can be compared.

Every society needs unification and control of its economic activity. Above all it needs a means to discover and to correct, before they have gone too far, mistakes in the direction of economic effort and in the allocation of economic resources. In a static economy, such as that of a primitive tribe, tradition hallowed by age and fortified by religious rites is sufficient for this purpose. But in an expanding economy there must be a governor in the system itself to prevent misdirection and to correct mistakes promptly. Otherwise, an error once made, might be persisted in until it results in economic catastrophe.

The market discharges these functions by making price, that is, an economically rational value, the organizing principle of economic life. The claims to scarce goods—income—are distributed according to the individual's contribution to economic production; in theory at least there is no other basis. Human effort is reduced to a common denominator by price also; maximum economic efficiency in terms of cost and price determines the organization and co-ordination of human effort under the market system. And the constant check of cost by price in a competitive market is intended to supply an immediate, permanent and automatic control for all economic activity.

This concept of price as the economically rational value is in turn based on the belief that the proper end of economic activity is the satisfaction of the economic wants of the individual. The economic wants of the individual are the ultimate criterion of economic production, his decision how to allocate his purchasing power between competing goods is the ultimate director of the market and of production under the market system.

A good many of the traditional arguments for and against the market are mere shadow-boxing. They deal with the market as a theoretical abstraction claiming both perfection and universality. But the market is nothing of the sort. It is a man-made social institution, operating not in a vacuum but in society. This society has many other concerns beside economic ones, and many other responsibilities beside the satisfaction of the individual citizen's economic wants and needs. Herbert Spencer, seventy years ago, overlooked this in his condemnation of social services such as municipal fire brigades or free schools as "socialistic" and as destructive of the market system; so did the English Socialist * who in our days "proved" the market to be a failure by showing that the behavior of people in the market was not exclusively determined by economic rationality.

The functioning market of a going free-enterprise society differs considerably from the theorem of the textbooks. In a functioning market, competition is not and cannot be perfect. Even if kept free from major monopolistic attempts, no economy could or should realize the ideal market of absolute competition. It must be full of small, local monopolies and

---

* Barbara Wooton whose book *Lament for Economics* enjoyed considerable popularity during the Depression.

near-monopolies. The restaurant opposite the court house enjoys something of a monopoly on the provision of lunches to lawyers and other people who have business at court; equally monopolistic is the advantage of the drug-store owner whose brother happens to be the small town's leading doctor. Almost nobody buys in a completely free market except, perhaps, the professional purchasing agent of a very large buyer—and even if he awards the contract to the lowest bidder, the field of competition is usually severely limited by geography and communication.

More important is the fact that the individual consumer of the market-theory does not exist. Wants are as much an expression of noneconomic needs and desires as of economic ones. Social preferences differ from country to country, from region to region, from class to class. A handmade dress or suit which, to the colored share cropper in the Deep South, is a mark of social and economic inferiority, is a badge of distinction on Park Avenue. Perfume will sell better at five dollars than at fifty cents even though the contents of the bottle may be the same. Social prestige, habit, tradition, fears and hopes, fashions, the desire to "keep up with the Joneses" are all powerful determinants of individual economic action though all of them are economically irrational.

Economic rewards, that is, incomes, are also not distributed primarily according to the recipient's contribution to economic production. Not only does every society give noneconomic rewards in the form of prestige, power, titles, etc., which are often more ardently desired than money or goods. Every society must reward thousands of services which, in terms of strict economics, are unproductive—ranging all the way from the priest to the gambler. Economic services proper are rewarded as much according to the social esteem in which the occupation or profession is held as by their economic contribution. Physically dirty jobs, or jobs in which personal service is given, are underpaid everywhere. Jobs which are conspicuously in the public eye, are equally over-paid. Where the connection between the work and its economic effect is indirect and difficult to measure, social custom decides—as shown by the relative economic position of research physicist and corporation lawyer. For social reasons the poorest groups of our population, such as the cotton share croppers are paid much higher wages than economic efficiency would ever justify. Seen purely as a factor in economic production, the cotton share cropper contributes about four or five weeks of unskilled labor during the entire year; for cotton needs little cultivation except at picking time. Regarded as a wage for four to five weeks of work, that is, regarded only on the basis of economic rationality, the $200 or $300 received by the share cropper every year is fabulously high and completely unjustifiable. Yet, everybody will protest, rightly, that the share cropper's income should be a good deal higher than it is if he is to have a minimum standard of living and that it is ludicrous to apply economic rationality in judging his income.

The market as a concrete institution of a free-enterprise society can therefore be only an approximation of the market of the textbooks—and not a very close approximation either. But this is sufficient for it to discharge its main functions. That there is no really perfect competition is of considerable importance to the economic analyst or to the businessman who contemplates the purchase of a property. Nevertheless the incomplete and partial competition of the actual market provides a sufficient check on economic inefficiency and on economic mistakes. That consumers do not act according to economic rationality, indeed that they do not want to act so, is obvious. Modern advertising openly exploits this fact; and no one would deny that it often abuses the consumer's ignorance, his gullibility or his fears, hopes and day dreams. Yet, with all the abuses, the consumer's dollar is still the determinant of economic action. This means that, whatever the limitations on economically rational behavior, the actual market still performs its twin tasks of allocating scarce goods and of integrating individual economic efforts into the teamwork of production.

For this reason, the really important arguments are not those that deal with the failure of the market to measure up to the ideal, but those that attack the very principles on which it is based. We shall here be concerned with two such arguments *: (1) that the market is socially destructive because it subordinates everything to the economic criterion, that is to price; and (2) that the market is socially destructive because it subordinates all economic considerations and concerns to the satisfaction of the individual's economic wants. What makes these arguments important is that their premises are correct; the market does subordinate all social activity to price, and all economic activity to the satisfaction of the individual's wants. But is it therefore antisocial?

Ours is certainly a materialist age in which economic goals have become deified. And one may well feel that the Occident is giving up all the real values, all its heritage, all the things that make for the Good Life, to chase the phantom of the rising standard of living. The argument may seem a little weak to those who have seen real poverty—the poverty of preindustrial countries; but even they will admit that material goals such as our culture glories in, are not the highest goals of human endeavor. But what is the alternative? Unless we

---

* There is a third major argument against the market system: that it is unable to overcome depression and unemployment. This is so important a point today—and differs also so completely from the arguments discussed here—that we shall devote to it the whole of the next section.

know what to put in the place of the economic goals, we simply cannot act. Before we can throw out a going system, however bad, we must have something better to put in its place. The argument that things could not possibly be worse and that any change must be a change for the good, is always nonsense in politics.

Of the making of utopias there is no end; and they are useful things as they fire the imagination of men and give them lights to steer by. But in politics the question is not what is ideally desirable. It is which of the possible solutions is best. And war is today the only possible alternative to economic progress as the organizing principle of social life in the Western world. This was the only goal which Hitler's Nazi Germany, the most thorough attempt at a noneconomic society made so far, could find. The Nazi leaders may have wanted war from the start—some certainly did. But the tremendous popular appeal of Nazism was to the vague but powerful revolt against economic goals in the German people. The tragedy of Nazism was not that it provided a new outlet for man's old urge for war. But it perverted idealistic and romantic movements which had rejected economic goals as too crass and too materialistic, into the crassest materialism of the belief in war and conquest precisely because these movements were romantic ones, that is, purely negative ones.

There is no evidence that another attempt made elsewhere would lead to a different result. To make economic progress the goal of social effort may be as bad and as deleterious as the critics say it is; and the subordination of other social considerations to profit can certainly be overdone, and often is. But the job of social integration and that of allocating scarce goods has to be done. And certainly economic progress as an organizing principle is more constructive and more beneficial socially than total war.

If we accept economic progress as a social good—even if only *faute de mieux*—we must also accept price as socially constructive; it is a simple, dependable and economically rational mechanism. A society that strives for economic goals has to base its economic system on price, if it is not to live in constant tension. But for price it would have to rest on political, that is extra-economic fiat. In the market system, economic activity is determined by the same factors which inevitably determine productivity and efficiency in any economic or social system, namely, the cost factors of labor, rate of capital accumulation, etc. In this sense—and in this sense alone—the market system is a "natural" system; and for this reason the subordination of other criteria to that of price gives the greatest social stability and the least social friction to a society that believes in economic goals. The Soviet Union, while it does not know a market in our sense, subordinates economic activity to price and cost just as does a capitalist economy; for it too professes the belief in economic goals. The only difference is that the price is set by the state instead of by the composite action of individual consumers.

The argument that the market is antisocial because it makes economics supreme, is based on esthetic or moral values. It is also usually an attack on society whatever its organizing principle, rather than on an economically organized society. The moral and esthetic critics would have been just as critical had they lived in the thirteenth instead of in the twentieth century; for every society must subordinate all other values to one guiding criterion of value. Hence their point is essentially a nonpolitical, even an antipolitical one.

The opposite is true of the second argument: that the market system is antisocial because it subordinates the needs and wants of the group to those of the individual. This is an argument from politics. It leads to the most important conclusions regarding the political functions and the political limitations of the market system.

The market system necessarily fails to satisfy group needs because it centers on the satisfaction of individual demands. It is the definition of the market that it is directed to and by the individual consumer. There is nothing very new or very startling in this statement; it was first made by no less an advocate of the market system than Adam Smith. Obviously, what concerns the survival of society as organized society is a matter for community action. Its satisfaction can only be achieved on the basis of community decisions and preferences, that is, on the basis of political decisions.

Herbert Spencer's demand that the market be universal, was a complete misunderstanding. The market can exist only as an institution of a going society. To make it absolute and universal means, however, to abolish organized society. Anarchism may be defensible on philosophical grounds; but it can never be the policy of a society whose first duty is to its own survival.

A complete misunderstanding also underlies the demand so popular today that we abolish the market because it cannot make political decisions and that we replace it by "economic planning." This appeal rests on the assertion that under a "planned economy" the *economic* system will automatically and infallibly give us the right and necessary *political* decisions. This is sheer nonsense and a dangerous bit of quackery.

No economic system no matter how it is organized can give us the right political decisions. Political decisions must always be made by political organs; and needless to say they can never be infallible or automatic. The inadequacy of military preparation in England or in the United States before the war—clearly a danger to the survival of those countries—was not the result of the market system but of the unwillingness of leaders and voters in the democracies to make the decision for war. Once this decision was taken the market delivered the war goods without trouble. Only our present tendency to search for an "automatic system" that will take the burden of responsible political decisions off the shoulders of the citizens can explain the appeal of "economic planning" as a panacea. This tendency is not confined to the sphere of economic policies; it is very much in evidence, for instance, in the field of international politics and international organization. It is actually nothing but a reformulation of Herbert Spencer's search for the infallible remedy against the burden of responsibility, watchfulness and decisions. And it is a grave threat to the survival of a free society which can only rest on the political responsibility and decisions of the citizen. An "infallible" and "automatic" system is simply a tyranny.

The campaign for "economic planning" is thus directed not against the market as an economic institution but against free government. It is really an argument for the absolutism of a Leader, or for the rule of the bureaucratic expert. Stripped of its sales talk, the argument for "economic planning" bluntly asserts that under present-day conditions no industrial society can have a free government and survive.

The absolutists of the market, and the absolutists of economic planning, both fail to see that the market system by its very foundation in the satisfactions of the individual implies two coexistent and equally important spheres of social life. The one is the individual sphere in which organized society exists only as a tool for the satisfaction of individual ideals, aspirations, needs and wants; the other is that of organized society in which the individual exists only as a tool— the term "member" is a highly appropriate one—for the sake of society's survival and for its ends. Both spheres are essential to the nature of man. Indeed without them, there could be no human society; there could only be the beehive or the madhouse. The question—the real question of economic policy—is where to draw the line and how to make one sphere balance and support the other.

Social Needs

If we turn first to the sphere of social needs which the market cannot satisfy, there are definite areas from which it has to be excluded, and to which the individual's economic needs and wants are completely irrelevant. The classical examples are the administration of justice and the maintenance of internal order. Another one, particularly important in the development of the United States, are the "internal improvements" which through collective action establish the framework for more effective individual action. The TVA is the best contemporary illustration. But the most important case is modern war. Total war is the test of a society's capacity to survive. In it the individual must be completely subordinated to society—not only in his needs and wants but in his very existence. Modern war is the absolute antithesis of the market. If we were to live in perpetual total war, or only perpetually under its threat, the market system could not be maintained. The really decisive encroachments on the free-enterprise system during the last two generations have been the result of the gradual degeneration of modern society into a total-war society.

The determination of the areas from which the market must be excluded has never presented much of a political problem. It is a simple matter of obvious necessity. All that has to be said here about these problems is that it is in the best interest of society to make a clear decision which areas are purely political, to formulate unambiguous policies for their administration, and to establish strong organs of government to carry out these policies. Also the attempt must be made to utilize the citizen's imagination and initiative to their fullest extent in these spheres.

Problems of economic policy proper only begin when we try to establish the limitations on the operation of the market in those areas where the market can and should operate but cannot be allowed full sway in the interest of social stability.

Everything in the market is a "commodity." Everything is a factor in production to be organized according to economic rationality and valued according to its price on the market. But no society can allow labor, physical resources of land or equipment and money to be treated as "commodities." Labor is man. Land and capital equipment are his environment and his productive resources. Money and credit are the social organization itself which brings together man and his resources. Clearly, all three must be preserved for society to survive. The market cannot be allowed to destroy them nor to destroy their stability.* To limit the operations of the market for the sake of the maintenance of the social fabric has been the purpose of most of our economic policy in the last hundred years. It is the rationale for the regulation of work and employment, of the labor of women and children, of the conservation of natural resources, of central banking, of slum clearance, but also for the supervision of the trade in narcotic drugs.

A special problem—in itself of considerable magnitude

---

* This is a summary of the main point of Karl Polanyi's *The Great Transformation* (New York 1944). My only quarrel with this profound book is that the author falls himself prey to the economic absolutism he so deplores in others. Not only does he fail to see the role of war in the shrinking of the market sphere, he believes that the market must either be absolute and universal, or cannot be at all. Hence he concludes from the necessity of limitations on the operations of the market that the market has no sphere at all in which it can exist and operate. I see no logical or political justification for this conclusion.

and difficulty—is the limitation of the effect of economic change on the social fabric. The whole purpose of the market system is change, namely economic expansion. But society requires a considerable stability and predictability to survive. Above all the individual can only function in a social habitat with which he is familiar, which he understands and for which he has traditions. Even in this most mobile country, the "mobility of labor"—to use the economist's term—is very low. The Oklahoma farmer, "tractored" off his land becomes an "Okie," without social roots, disintegrated and himself a disintegrating force. The worker in a town that has lost its industries, cannot simply pull up stakes and go elsewhere. He is tied by hundreds of bonds—family, home ownership, friends, church, even by his debts. And our greatest social postwar problem will be the social effect of economically necessary change on the social unit of the family farm. Especially pressing will be the problem of the millions of Southern cotton share croppers whose whole existence is threatened by the mechanical cotton picker. No doubt, the replacement of the economically most inefficient share cropper by the efficient machine should eventually result in a higher income for all, including the displaced share croppers or their descendants. But where will the five or eight million share croppers go, and what will they do? And what about the social and economic fabric of the South of which they have been the warp? Surely a sudden displacement of the share croppers would be a social and political catastrophe not only for the South but for the whole country. At the same time to maintain by political means the socially and economically obsolete system of cotton share cropping in the face of technological advance can only result eventually in even worse catastrophe; with every year the adjustment will become more difficult, the status quo less tenable. In dealing with the social effects of economic change we clearly have not only to solve the problem of limiting the market but that of making it operate as well.

Where the line has to be drawn that limits the market, and how it is to be drawn can only be decided if we juxtapose the political and social functions of the market to its limitations. As the example of the cotton sha1 ? cropper shows, the economic rationality of price supplies a constant gauge of political decisions affecting the economic sphere. If we decide to maintain the cotton share cropper in spite of his economic obsolescence, the market will show us not only how much this decision costs in terms of national wealth and income but also how great a discrepancy develops between economic and social rationality. Without such a yardstick we simply could not have a policy at all. We would either have to let loose the technological forces all at once and risk social upheaval now, or keep the machine out altogether and ensure eventual total collapse. With the market as a yardstick we can have a policy of gradual adjustment, difficult though it will be. The existence of the market is thus a prerequisite to any policy that aims at controlling the impact of change, at least as long as we want economic expansion.

There can be no adequate substitute for the market in this function, precisely because it is based on the decisions of the individual consumer. Not that the individual in his economic decisions is necessarily wiser or less given to mistakes than would be a well-trained economic expert. But the mistakes of the individual are small mistakes because his area of operation is small; and because there are so many individuals, their small mistakes, setbacks and catastrophes tend to balance each other. With a few economic dictators in command—such as a group of economic planners—the economy would proceed in a series of violent fluctuations and with the constant risk of catastrophic mistakes. It is no accident that the Soviet economy works on the highest profit margin of any industrial country; the risk of catastrophic mistakes, such as led to the great famines of the early thirties, is very much greater under a Five-Years Plan than in an economy which is ruled by those millions of very small bosses, the consumers.

In a society like ours which believes in economic goals, we could not have a successful social policy unless we had the principle of economic rationality which the market gives in price. The very delineation of the areas where the market cannot be allowed to operate freely depends on a functioning economic yardstick. The interests of society for the sake of which we have to limit the market are by no means harmonious. What is more important for society—to abolish slums through cheap housing or to maintain the social security and traditions of construction workers through restrictions on methods and materials? A decision can only be reached if these conflicting interests can be expressed in the same terms, that is, in terms of their effect on costs and prices. Without the common denominator of price, every single decision of social policy would be a political duel beyond compromise, and to be decided solely by political pressure. Above all, without the yardstick of price, we could not measure the effect of a social policy on economic efficiency and productivity. And these effects are a genuine concern of policy not only in any society that strives for economic expansion but in any society that wants to survive. For the efficient utilization of its economic resources is a prerequisite to the physical survival of a society and of its members.

The Individual Wants

So far there has been little or nothing in our argument with which the confirmed socialist could not have agreed. But at this point he would take issue with us: "Nothing you have said so far, is really an argument for the market, that is for basing economic decisions on the whims and preferences of the individual consumer. You have only shown that in a society that strives for economic expansion, economic policies and decisions must be based on economic rationality, that is, on price. I fully agree; but you don't need a market to have price. Look at the Soviet Union which subordinates economic decisions to price without subordinating them to the individual consumer. You argue that a price that is based on competition, that is, on the decisions of a multitude of small consumers, is a more reliable yardstick and corrective than a price that is based on the calculations of economic experts under an over-all plan. I think that you tend to overestimate the efficiency of market competition and to underestimate the possibilities of "socialist competition," that is, measurement and correction based on the objective yardstick of cost accounting. But even if you should be right, it would prove only that a socialist system would need a somewhat larger risk-premium in the form of a higher profit margin. That, however, is a very minor matter compared to the tremendous advantage a socialist system gives in terms of social strength by making the satisfaction of society's survival needs paramount."

Our hypothetical socialist is quite right: everything said so far dealt with price and cost rather than with the specific price of the market, that is with price determined by individual demand. There is only one thing he overlooked—a society which considers economic goals to be social ends, can be a *free so-*

ciety only if its major economic decisions are made on the basis of the individual's economic wants, that is, in and through a market.

This point is usually presented today in the argument that a collectivist economy would demand an absolute government. This is true; but why is it true? Why is the socialist counterargument incorrect that freedom could and would be preserved through the popular control of the economic organs of the government? The answer is that no society can be free in which the citizen's self-interest in the socially constitutive sphere is in continuous and inevitable conflict with the self-interest of society. If this happens the citizen must be prevented from following his self-interest. His actions in the very sphere in which lie the social goals, must be denied, controlled or suppressed. Government must be supreme and absolute; the citizen cannot be allowed to control, direct and supervise it; he cannot be allowed even to participate in it except, perhaps, in such shams as the Nazi "plebiscites."

In a society striving for economic expansion, the socially constitutive sphere is the economic one. Such a society therefore can only be free if the individual citizen's economic desires and decisions are socially effective and the determinant of the society's economy, that is, based on the market. If, as all collectivists assert, the individual's economic decisions are antisocial and cannot be allowed to rule the economy, social good and individual good in an economic society would be in basic conflict. The government would certainly have to be in full control of the economy, and all economic decisions would have to be taken on the basis of the good of the group, that is, by political fiat. In that case, a society striving for economic goals could never be a free society. It would have to have an absolute government over which the antisocial self-interest of the individual could not be allowed any control.

The relationship between the self-interest of the citizen and the interest of society is the most fundamental question of a free society. For there is no doubt that these two interests are never the same. Plato and Rousseau attempted to resolve the conflict by educating away the self-interest of the citizen, the philosophical anarchists such as Herbert Spencer by denying the reality of society. Neither attempt can be successful. But the market, however limited and incomplete, endows the economic self-interest of the individual with social efficiency and effectiveness. Hence the market, that is the use of the individual's economic decision as the governor of the economy, makes possible a free government in a society striving for economic goals.

Freedom is an article of faith, and not a law of physics. It is perfectly possible, therefore, not to believe in it. If the collectivists have no faith in it they cannot be proven wrong. Also, freedom does not come by itself but requires great and constant human effort. It is perfectly possible to hold—particularly for those who do not believe in freedom anyhow —that despotism is much easier. But one argument is impermissible—that a free society is less efficient and less stable than a despotic one. Precisely because in a free society there is no conflict between the desires and decisions of the individual and those of society, a free society suffers far less from friction and has far greater stability and far greater reserves of vitality than a despotic one. For it uses the self-interest of the citizen in the social interest instead of fighting it constantly. This is only a secondary argument for those who, like the author, believe in freedom as an article of faith and as commanded by the nature of God and of man. But since we have been concerned in this chapter with social stability and survival, we might point out that the market contributes to both because it makes possible a free economic society.

As long as we accept economic progress as a social good, the market is thus both, indispensable to a free society and indispensable to economic stability and functioning. Without price, that is without economic rationality, as the determinant of economic action, we could not have an economic society. Without market price we could not have freedom in an economic society. While the social interest demands limitation of price and market, it also demands the fullest possible utilization of the political and social potentialities of the market. Hence, regulation and intervention in these fields should never take the form of direct political control, and of substituting political fiat for market action. It should always be confined to the setting of the limits within which the market is given full play. There can be—and there is—considerable disagreement where those limits should lie in specific cases. They must be broad enough to allow the market its work of correction and integration; society's need to impose a limit on the market for the sake of a social interest in need of protection should always be weighed against the effect of the limitation on the operation of the market and on society's interest in economically efficient production. The market is neither a perfect nor an all-embracing institution. But within its limits it operates in the social interest.

3

IS FULL EMPLOYMENT POSSIBLE?

THE questions discussed so far—monopoly and bigness, profitability, market and market price, profit motive—have been with us for over a century. For the most part this chapter has done little but sum up a traditional debate. But, as has become clear during the last ten or twenty years, the future of the industrial system will not be decided by the answer we give to the classical questions of economic policy, but by its ability to provide full employment. If the free-enterprise system fails to maintain full employment, it will not survive, whatever its other advantages. If it solves the full-employment problem it will have the support of the great majority of the people in this country. Full employment has become the touchstone of America's economic system and the focus of our economic policy.

A great deal can be said against the current belief that full employment is the greatest economic good, and that unemployment is the greatest economic evil. Catastrophes rarely occur twice in the same manner. And the means adopted after one catastrophe to prevent its recurrence are usually ineffective against the next. Hence it may well be that in concentrating on the prevention and cure of unemployment, we are preparing against the last depression rather than against the next one. Nevertheless, it is right to see in employment a crucial test of the social efficiency of our economic system. Long-term unemployment has not only disastrous economic consequences; it endangers the very cohesion of society. The chronically unemployed has been deprived, without fault of his own, of his full citizenship, of his standing in the community, and of his self-respect. A society in which citizenship, standing, and self-respect depend upon such uncontrollable and incomprehensible forces as those unleashed by a depression, cannot possibly hold together or make sense to its members. No industrial society today can tolerate long-term unemployment or can afford to run the risks inherent in it. Industrial society, as this last war has proved, can stand severe economic dislocations and shocks if only reasonably full employment is guaranteed. We must therefore subordinate all the questions discussed so far in this chapter to the one: can full employment be obtained under the free-enterprise system with its large corporations?

"Full employment" is as ambiguous a term as such slogans usually are. If we ask whether the free-enterprise system can guarantee every man the job he wants to have or is qualified to do, the answer is a straight "No"; nor can any other system give such a guarantee. Nor could we provide a permanent surplus of jobs—the demand made by Sir William Beveridge among others. The resulting inflationary pressure would soon cut both productive efficiency and purchasing power and thus bring about the very unemployment we try to prevent. Altogether we would not want to eliminate economic fluctuations. Risks can be abandoned only if we also give up the chances. Complete stability means complete rigidity and stagnation. What we want is to prevent large-scale, long-term unemployment and to give all men with the ability and the will to work a reasonable opportunity to support themselves by their own labor. The risks and fluctuations of a normal labor market are perfectly bearable socially and economically. But we cannot stand the abnormal labor-market of a catastrophic depression.

So much has been written about full employment and the

prevention and control of economic depressions that the lay-man as well as the economist finds himself lost in the maze. Apparently, no two writers ever agree on the nature of the problem nor on its cure. Nevertheless, out of this copious and emotional discussion, several major conclusions have emerged.

First, it has become quite clear to everybody but a few economic theoreticians battling over technicalities, that it is not of first importance to know the *economic* causes of de-pressions. Not only does it seem highly probable that there is no one single cause of economic depressions but a multi-plicity of interlocking causes. It has also become almost cer-tain that none of the so-called causes—"tentative hypotheses" would be a more nearly accurate way of describing them— are really responsible for the depression. They serve only as the release. The real root of a depression is the structural complexity of the modern industrial system—that is, some-thing we cannot cure or avoid. It would be just as reasonable to forbid people to use fire for heating, light and cooking in order to avoid burning down the house, as to try to avoid economic complexity to escape depressions. Economic com-plexity is a condition of productivity. We know also that the paralysis which tends to afflict a modern economy in a de-pression, and which makes it a chronic depression, is not economic in nature. It is caused above all by the social dis-locations and psychological shock of the depression itself. Economic policy must thus concentrate less on eliminating the economic causes of depressions, whatever they may be, than on overcoming the depression-caused inability to get going again.

The experience of the last twenty years has shown us that the traditional counsel to let the economy cure itself has be-come irrelevant. It may be perfectly true that a depression, if left alone, will ultimately provide its own cure. But the patient will have died of exposure and shock by that time. Modern industrial society simply cannot stand the social wreckage of prolonged unemployment and stagnation. However correct the economic theory of the advocates of a "hands off" policy may be, they fail to understand that a major depression is primarily a social and political threat. Every industrial country must therefore adopt a policy of positive action and intervention in case of depression.

Further, while we know very little about the causes of a depression, we do know a good deal about the cure. It has taken us a long time to learn the obvious—that chronic unemployment is the same thing as a failure to employ our productive resources to their full capacity. Once that is clear, however, we can see that the way out is to produce.

A depression will not occur as long as the production of capital goods is maintained. In any depression, whatever its cause, employment will be restored by a rise in the production of capital goods to the level needed to sustain a normal economy. Though only a part—normally about a quarter—of a nation's industrial volume, the production of capital goods determines total business. The largest volume of consumer goods production, on the other hand, will never by itself overcome a depression or restore employment; all it can do—as we saw in 1936-7—is to create a deceptive "prosperity without employment." We have but to contrast the failure of all attempts to overcome unemployment by doctoring its causes or by subsidizing consumption—such as the New Deal in this country or the policy of the National Government in England from 1931 to 1938—with the success of all policies which simply put capital goods industries to work such as those in Soviet Russia, in Nazi Germany, and finally, after the outbreak of the war, in the democracies. And in a country which like the United States is largely independent of foreign supplies and of foreign markets, reasonably full production is always physically and economically possible given the will and the imagination.

It follows that all attempts to solve unemployment by indirect means are completely inadequate. This applies particularly to monetary policies, such as were the arcana of the New Deal. We have learned a great deal about monetary policy since 1914. One of the main lessons has been that monetary policy is only an auxiliary, though a very important one. Failure on the part of the lay public to understand this may become a real danger at the onset of another depression as it may force the government of the day, whether Republican or Democratic, to fall back automatically on New Deal monetary policies as the "safe" and "traditional" course. But while these policies by their very novelty and incomprehensibility had a certain psychological effect in the nineteen-thirties, they will fail miserably the next time they are tried—thus inviting the demagogue to ride to power on the popular demand for a working depression policy.

It is often asserted that depression and unemployment are "capitalist" phenomena and could not possibly occur under a socialist system. But everything we have learned about the anatomy and pathology of the depression contradicts the claim that economic fluctuations depend on the ownership of a society's economic resources. A socialist system is subject to the same economic stresses and strains as a free-enterprise system of comparable industrial structure. What matters is not that the economy in a socialist state is socialist but that the government is absolute. For that enables it to intervene directly into the allocation of economic resources between production of capital goods and production of consumers' goods. It is the increase of capital investment—that is expenditures for the production of capital goods—which keeps production as a whole going. If the free-enterprise system finds a way to keep up the rate of capital investment in the face of a depression it can do as well as any socialist state, and without giving the government absolute powers.

But even though the absolute government of a socialist state has the power to order the production of capital goods, it knows as little as the government or the businessmen of a capitalist country what capital goods to produce. Actually no socialist state to date has really solved the problem. Neither Soviet Russia nor Nazi Germany have been able to find any other outlet for their forced capital investments but war production; nor, so far, have the democracies. The last depression was overcome everywhere only by producing for war. If war production should remain the only way out of a long-term depression, industrial society would be reduced to the choice between suicide through total war or suicide through total depression.

The Business Cycle

The first problem of a full-employment policy is to generate capital-goods production during a cyclical depression. In the last cyclical depression the New Deal tried to stimulate the production of producers' goods by subsidizing the consumption of consumers' goods. It failed because the existing producers' goods equipment was sufficient to accommodate substantial increases in consumer-demand resulting from government spending. There is no reason to believe—in fact, there is every reason to disbelieve—that any repetition of the New Deal policies, even on a much more sweeping scale would have a different result. That is, indeed, openly admitted in the new theories of the same economists whose ideas were responsible for the New Deal policies. Instead of demanding deficit spending to stimulate consumer expenditure their new program calls for deficit spending on producers' goods in the form of a large and well-prepared program of public works.*

The thinking that has gone into this program is far more realistic than most of the ideas so far produced by private enterprise. At least the government economists squarely face the issue of production. It should also be said that a program of public works on a sufficiently large scale might have a fair chance of overcoming unemployment provided it is accepted by the people; after all, economically speaking, war production was nothing but a public works program. There is no doubt that we shall adopt such a program of government-financed and government-run public works, if there is no other way out of a depression.

It would be pointless to deny that the case for a government-sponsored public-works program is a strong one. But it does not really answer the question what public works we shall produce. Many of our planners seem to believe that all that is needed is a mechanism, and that the decision what to do with it will take care of itself. This makes it appear more than likely that, in an emergency, the public works actually undertaken will necessarily consist of armaments production. Everybody is in favor of national defense; patriotism—or its imitation—is always safe in politics. It is also the one large-scale production program which we have the experience to organize and run. Finally, it can go on forever as no country bent on arming itself has ever had a strong enough army or a large enough navy.

This should not be mistaken as an argument against a strong peacetime defense program. On the contrary, a con-

---

* The best short statement of this program was Mr. Henry Wallace's testimony before the Senate Commerce Committee in January, 1945 on the occasion of his nomination as Secretary of Commerce.

sistent policy of national preparedness is certainly necessary and desirable. But it would be disastrous—above all to the national defense of the country—if armaments were to become the means of providing employment rather than the outcome of a considered national defense policy. It certainly would not be in the interest of national defense to subordinate it to the requirements of the domestic economy. Nothing could be less conducive to peace or to security. For if this country—or any other of the great powers—were to make its defense program a function of its domestic employment situation, it would become impossible to conduct a constructive and well thought-out foreign policy or to develop any lasting international collaboration.

Moreover, the almost complete control of capital investment by the government that is implied in such a program must corrupt our system of government. Political power would become the main means to economic advancement and gain. The government itself would become the football of selfish interests out to divert the stream of government cash into their pockets. It is no accident that the rise in the number of pressure groups during the last twenty years paralleled the extension of government control and intervention in economic life. It is also no coincidence that the very planners who are most convinced that a government program of public works is the only salvation of popular government, are also the people who proclaim most loudly that we must leave policy making and administration to the expert bureaucrat rather than to submit them to popular discussion and decision.

Finally, the advocates of a government-sponsored public-works program tend to forget that such a program would have to be justified as an "emergency measure" like the New Deal spending policies. Even if the government planners call their program a "plan to promote free enterprise," as has lately become the fashion, public works would be regarded as a temporary expedient. This would revive the tension between the beliefs of a large part of the population and the practices of their government, which has been such a marked feature of the New Deal. Such a cleavage tends to disorganize not only the political but also the economic system. And like the New Deal's "spending-lending," a program of public works may well fail to get the economy going again; its employment-creating effect would be offset by a steady shrinkage in the private sector of the economy. The politics of a public-works program might thus easily defeat the economics. Recovery would be only apparent as it was in 1937, and not real. We would become dependent upon ever-increasing "shots in the arm" like a drug addict, and might finally be forced into state-socialism by default.

This should not be mistaken for an argument against public works as such. The old American tradition of "internal improvements," in which the Tennessee Valley Authority stands, is an excellent one. There is plenty of room in this country for a large-scale program of "internal improvements"—highways, irrigation and power projects, reforestation or waterways. However, these necessary and beneficial projects could only be harmed grievously by being subordinated to the employment needs of the economy instead of being undertaken in the national interest. Their usefulness and their benefits would seriously be impaired were they to be made political projects designed not to strengthen America's permanent economic structure but to provide emergency relief. To be efficient and successful a public-works program must not be subordinated to political or social considerations alien to it. The TVA is an example. It succeeded only after it had ceased to be run primarily as an experiment in "planned living" and as a stick with which to beat business, and concentrated—in collaboration with business—on its own jobs: flood control, power supply, land rehabilitation.

A good many of the advocates of planning admit all this. But they contend that there is no alternative and that only the government can effectively provide production and employment in a depression. It was indeed true that only the government could have provided the consumer purchasing power on which the "old" New Deal based itself. But investment in producers' goods is something very different.

Challenge to Business Leaders

It is perhaps the greatest weakness of American business leaders today that they have not seriously come to grips with the question of full employment. If the large corporations do not offer a constructive and positive full-employment policy, they concede defeat without a fight. The demand to let nature take its course is not a policy at all. Indeed it amounts to an abdication of the leadership which Big Business claims. It is an admission that only the government can do something constructive. There are some signs that the large corporations are beginning to realize their responsibility, and that they are coming out of the state of shock which has paralyzed their social and political imagination since the Depression. Signs of a new attitude are the concern of business leaders with reconversion, resettlement of dislocated workers, and re-employment of veterans, and the work of groups such as the Committee for Economic Development. But the real problem has yet to be tackled and tackled right away.

Actually the challenge of unemployment provides business with one of its greatest chances. It is possible to provide full employment on a free-enterprise basis, notwithstanding the contrary views of the planners. The following pages do not pretend to present solutions. They only try to show how the problem might be attacked and from what angle.

Any attempt to work out a full-employment policy must start with the realization that the advocates of government-sponsored public works are right in two of their fundamental assertions. The problem of unemployment has to be attacked directly by providing work for the producers' goods industries. Also in a modern industrial economy the time unit of economic life is not the calendar year but the business cycle of seven to fifteen years. On this realization rests the demand of our planners that government base its policies on a ten-year "average" of capital investment. The business cycle is roughly equal to the average life-span of capital equipment during which it has to pay for itself and at the end of which it has to be replaced. Ten to fifteen years is also the average development period of new industries, new products, and new processes, from the laboratory stage to that of successful commercial production. For the farmer the calendar year is indeed much more than a convenient measurement; his production cycle actually runs from harvest to harvest. But to apply the farmer's unit of economic life to an industrial economy, except as a conventional measurement, cannot be justified; yet we let the calendar year determine our economic thinking and our economic policy. The proposal of the advocates of public works to spread the capital investment of an economy over the period of the business cycle is, therefore, essentially sound. But does it really require government control and large-scale deficit financing to accomplish a reform of the measuring unit?

We would achieve practically all that is promised by the public-works program—and achieve it on the basis of free enterprise—by an elementary reform of our fiscal system which would make it conform to the facts of modern economic life.

Our fiscal policy today applies the convention of the calendar year like a strait jacket to our industrial economy which makes practically impossible business investments in bad years. Our revenue laws all but completely separate the financial results of one year from the financial results of another year. January first, or the beginning of the new accounting year, are points at which, according to the fiction on which we base fiscal policy, industrial life starts all over again from scratch. The one highly inadequate exception is in the provision which allows the deduction of losses incurred during the past two years from current profits—and even that is regarded as an unjustifiable concession by the fiscal mind.

The hold which a completely obsolete time-convention has on our fiscal policy shows even more in our failure to grasp the obvious fact that a new business during its first years is not an economic adult but an economic child, who needs special protection. Nobody would put a soldier's pack, complete with rifle and tent, on the shoulders of a six year old and expect him to be able to go through a twenty-mile forced march; yet, in its treatment of new ventures, our fiscal system does just that.*

A change from an annual basis of taxation to a cyclical one would not, of course, replace annual tax payments by a payment made once every ten years on the over-all profit of a cyclical period. But just as we have succeeded in the payment of the individual income tax to combine "pay as you go" taxes with an ultimate assessment of an annual tax, we can easily combine annual business taxes on a preliminary pro rata basis

---

* It hardly needs emphasizing that this is not an attack on New Deal fiscal policy, critical as I am of it. The calendar-year approach was used in just the same way and with the same results under Herbert Hoover.

with a final adjustment payment once every ten or twelve years. While payments would be annual the basis would be cyclical returns.

A cyclical approach to the taxation of business would result in taxes being levied on the actual profit rather than on the fictitious figure of the "annual profit." This would make it possible to use cyclical taxation to bring about capital investment in depression years. Today we tax all annual profits beyond an often insufficient provision for depreciation. Thus business—especially with the present, almost confiscatory tax rates—can normally neither provide for the risks inherent in expansion nor accumulate the capital reserve with which to finance it.

Under a system of cyclical taxes there would be no conceivable reason why reserves made out of annual profit should be limited to minimum depreciation needs. We could allow business, whether big or small, to set aside for future contingencies as much as they consider advisable—if they set aside too much, the government would regain its lost tax income a few years later anyhow. And that would make it possible to encourage and to reward the setting aside of reserves out of current profits as a basis for a positive unemployment policy.

The Employment Fund

To prevent unemployment, business should be exempted from taxes on reserves for future contingencies set aside out of current profits. These reserves would become taxable, however, unless they were actually used within a specified period —say ten years—either to offset losses or for employment-creating capital investments, such as investments in new equipment, new plants, new products and processes. We should put a positive reward on the use of such reserves for employment-creating investments in depression times—perhaps something like a discount of ten cents on the current tax for every dollar spent productively during a business recession or depression. At the same time we should penalize heavily the hoarding of these reserves in times of slack employment.

By means of such a policy, we would force business to work out long-term plans for capital investment. This would on the one hand lessen the danger of overspeculation or boom. On the other hand it would greatly reduce the danger of defeatist underinvestment in a depression, that is at a time when without such plans and without a concept of a long-term rate of business profitability, nobody dares to invest. We would also create in a few years a revolving fund available for capital investment that would be more than ample to provide the necessary expenditure in producers' goods even during the worst depression year. Let us assume corporation profits before taxes of twelve billion dollars a year—a very low estimate which implies a sharp falling off of business volume in the postwar period. We could then expect annual reserves of at least three billion dollars over and above the depreciation provisions. Within five years (except during a depression) we would have accumulated a capital investment fund of fifteen billion dollars which is more than the amount of capital expenditure that, if spent in 1932, would have converted a period of intense depression and unemployment into one of high business volume and full employment. Actually, if such a fund existed and were used, we should never have to fear a collapse like that of 1932. The existence of the fund alone, and its impact on the economy in the early stages of a depression should be enough to prevent the psychological collapse which makes a depression chronic. In fine, such a fund without costing the taxpayer one cent,* would perform efficiently and effectively the job that the government planners propose to perform by means of deficit-financed public works; and it would do so without any of the social and political dangers inherent in public works.

To give such a policy maximum effectiveness, the funds set aside for capital investment might serve as the basis for a guarantee of employment in poor years. Everybody knows that unemployment insurance is not an insurance against unemployment at all. It gives money instead of a job; but money payments, even if the rates are high, do not make good the loss of standing in family and community and the loss of self-respect which follows the loss of work. Also, no unemployment insurance can possibly provide against more than temporary unemployment.

Our Social Security laws admit that frankly; yet the rate the law aims at is based on the fantastic attempt to provide by insurance against a general catastrophe—about as sensible as if marine insurance rates were to be based on the risk of simultaneous and total loss of all ships. The resultant compromise-rate between a premium that would correspond to the normal risk of temporary unemployment in a going economy, and the rate that would correspond to the risk of general and permanent unemployment—which on an actuarial basis might approach a premium several times the current wage—is far too high for the ordinary insurance purpose and ridiculously low for the pretended purpose. Small wonder that the application of this legal rate has had to be postponed year after year. The same criticism applies to the Beveridge plan.

---

* Any part of the fund not used for employment-creating investment, would become taxable at the full rate within ten years; thus tax payment would only be postponed. And that part that is being used would simply take the place of government expenditure—likely to be much larger than the uncollected tax— which would otherwise be needed in depression years.

This does not mean that unemployment insurance is worthless; but it applies properly to transitory short-term unemployment in a going economy. Any need over and above that would have to be satisfied out of reserve funds which actually provide jobs. Such a reservoir could be created if business were permitted to set aside, free of taxation, funds earmarked for employment-creating purposes. If such funds exist, business could guarantee jobs to its workers—not indefinitely, and not to all, but for a considerable period varying with the length of service.

Moreover, such an investment and employment reservoir might have a marked and beneficial effect on union wage policies. At present the union automatically demands an increase in wage rates in good years, even when living costs are not rising. Yet it also fights against any decrease of the wage rate in bad years. The wage structure thus acquires a rigidity which is one of the greatest obstacles to recovery in a depression; for it prevents an adaptation of industry's major cost factor to economic conditions.

Intelligent union leaders know very well that this policy is harmful not only to the economy but to labor itself. But under present conditions they could not change it. One reason is that the more members of a worker's family are out of work, the greater the demands on the pay checks of those who still have a job. For the worker the economic unit is the family, and the income that matters is family income. This was shown clearly in the early years of the Nazi regime in Germany. Hitler cut wage rates sharply below the union-maintained levels of 1932. At the same time armaments production and the building up of a huge army and an equally huge bureaucracy soon restored employment. As a result, the average German worker felt that his income, that is, family income, had been increased by the Nazi regime which greatly puzzled foreign observers who only saw the slash in the individual worker's pay check.

If only one out of three working members of a family becomes unemployed, the family income is cut by one third—and few working-class families have enough of a margin in their budget to stand such a cut without undergoing real hardships. To maintain the wage of the two members who are still employed, thus appears the least that can be done for the worker. If there only would be a reasonable chance that numerical employment could be maintained, labor might be able and willing to agree to take cuts in the wage rate during bad times; and an investment and employment reservoir would provide the assurance of maintaining numerical employment.

In addition, such a reserve fund might answer labor's main argument for economically unjustified wage increases in good years—that the worker has to provide an emergency fund during good years in view of the uncertain nature of his employment. Altogether an employment reserve would give the worker a feeling of security which should go a long way towards counteracting that psychological defeatism which is so largely responsible for the depression's tendency to become permanent.

There are probably serious objections to this plan; certainly a great deal of expert work would have to be done before it could be put into action. But it is not offered as a final solution, nor is it pretended that by itself it will be sufficient. It is presented only to show that it is possible to control cyclical depressions in a free-enterprise economy, provided industry and government use imagination and initiative.

Expansion

A full-employment policy must not only overcome cyclical depressions. It must also provide for the constant expansion of our economy to keep step both with the increase in the working population and with the continuous increase in productivity per man-hour which may cause technological unemployment. During the last ten years, it has become popular to assert that ours is a "mature economy" which can no longer rely on automatic expansion and which must substitute government action and control for our traditional trust in natural growth.

This assertion rests on two premises: that American expansion in the past was largely based on the appropriation and overrapid exploitation of nature's bounties which can no longer be continued without serious depletion of the nation's natural capital; and that the major areas of economic expansion lie in fields which cannot be adequately worked on the basis of our existing system of distribution. These premises are, broadly speaking, correct; the question is only whether they lead to the conclusion that economic expansion is to be obtained only from government intervention and control.

It is certainly true that in the interest of its national survival this country can no longer permit the depletion of such resources as soil, forests or petroleum. The main source of future expansion must be the accumulated reserves of created capital, that is, profits, and the initiative and imagination of the country's inhabitants. To say that a country in this position has reached the state of maturity in which its economy cannot grow is nonsense. According to this assertion a country like Germany could never have become a major industrial producer. Her industry was built up in the fifty years before the first World War with meagre and carefully husbanded natural resources.

The correct conclusion, as has been said once before, is that in the future we will have to rely to a greater extent on the capital accumulated out of current profits. Even if we assume that the rate of expansion in the future will be less than it has been in the past, we shall need a higher profit margin coupled with a fiscal policy which puts positive rewards on the use of profits for future expansion.

We must also adopt a new policy of conservation towards young and growing businesses. We have become conservation-conscious in respect to the resources supplied by nature. But we are still unbelievably spendthrift with the resources supplied by man, that is, imagination, courage and initiative. In the future, these man-made economic assets will become the more important, the more we have to conserve our natural resources. If we do not protect and conserve these assets we shall exploit and exhaust them even more rapidly than we have been depleting our resources of iron ore or petroleum. While we may expect human ingenuity, initiative and imagination to find substitutes for exhausted natural resources—within limits, of course—there is no substitute for the human resources of a society once they have been choked off. Hence the argument of the mature economy does not lead to a demand for government planning or control but on the contrary to a demand for the encouragement and rewarding of individual enterprise and initiative.

Our present fiscal policy does its best to stifle new ventures. Instead of building them up, it loads on their shoulders the full burden of a grown and established business. New ventures should be exempted from taxation entirely for the first decade, at least they should be allowed to deduct in full all loss incurred during that formative period. At the same time—and this is largely a task for private business—we have to make it possible for such new ventures to obtain equity capital. Today—as a result of our tax policies as well as of a bureaucratic approach to banking policy—there are no sources of capital for new ventures. That such capital can be supplied, is shown by the fact that General Motors successfully supplies equity capital to dealers within the limits of ordinary banking risks and profits. But before this example could be copied on a large scale, we would have to alter radically our fiscal mentality and policy.

The doctrine of the mature economy asserts that the major areas of economic expansion open to us today cannot be worked satisfactorily under the present distribution system. This assertion leaves out entirely the possibility of developing new major industries—aviation, electronics, new sources of energy—which so far in the history of modern economic life have always sprung up to confound the prophets of stagnation. But no policy can reasonably be based upon the assumption that we will get new industries in the future because we have always got them in the past. We therefore have to agree that the greatest unfulfilled needs of our economy, except for war-created shortages, may lie in areas such as housing, where private enterprise has not so far built up a distributive system capable of satisfying the tremendous latent demand. The reason for this is that our distribution system is largely geared to individual market action alone. Demands like that for housing cannot however be easily satisfied by the isolated action of the individual in the market.

We know that houses can be built very cheaply—cheap enough to bring good new housing within reach of all but a small portion of the population—provided that they are mass-produced and mass-assembled. This means the removal of those union restrictions which today prevent the use of efficient building methods and of cheap building materials. It also means that cheap housing can only be achieved if a large number of units are put up at the same time together with an organized system of transportation and sewage disposal, with hospitals, schools and stores. The economics of housing are not so very different from those of railroad transportation, or electric power supply, none of which can be provided for an isolated individual consumer though the economic satisfaction they give is individual, not group, satisfaction. The question is only how to organize this community action for individual satisfaction, that is, how to make possible mass production and mass assembly.

Compared to other economic problems solved successfully in the past, this problem of organization is a simple matter. One way to solve it was shown by the insurance company that built the New York housing development of Parkchester. Community projects can be financed by institutions like insurance companies or savings banks, which administer the accumulated savings of the community. Another way would be through the organization of local co-operatives for specific local projects. This would require positive action on the part of the government in the form of special tax exemptions. The government would also have to supply expert advice and assistance, perhaps modeled after that most successful of all government agencies, the County Farm Agent. It will be necessary in poorer regions to supplement local capital resources with loans and grants-in-aid from the government. But while there is a fertile field for federal encouragement, advice and help, there does not seem to be any necessity for large-scale direct government action in order to make effective the latent demands of our economy on the satisfaction of which economic expansion seems to depend.

The Economic Policy of a Free-Enterprise Society

To sum up: If we have no workable policy to overcome serious long-term unemployment the government will assume control of the national capital-goods investment in the next major depression. We will be forced into a collectivist economy. This is inevitable not only because of the popular pressure for a working depression policy, but also because long-term mass-unemployment threatens the cohesion and survival of the social fabric. And the first duty of any government is to the survival of the body politic.

But we can overcome a depression and provide employment as well or better within the framework of a free-enterprise system. In the first place, the mere switch to collectivism would not automatically eliminate depression and the need for a depression policy, as some of the advocates of planning contend. We would still have to solve all the problems of procuring and maintaining capital-goods investments. For the depression itself is not just the result of the structure of the free-enterprise system. Secondly, the only way to overcome a depression, to increase capital investment to its normal level, is as open to a free-enterprise system as to a collectivist one. The questions involved are all of a technical nature, and can be solved under any system provided the economic resources are given. If we succeed in mobilizing the resources of a free-enterprise economy to maintain and to expand capital investment, we shall not only avoid the economic, social and political dangers of the collectivist solution. We shall have made sure that there is always an answer to that most urgent and so far unanswered question: what capital goods shall we produce? The answer will not be armaments, as seems almost inevitable under a collectivist government, but production that is based on the needs of the individual consumer and that leads to greater national wealth.

There is no inherent and unavoidable conflict between the basic requirements of social stability and functioning and the basic requirements of corporate stability and functioning;

harmony can be established between the needs of society and the purposes and needs of the large corporation. There will, of course, always be much room for disagreements on specific issues and on the exact line to follow in each concrete case. But this conflict need not extend to fundamentals. A free-enterprise economy which organizes its industrial resources in large corporations, and a stable and strong society are not only compatible, they are complementary. Above all, profit and profitability are not inimical to the best interests of society but essential to its well-being and very existence. Profit is society's insurance against the risks of economic life. And as the only source of capital formation, it is the basis both of all economic expansion and of any workable depression and full-employment policy.

There are five pillars on which an economic policy for a free-enterprise society rests.

(1) It must have a working full-employment policy. Without reasonable full and stable employment, we could actually not have an economic policy at all but would be forced to rely on improvisations and emergency measures. Without such a policy, free enterprise will not be maintained in any industrial country whatever the arguments against its abandonment or against collectivism. On the other hand, we can say that as far as this country is concerned, no successful full-employment policy can be worked out except on the basis of the free-enterprise system. Any full-employment policy based on collectivist principles seems likely, for a considerable time to come, to run afoul of the beliefs and desires of the American people and might thus well be reduced to ineffectiveness. A full-employment policy which promises to overcome the nightmare of chronic unemployment, and which at the same time bases itself on the free-enterprise system, is the only one that can be effective in this country. To show that such a policy

can be attained has been the purpose of the preceding pages. To work it out is the most urgent task of domestic policy—a task for government and business alike.

(2) A workable economic policy requires the clear determination of those spheres in which the survival interest of society demands collective political rather than individual economic action. In these spheres the government must assume direct control and must pursue a vigorous, constructive policy. National defense or the administration of justice are obvious examples, as are the "internal improvements" which set the frame for individual economic action. These tasks should be worked out clearly and should be made the unambiguous responsibility of strong government agencies equipped for decisive action. They should be seen not as competing with, but as complementary to, the sphere of free enterprise and of individual decision.

(3) There are some very important areas of economic life which, in the interest of economic efficiency, should be organized on the basis of economic rationality, that is on and by market price, but which must also be protected against the market in the interest of social stability or of social justice. The clearest examples in this country today are to be found in farming where the family farm has to be protected for social reasons against the full and immediate effects of technological progress which threatens to destroy it.

How much political intervention is desirable—if it is desirable at all—is a question that has to be decided pragmatically from issue to issue. But whatever the decision is, political action in such matters should not take the form of direct control and intervention. Government should confine itself to establishing the limits within which the free-enterprise system and the market are allowed to operate freely. Both for political and for economic reasons the proper and efficient economic regulation must not work through administrative control and interference but through the legislative and judicial determination of the limits and conditions under which business is to operate.

(4) One of the most important tasks of such regulation—and one which is in the interest of free enterprise itself—is the prevention of monopoly. But we have to be careful not to confuse monopoly which is always antisocial, with mere bigness which can be made into a social asset through decentralization. We also have to differentiate between genuinely monopolistic practices and attempts on the part of business to promote social stability through long-term price, sales and employment policies which by attempting to put economic action on the basis of the business cycle—instead of the calendar year or the season—promote the best interests of society.

(5) Finally, we should center our economic policy on the conservation of our human and man-made economic assets. This means the adoption of a fiscal policy and mentality which encourages the accumulation of capital resources for future capital investments. It also means adopting a positive policy of stimulation and encouragement for new ventures and for young enterprises and the supply of equity capital to them on a free-enterprise basis.

One reservation must, however, be made to our statement that there is no conflict between the needs of free enterprise and those of modern industrial society. The harmony without which there can be no free-enterprise economic policy is possible only as long as (a) our society continues to believe in economic progress as good, and (b) as long as social survival does not demand full control of the entire economy by the state. A free-enterprise society would become impossible if we had to live under total depression or total war.

If we do not succeed in overcoming depressions our society will almost certainly make economic security rather than economic progress the goal of economic activity. This could be accomplished only by the elimination of risk and chance, the abolition of change—and with it of expansion—and the "freezing" of productive techniques. It would also mean that the goal of economic activity is no longer seen in the satisfaction of the economic wants of the individual consumer. The profit motive as the mechanism through which individual actions are made socially effective, and the market as the institution of economic rationality, would both cease to make sense socially. The free-enterprise system would no longer fulfill basic social needs in fulfilling itself; its needs and requirements would appear to be in conflict to society's needs. Also, the government would be forced to take control of the economy if we do not succeed in overcoming depressions otherwise. For if mass unemployment becomes chronic the survival of society demands collective political control over the whole of economic life.

A much more serious threat is that of total war. Not only can we overcome depressions on the basis and with the resources of the free-enterprise system. There will also be powerful political resistance against a collectivist depression policy—although it is unlikely to prevail if the depression lasts long enough. If we have to live under the threat of total war we shall, however, not only have political pressure for complete state control. The objective requirements of modern total war are such that it requires that all economic goals be subordinated to the collective goal of national survival, and that all economic activity be controlled by the central government. To let the economic wants of the individual consumer decide production and distribution becomes absolutely impossible under the technological conditions of modern warfare. For even the wealthiest and strongest country is forced to devote more than half of the nation's resources to war production which has to be under centralized government control. By contrast, nineteenth century warfare rarely employed more than one eighth of a belligerent's productive resources, usually much less. And it is unlikely that the rapidly expanding military and naval technology of the late seventeenth and early eighteenth century which a historian of Tawney's rank holds largely responsible for the rise of Enlightened Despotism and centralized government, ever absorbed more than a quarter of the resources of a major country not excluding France during the ruinous wars of Louis XIV. According to Delbrueck, Germany's foremost historian of warfare, Frederick the Great amazed everybody in his "total Wars," by mobilizing almost one third of the economic resources of his poor and backward Prussia for war purposes. Indeed our time is unprecedented both in the demands military technology makes upon the economy and in the ability "totally" to organize the economy for the satisfaction of the demands. But even if civilization should survive free enterprise would certainly be a casualty in the first "atomic war."

To develop in this country an economic policy which will give us a functioning industrial society based on free enterprise and the modern corporation, will not eliminate war. But it will greatly contribute towards world peace and stability— perhaps more and more directly than anything else in the United States could do by itself.

EPILOGUE (1972)

General Motors Revisited

WHEN this book first appeared, a quarter-century ago, it was considered by many readers and reviewers as being "pro-business" and "pro-General Motors." But this was not the reaction of General Motors managers themselves. On the contrary, they resented the book as being sharply critical, indeed unfairly critical, of General Motors. And they rejected it altogether as being fundamentally "anti-business."

Outside of General Motors, managers—in businesses but also in such nonbusiness institutions as government agencies and hospitals—speedily adopted *Concept of the Corporation* and used it in their own work and in their own organization. One of the earliest users was an automobile company. But it was not General Motors. It was Ford. According to company spokesmen, Henry Ford, II, based his approach to the revival and reorganization of the moribund Ford Motor Company he took over in 1946—the very year the book appeared—on the principles and concepts of *Concept of the Corporation.*

But within GM the book was pointedly ignored. It has never been referred to, to the best of my knowledge, in any speech, article, or book by a General Motors executive.* The

* The most telling example is the book Alfred P. Sloan, Jr.—the architect of General Motors and in many ways the "hero" of *Concept of the Corporation*—published on GM and on its organization many years after *Concept of the* N.Y., Doubleday, 1964) *Concept of the Corporation* is not mentioned at all, *Corporation* had appeared. In *My Years with General Motors* (Garden City, even though it was Sloan who had originally urged me to do the study and had followed every stage of the work with keen interest. But the end result was clearly not to his liking.

291

book was not, to the best of my knowledge, ever distributed at GM, nor were GM managers encouraged to read it. It certainly did not have the slightest impact on GM structure or on GM policies.

Yet my relations with GM managers during the period at which I worked at the book, a period of two years, were both close and friendly. I more or less lived within GM for the better part of two years, visited at every major division and most of the larger plants, talked at least once with every senior member of management and with countless men all the way down to first line foreman—and all this with little friction or unpleasantness. Indeed, my personal stock within GM, up to the moment the book appeared, stood apparently very high. At least I found out, a few years later, that some fairly senior executives had seriously proposed my being invited to join GM in an important management position. Yet the book itself was anything but welcome; and after it had come out, the author also soon ceased to be welcome.

I relate this bit of ancient history not because it matters by itself. It does, I believe, give a clue to the curious subsequent history and the present ambiguous position of GM, the world's largest manufacturing company. In the last twenty-five years GM has been, in one way, an astounding success. But in this period GM has also, looked at another way, become a resounding failure. As a business and in terms of sales and profits, GM, at least until the very late 'sixties, went from success to success, piling up one record after another. Its position in the American automotive industry actually became even stronger than it was in earlier years. Yet, at the same time, GM as an institution has become the target of discontent and widespread hostility, from Ralph Nader to the environmentalists, from the "liberals" interested in race relations to the "radicals" opposed to any form of institutional organization. GM has almost attained to the unique distinction of being the perfect American "villain." The reaction inside GM to this book when it first came out foreshadowed, I think, both GM's success as a business and, at the same time, GM's failure as an institution.

The General Motors managers who resisted and resented this book included probably most of the men then in top positions, that is, staff vice-presidents, group executives, or heads of the large divisions. The group included at least two, if not all, of the three men who have occupied the chair of GM's chief executive since Alfred P. Sloan, Jr., vacated it shortly after the book was published. And many of these men talked to me quite candidly about their objections. Only one, let me add, tried to persuade me to change my position. The others fully accepted my right to my opinions; but, for that reason, they felt that they had to explain to me why they thought that I was both wrong and "subversive."

The first thing practically all of them said was: "You want us to re-examine our basic principles. Your book is full of suggestions for changes in specific policies. But above all, if I read you right, you believe that the time has come for GM again to think through carefully its basic objectives and its basic structure, and to attempt major constitutional reform. This is dead wrong. The validity and effectiveness of our objectives, our organization, our policies, are proven by their success. They not only enabled us to become the world's largest and most profitable manufacturing company. They enabled us successfully to compete in very different markets, such as those of Europe. They enabled us to switch from peacetime production to war production and to do things none of us had ever done before; and you yourself point out that of all major producers in the American war effort, GM has by far the best record. And now you ask us to throw all this away, just as we are about to return to the very conditions of a peacetime economy for which these policies were developed and in which they have proved themselves. This is not just folly. This is frivolous."

They were essentially right in their suspicion that I thought the time for change had come for GM. It was not only that I believed that policies after having been in effect for twenty-five years can always stand a hard critical look. The time seemed to me to be propitious for basic changes. The war years had cut the continuity of GM's objectives and organization. Not one GM plant produced any product it had made in the peacetime years. Now, with conversion to peacetime production imminent—for the book was completed in the months of final victory in World War II—changes, even sharp changes, in concept and direction, might have been carried out with a minimum of disturbance. At the same time, the top management that had been leading GM for a quarter of a century, the top management of Alfred P. Sloan, Jr., was about to retire. Sloan, indeed, had been ready for retirement before America went into World War II, and only postponed this step "for the duration."* By the time the book came out, he was well past seventy. And with Sloan, as everybody knew, most of the "old guard" would go, as indeed they did. Such a change-over is, of course, an ideal time for basic rethinking of direction and structure in a business. Indeed a new management, coming in after such a long tenure by a predecessor, can be expected to make fairly drastic changes.

This, the critics conceded. And yet they felt strongly that to suggest that GM and its policies might be in need of change

---

* He did indeed retire as chief executive officer shortly after the book came out, even though he stayed on as a vigorous, effective, and most influential chairman for another ten years, until 1955.

was to be critical, if not indeed hostile, to GM. As they saw it, my mission had been to set out clearly the basic principles on which past achievement had been built so that Sloan's successors could faithfully follow Sloan's policies. Yet I had come out with the opposite conclusion from the one which my own facts implied—or so it seemed to them. I had concluded, and indeed had said openly in quite a few places, that change rather than faithful continuity was what GM needed.

But much worse, my critics felt, was the underlying "hostility to business" which my book revealed to them. How else, they argued, could one explain my criticism of GM policies in such areas as labor relations, the relations between the company and the major cities in which its plants were located (what today we might call "environmental relations"), public relations, public affairs, and so on? How else could one explain the criticism of the internal structure of the big divisions such as Chevrolet, except as criticism of "business" itself? I had, they told me, not even attempted to base these criticisms on "rational" arguments. I had not even attempted to say that the existing policies were not in the interests of GM, did not help in producing better and cheaper products for the customer, a larger profit for the company, or better jobs for employees on all levels. On the contrary, I had clearly accepted the fact that the existing policies were optimal for all major parties to GM itself—workers, managers, stockholders, and dealers. I had criticized these policies because I had adjudged them as not fully acceptable to the "outsiders," e.g., society and community. I had, in other words, asked GM to assume authority in matters in which it had no authority, and to step beyond being a "business" with a clear and defined area of authority and responsibility. Instead I had asked GM to make political judgments, to make moral judgments, to make value judgments—all areas in which a business had absolutely no business to be and in which it would be clearly beyond the limits of its authority as well as of its competence.

At the very least, my GM critics argued, this showed that I did not understand business. This interpretation would be further strengthened, my critics said in all friendship, by the private "farewell letter" I had written to the top management people in GM after I had finished writing the study. In that letter I had, among other things, suggested that GM set up a Customer Relations Council and put customer representatives on it, parallel to the Dealer Relations Council which GM had set up earlier and which I had discussed in the book. This, my critics in GM management pointed out, showed that I did not understand that in respect to its dealers GM had indeed power. Therefore it had to assume responsibility and had to make sure that the dealers were adequately represented. But over customers GM had no power. Instead, the customer had power over GM. He could not only not buy a GM car and go to Ford or Chrysler—and, in those days, several others such as Packard or Hudson—he could also postpone buying a new car almost indefinitely. And he could, of course, not buy a car at all. The customer had the power; and he voted with his pocketbook, which gave him more than ample representation.

My critics did not dispute that it would be a good idea to get customer opinion. They pointed to the tremendous attempts GM had made for years to survey, poll, and interview customers—and GM indeed has the oldest and the most extensive customer research activity in business. But to ask the customer to take responsibility for advising GM and for becoming a party to GM decisions was, in effect, abdication of GM's responsibility, and at the same time a usurpation of authority where GM had no authority. It was an attempt, frankly, at manipulating the customer which was both illegitimate and despicable.

Not every one of the GM managers who gave me their objections to my book presented his thinking in so intellectual an argument. But they all felt that I was fundamentally "out of sympathy" with the basic ethos of business, and, in effect, demanded of a business an assumption of political and moral authority way beyond business' authority or competence.

The history of GM since 1946 shows the fundamental impacts of these basic attitudes which the senior managers of GM expressed in criticizing *Concept of the Corporation*, all of twenty-five years ago. There is, first, the undeniable success— undeniable at least in the United States, and persisting into the late 'sixties at least. This success has clearly been based on applying, without much change, the basic policies Alfred P. Sloan, Jr., had developed around 1922. It has been based on staying within the same structure with the same concepts.

The last twenty-five years have been years in which almost every large business has undergone major changes in organization—except GM. GM's organization today is essentially what I studied twenty-five years earlier. The only change, if indeed it can be called a "change," has been to put together, in 1971, all assembly operations into an Assembly Division— but this was already prefigured in the 1946 organization and was in fact put into effect for all divisions—except the largest, Chevrolet, and the smallest, Cadillac—right after the end of World War II. GM has not even changed its structure in respect to the automotive business outside of the United States. Where most other large companies have organized themselves as "multinational" companies, GM—which went "multinational" far earlier than most, in the early 'twenties—is still an "American" company with "overseas affiliates."

The GM "concept of the corporation" and its principles of organization have in these twenty-five years become the models of organization worldwide. When I wrote this book, General

Motors was unique in its organizational concepts and structure. Today it is the rare business that has not been made over
in the image of GM.

The crucial event here was probably the decision of the
Ford Motor Company in 1946 to remodel itself after General
Motors.

Then, a few years later, another giant of U. S. manufacturing, the General Electric Company, embarked on the road to
decentralization and worked out its own adaption of the General Motors pattern. From then on, large business after large
business—and many small and middle-sized ones as well—
have adopted the General Motors concept, not only in their
organizational structure but also in respect to measurements
and controls, to the way they define their business, and to the
way they develop business strategy.

The development has not stopped at America's frontiers.
Late in 1963, for instance, the world's second largest chemical
company, Britain's Imperial Chemical Industries, adopted
every important feature of the General Motors system; decentralization into autonomous divisions, each a business of its
own; full responsibility of the divisional manager for the performance of his division; and top management control of
policy, of capital expenditures, and of upper-level promotions.

Imperial Chemicals was somewhat late—the other big industrial businesses of the Free World, in Western Europe as
well as in Japan, had, by and large, adapted the General
Motors concept and structure to their conditions and needs
well before 1963. Even in Soviet Russia, the basic trend of
industrial organization has been along the trail which General
Motors first blazed, with "decentralization" as the slogan.

In other words, my critics were right—up to a point—in
saying in 1946: "We have the answers; don't ask new questions."

To the extent to which they did then what others have learned to do since, they have been rewarded with success.

We have, of course, learned quite a few things about decentralization, and the related ideas, as a result of this large-scale experimentation with corporate structure and policies. We have learned first that one can set up a decentralized division only if there is a genuine business entity with its own products and its own market—that is, a unit which can truly show profit and loss. Where such distinct business cannot be identified within a company, true decentralization is not possible. This limits the scope of decentralization; major materials businesses—an aluminum company or a paper company—are not really capable of being decentralized. But it may not be accident that those industries which cannot effectively set up reasonably small economic units with true local responsibility have generally shown much poorer results during these last twenty years than the businesses, much larger in number, which can be and have been decentralized.

The second lesson we have learned is that decentralization does not mean weakening central management. On the contrary, it is a means of strengthening the top management of the corporation by enabling it to concentrate on its own corporate tasks—to make the major entrepreneurial decisions, to set policy, to allocate capital, and to develop and place key personnel. In the decentralized business central management does not have to get into the details of daily operations. These are the responsibilities of the divisional managements and can, and should, be left to them.

This, however, means that decentralization will work only where the central corporate management has available adequate information and dependable knowledge regarding the company's businesses. Information and knowledge set the limits to decentralization. One cannot successfully decentralize what one cannot control through impersonal, indirect information. For a management that decentralizes deprives itself thereby of the direct daily experiences. It has to be able to rely on reports and figures—in short, on impersonal and indirect information. Any attempt to decentralize beyond the limits of information leads to trouble. It may even lead to disaster. This at least is the lesson taught by such experiences as that of the General Dynamics Corporation. A giant company in the defense and space industry, it managed, in the late 'fifties, to lose the incredible sum of 500 million dollars —the largest loss ever sustained till then by any business—in an attempt to develop a jet passenger plane. And the main reason for this catastrophe was decentralization without adequate central-management information.

This experience would not have surprised the men who designed the General Motors structure all of fifty years ago. Nor would it have surprised any reader of this book. Still, today we understand these limitations a great deal better than we did twenty-five years ago. On the one hand, we have learned that decentralization, where it can be applied, has tremendous impact. It liberates energies. It creates responsibility. It develops tomorrow's managers. And it frees top management for the top management job. At the same time, however, we also know that decentralization without a genuine market check is not effective. And we know that decentralization makes hard demands on the information and measurements systems of a business. But the people at GM can justly claim that they knew all this in 1946; and it is not their fault that it took the others so long to learn it.

In another area we have also learned a great deal beyond what we knew when this book was written.

If the worldwide trend toward the General Motors model bore out the conclusions of this book, another trend has shown how limited in its vision the book was in so important an area as that of the structure of industrial society. Throughout *Concept of the Corporation* it is taken for granted that there are essentially two major groups in the business enterprise: the "workers" and the "managers." In this respect the book simply repeated what had been commonplace for a century. But the commonplace had ceased to be valid before the book was written, though during the days of World War II this change was obscured by a tremendous temporary increase in the number of manual workers.

By now we know that there are three groups in industrial society: the "workers," that is, the men who work with their hands, whether their job is skilled or unskilled; the "managers"; and thirdly, the large and growing group of employed professionals who work with their knowledge rather than with their hands—the engineers and accountants, scientists and salesmen, market researchers and production schedulers.

These people are employed. Yet they do not consider themselves "workers," nor are they considered as such by society. They are not "bosses." But they see themselves as "members of management" and are clearly seen as such by everybody else. They are not "capitalists"; they do not own the businesses in which they work. But they are "capitalists" in that, through pension funds and investment trusts, they own American industry, by and large.

This group is already larger than that of the old-style "worker." Indeed, the manual worker has been declining, both in total numbers and as a proportion of the population, since the end of World War II. On the other hand, the "knowledge workers" of the professional middle class are doubling in number about every eight years or so. They are rapidly becoming the representative and most important group both in business and in our society. The largest single occupational group in the United States today is, for instance, the teaching profession. The teacher is almost the prototype of the employed middle-class professional. Yet there is almost no mention of this group in *Concept of the Corporation,* just as there was very little attention paid to it in the America of 1940 or 1945.

The principal factor in this development has been the business corporation. It was the first social institution that learned how to bring together a diversity of knowledges in a common effort. The large business corporation, such as General Motors, was the first large-scale knowledge organization. It developed an almost insatiable appetite for all kinds of knowledge and conceptual skill. It provided the thrust which is rapidly making a college education as common as a high school education was forty years ago, and more common than any type of schooling was less than a century ago. Without jobs for educated men and women, there would be no "educational revolution." But, in turn, the fact that the modern corporation is a knowledge organization (as are increasingly all other large-scale organizations, the government agency, the armed services, the modern hospital, and so on) changes the nature of the work. Automation, for instance, is the substitution of knowledge work for manual work and of conceptual skills for manual skills.

This change has altered the social relationships both within the corporation and within society. It also has created a very different problem for management. The great challenge to management today is to make productive the tremendous new resource, the knowledge worker. This, rather than the productivity of the manual worker, is the key to economic growth and economic performance in today's society.

In World War II, as in the decades before it, the ability to train manual workers and to obtain performance from them was the key to productivity. In today's economy, it is the contribution of the man of knowledge, the scientist or the engineer, that determines the strength of a country.

And the social problem of the twentieth century is no longer the role and function of the industrial workers, the "proletariat," but rather the role and function of the employed professionals, the technical and managerial middle class, the knowledge workers.

But this shift strengthened rather than weakened the basic General Motors concept. GM is still essentially an organization of blue-collar workers—that is, a production organization. And yet from the beginning the organization of GM was conceived as an organization of management and managers. GM all along took the approach that management is rational work. And as early as the nineteen-twenties GM tried to think through how one organizes the rewards for managers and also how one fits nonmanagers, that is, professional specialists, into a management structure.

Whether the GM model will be adequate for the future is another matter. We know already that it is not the "final answer." We know that the basic problems of organization in the large institution, and especially in the large business, are not problems which GM faced. GM never pretended to be "multinational," let alone "multicultural." This probably explains in large measure why, outside the United States, GM has not been nearly the success it has been inside the country —though it has not been doing too badly in other parts of the world. Most other large businesses are increasingly "multinational." This is true not only of companies based in the United States, but increasingly also of companies based in all other developed and advanced countries such as Sweden, Germany, or Japan. And there GM does not provide the answers to the pressing questions of organization, of relationships, of structure, which we will have to solve to make the multinational corporation truly productive and perhaps even to save it from nationalist pressures.

GM has been all along a "managerial" company rather than an "innovative" one. The basic innovations in the automobile industry were all made before 1914, before GM got started. There is no feature on any car on the market today that could not have been obtained as optional or standard equipment on some car offered commercially before 1914 (except only air conditioning and electric push-buttons to open and close the windows). It is only now, under the pressure of safety demands and of concern with environment and pollution that the automobile industry is forced into new engineering thinking.

But we will need to understand increasingly how to organize and to manage innovative organizations. And for this the GM model is not adequate and may not even be appropriate.

Also GM is, of course, a manufacturing company. In 1946 manufacturing was *the* central business activity. Today it is *a* central business activity. And more and more businesses are not "manufacturing businesses"—they are financial businesses, services businesses, distribution businesses, transportation businesses, and so on. Also we now realize that we face a tremendous problem of organizing and managing the nonbusiness institutions, the government agency, the research laboratory, hospital, the university, and so on. And for this, again, GM, while a highly stimulating model, is clearly not the "final answer."

And then, even though in 1946 GM seemed to be the very apex of complexity and diversity, it is, by comparison with today's businesses, a simple one-product business, using one technology and supplying one market. Today we not only have the "conglomerates." Even in businesses that control their growth and try to organize themselves on a rational principle rather than around financial manipulation, today's reality is one of a great many products, a great many technologies, and a great many markets. And this raises problems of diversity and complexity which go well beyond anything the GM model attempted to solve.

And yet, up to this day, the GM model has remained the one general model of organization for large institutions, and, of course, especially for large businesses. One may argue that GM should have taken the critical look at itself that I proposed twenty-five years ago. But, in retrospect, my critics within GM at that time have been proved right. Not to have changed anything has been the foundation for GM's success in terms of sales and profits.

But it also clearly has been the source of GM's failure as an institution. For today GM is clearly in deep trouble—not because its cars do not sell or because it lacks efficiency. GM is in trouble because it is seen increasingly by more and more people as deeply at odds with basic needs and basic values of society and community.

To a large extent, GM's present troubles would have happened no matter what GM management would have done or would have been. To a large extent what GM suffers from is the end of the old love affair between the automobile and the American public. After fifty years of passionate addiction to the automobile, the ardor of the American public has cooled. The automobile is still a utility for most of us, but it is no longer a "symbol," no longer a psychological and emotional value beyond almost any other in our material civilization. Outside of the United States this has not yet happened. On the contrary, where the automobile has not yet become universal, the passion burns as brightly as it ever did in this country. But it is clear that sooner or later the same cooling off will happen—and in Europe and in Japan there are the first signs that it is about to happen.

Old love affairs do not "fade away." They end in bitterness, in bickering and recrimination, and in fault-finding. And this one is no exception.

Actually GM managers could well argue that they are being lambasted today for the sins they did not commit, and indeed, in many cases, for their virtues. GM is the very target of the campaigns to make the automobile safer. Yet GM could well argue that, historically, it has been in the forefront of the campaign to reduce automotive accidents—it has spent countless dollars and tremendous energies on making highways safer and making drivers drive more safely. GM could equally claim that it was in the forefront in the drive to give employment opportunities to minority groups, and that it did so, and did so as a matter of deliberate policy, thirty years ago, when most other businesses did not hire blacks except for the most menial jobs. GM could equally claim—and prove—that it began to work on such matters as traffic sprawl and traffic congestion in cities where it had plants, long before anybody talked about "traffic planning."

But rational arguments are wasted in a lovers' quarrel. And to the extent to which GM is the victim of our disenchantment with our old love, the automobile, there is probably nothing management could or should do except wait out the storm and hope that it will blow itself out—as it well may do.

But this is only a small part of the story. The failure of GM as an institution—for failure it is—is to a large extent the result of the very attitude which led my critics within GM management to reject this book as "hostile to business." It is an attitude one might call "technocratic." It is an attitude which says: "We are the experts and within our area of competence, we make the decisions. Other areas are not our business. They are the business of other people."

The attitude is best exemplified in Alfred P. Sloan, Jr.'s, own book, *My Years with General Motors* (perhaps the most interesting, most revealing, but also the most frustrating book on business ever written by a businessman). For the book focuses exclusively on what went on within GM, even though it deals with the New Deal years. It focuses exclusively on policies, business decisions, and structure, even though Sloan himself was a master at working with and managing people, was personally exceedingly "people-focused" and an early practitioner of what now, following Douglas McGregor,* is usually called Theory Y. Yet there are no people in Sloan's book, no mention of Sloan's own great strength, the leadership of people, no discussion of relations with people, no mention of the time and attention he himself gave to placing people in the right jobs and to making their strengths effective. It is perhaps the most impersonal book of memoirs ever written—and this was clearly intentional. It is what Sloan meant by "professional management."

Sloan's book, at the same time, knows only one dimension: that of managing a business so that it can produce effectively, provide jobs, create markets and sales, and generate profits. Business in the community; business as a life rather than a livelihood; business as a neighbor; and business as a power center—these are all absent in Sloan's world. This too is what Sloan meant by "professional management."

And it is this "technocratic" view which the failure of GM as an institution these last twenty-five years puts into serious doubt. GM's present predicament is, above all, the failure of the "technocrat" approach to the management of institutions.

---

* See McGregor's book, *The Human Side of Enterprise* (McGraw-Hill, 1960).

Not so long ago, John Kenneth Galbraith, the Harvard economist, prophesied that institutions will be taken over by "technocrats." Indeed he advocated it. But if the GM experience of the last twenty-five years is a lesson, and indeed if the rebellion of the young means anything, this is not going to happen.

On the contrary, we will demand of our institutions that they take responsibility beyond their own performance and beyond their own contribution. We will demand this not only of business enterprise but of all other institutions as well—the university and the hospital, the government agency and the school. This, I submit, is one lesson from GM's history, one lesson from its success and one lesson from its failure.

It is a dangerous lesson. For my critics in GM's management twenty-five years ago were not unthinking, not unreasonable, not irresponsible men. Their argument that it is usurpation for an institution to "take responsibility" where it has no genuine authority and no true competence is not an irresponsible argument.

And yet it is today no longer a permissible argument. For today in our society of pluralist institutions, there is no longer one "political" agency which can make what are "political" decisions while the other institutions are "technical" and can confine themselves to their own area of competence. There is a great deal to be said against the present clamor for "responsibility on the part of business." Every time the demand is made that "business take responsibility" for this or that, one should ask: "Does business have the authority, and should it have it? Are we dealing with an impact of business or with something that is totally outside of business?" If business does not have and should not have authority—and in a great many areas it should not have it—then "responsibility" on the part of business should be treated with grave suspicion. It is not "responsibility"; it is lust for power. And if business is not competent in an area—and business is hardly competent in such areas as the arts, education, or even civil rights—then business should, in its own interest as well as that of society, be most reluctant to take "responsibility." Responsibility without competence does damage. Responsibility without competence is irresponsibility.

And yet the attitude which my friends in General Motors took twenty-five years ago is no longer defensible. There is indeed danger to a free society if institutions arrogate to themselves "responsibility"—or have it wished on them—in areas in which their authority and their competence are murky. But in a pluralism such as we have built the opposite danger may be even greater; narrow construction of responsibility may result in the neglect of urgent community tasks.

In a way, the failure of General Motors as an institution highlights the most important problem of modern society: the problem of responsibility, of authority, and of competence of the large organization, whether a business, a hospital, or a university. The indiscriminate cry of "responsibility" is not only dangerous but plain silly. But clearly also the refusal to be anything but a "technocrat" is no longer possible and is indeed endangering both the individual institution itself and all of society.

If there is one lesson to be learned from revisiting General Motors twenty-five years later, it does not lie in the principles, the concepts, the structures of business enterprise, or of large-scale institutions altogether. Here, admittedly, we will have to learn a good deal. But we will also have to build on the foundation of General Motors, apply the same analysis, the same thinking, the same tools which Alfred P. Sloan, Jr., applied fifty years ago when he first designed the General Motors structure. And we will have the same objectives of

freedom under the law, of flexibility within order, of autonomy within responsibility that underlay his design.

The major lesson we can learn from revisiting General
Motors is that an institution, like an individual, is not an
island unto itself. It has to solve the basic problem of balancing the need for concentration and for self-limitation with
concern for its environment and compassion for its community. General Motors' success is clearly the success of the
"technocrat." But so is General Motors' failure.

INDEX

INDEX

313